Macmillan/McGraw-Hill Edition

McGRAW-HILL READING

McGraw-Hill
School Division

New York   Farmington

Contributors

The Princeton Review, Time Magazine

The Princeton Review is not
affiliated with Princeton
University or ETS.

McGraw-Hill School Division ⚛

A Division of The McGraw·Hill Companies

McGraw-Hill School Division
Two Penn Plaza
New York, New York 10121

Printed in the United States of America

ISBN 0-02-184742-8/K, U.2

2 3 4 5 6 7 8 9   043/073   04 03 02 01 00 99

McGraw-Hill
**McGraw-Hill
School Division**

New York   Farmington

McGraw-Hill Reading
Authors
Make the Difference...

Dr. James Flood

Ms. Angela Shelf Medearis

Dr. Jan E. Hasbrouck

Dr. Scott Paris

Dr. James V. Hoffman

Dr. Steven Stahl

Dr. Diane Lapp

Dr. Josefina Villamil Tinajero

Dr. Karen D. Wood

Contributing
Authors

Dr. Barbara Coulter

Ms. Frankie Dungan

Dr. Joseph B. Rubin

Dr. Carl B. Smith

Dr. Shirley Wright

Part 1

START TOGETHER

Focus on Reading and Skills

All students start with the SAME:

- Read Aloud
- Pretaught Skills
  Phonics
  Comprehension
- Build Background
- Selection Vocabulary

...Never hold a child back. Never leave a child behind.

Part 2

MEET INDIVIDUAL NEEDS

Read the Literature

Core Selection

Pupil Selection

Leveled Books

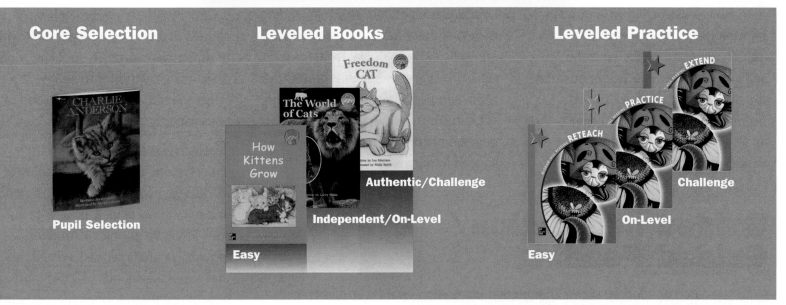

How Kittens Grow

The World of Cats

Freedom CAT

Authentic/Challenge

Independent/On-Level

Easy

Leveled Practice

EXTEND

PRACTICE

RETEACH

Challenge

On-Level

Easy

Examples Taken From Grade 2

Part 3

FINISH TOGETHER

Build Skills

All students finish with the SAME:

- Phonics
- Comprehension
- Vocabulary
- Study Skills
- Assessment

McGraw-Hill Reading
Applying the Research

Phonological Awareness

Phonological awareness is the ability to hear the sounds in spoken language. It includes the ability to separate spoken words into discrete sounds as well as the ability to blend sounds together to make words. A child with good phonological awareness can identify rhyming words, hear the separate syllables in a word, separate the first sound in a word (onset) from the rest of the word (rime), and blend sounds together to make words.

Recent research findings have strongly concluded that children with good phonological awareness skills are more likely to learn to read well. These skills can be improved through systematic, explicit instruction involving auditory practice. McGraw-Hill Reading develops these key skills by providing an explicit Phonological Awareness lesson in every selection at grades K-2. Motivating activities such as blending, segmenting, and rhyming help to develop children's awareness of the sounds in our language.

Guided Instruction/ Guided Reading

Research on reading shows that guided instruction enables students to develop as independent, strategic readers. The *reciprocal-teaching model* of Anne-Marie Palincsar encourages teachers to model strategic-thinking, questioning, clarifying, and problem-solving strategies for students as students read together with the teacher. In McGraw-Hill Reading, guided instruction for all Pupil Edition selections incorporates the Palincsar model by providing interactive questioning prompts. The *guided-reading model* of Gay Su Pinnell is also incorporated into the McGraw-Hill Reading program. Through the guided-reading lessons provided for the leveled books offered with the program, teachers can work with small groups of students of different ability levels, closely observing them as they read and providing support specific to their needs.

By adapting instruction to include successful models of teaching and the appropriate materials to deliver instruction, McGraw-Hill Reading enables teachers to offer the appropriate type of instruction for all students in the classroom.

Phonics

Our language system uses an alphabetic code to communicate meaning from writing. Phonics involves learning the phonemes or sounds that letters make and the symbols or letters that represent those sounds. Children learn to blend the sounds of letters to decode unknown or unfamiliar words. The goal of good phonics instruction is to enable students to read words accurately and automatically.

Research has clearly identified the critical role of phonics in the ability of readers to read fluently and with good understanding, as well as to write and spell. Effective phonics instruction requires carefully sequenced lessons that teach the sounds of letters and how to use these sounds to read words. The McGraw-Hill program provides daily explicit and systematic phonics instruction to teach the letter sounds and blending. There are three explicit Phonics and Decoding lessons for every selection. Daily Phonics Routines are provided for quick reinforcement, in addition to activities in the Phonics Workbook and technology components. This combination of direct skills instruction and applied practice leads to reading success.

Curriculum Connections

As in the child's real-world environment, boundaries between disciplines must be dissolved. Recent research emphasizes the need to make connections between and across subject areas. McGraw-Hill Reading is committed to this approach. Each reading selection offers activities that tie in with social studies, language arts, geography, science, mathematics, art, music, health, and physical education. The program threads numerous research and inquiry activities that encourage the child to use the library and the Internet to seek out information. Reading and language skills are applied to a variety of genres, balancing fiction and nonfiction.

Integrated Language Arts

Success in developing communication skills is greatly enhanced by integrating the language arts in connected and purposeful ways. This allows students to understand the need for proper writing, grammar, and spelling. McGraw-Hill Reading sets the stage for meaningful learning. Each week a full writing-process lesson is provided. This lesson is supported by a 5-day spelling plan, emphasizing spelling patterns and spelling rules, and a 5-day grammar plan, focusing on proper grammar, mechanics, and usage.

Meeting Individual Needs

Every classroom is a microcosm of a world composed of diverse individuals with unique needs and abilities. Research points out that such needs must be addressed with frequent intensive opportunities to learn with engaging materials. McGraw-Hill Reading makes reading a successful experience for every child by providing a rich collection of leveled books for easy, independent, and challenging reading. Leveled practice is provided in Reteach, Practice, and Extend skills books. To address various learning styles and language needs, the program offers alternative teaching strategies, prevention/intervention techniques, language support activities, and ESL teaching suggestions.

Assessment

Frequent assessment in the classroom makes it easier for teachers to identify problems and to find remedies for them. McGraw-Hill Reading makes assessment an important component of instruction. Formal and informal opportunities are a part of each lesson. Minilessons, prevention/intervention strategies, and informal checklists, as well as student self-assessments, provide many informal assessment opportunities. Formal assessments, such as weekly selection tests and criterion-referenced unit tests, help to monitor students' knowledge of important skills and concepts. McGraw-Hill Reading also addresses how to adapt instruction based on student performance with resources such as the Alternate Teaching Strategies. Weekly lessons on test preparation, including test preparation practice books, help students to transfer skills to new contexts and to become better test takers.

McGraw-Hill School **TECHNOLOGY**

*inter***NET** **CONNECTION** For information on research that supports this program, visit **www.mhschool.com/reading**

McGraw-Hill Reading

Theme Chart

MULTI-AGE Classroom

Using the same global themes at each grade level facilitates the use of materials in multi-age classrooms.

GRADE LEVEL	Experience Experiences can tell us about ourselves and our world.	Connections Making connections develops new understandings.
Kindergarten	**My World** We learn a lot from all the things we see and do at home and in school.	**All Kinds of Friends** When we work and play together, we learn more about ourselves.
Subtheme 1	At Home	Working Together
Subtheme 2	School Days	Playing Together
1	**Day by Day** Each day brings new experiences.	**Together Is Better** We like to share ideas and experiences with others.
2	**What's New?** With each day, we learn something new.	**Just Between Us** Family and friends help us see the world in new ways.
3	**Great Adventures** Life is made up of big and small experiences.	**Nature Links** Nature can give us new ideas.
4	**Reflections** Stories let us share the experiences of others.	**Something in Common** Sharing ideas can lead to meaningful cooperation.
5	**Time of My Life** We sometimes find memorable experiences in unexpected places.	**Building Bridges** Knowing what we have in common helps us appreciate our differences.
6	**Pathways** Reflecting on life's experiences can lead to new understandings.	**A Common Thread** A look beneath the surface may uncover hidden connections.

Themes: Kindergarten – Grade 6

Six Units IN EVERY GRADE

Expression	Inquiry	Problem Solving	Making Decisions
There are many styles and forms for expressing ourselves.	By exploring and asking questions, we make discoveries.	Analyzing information can help us solve problems.	Using what we know helps us evaluate situations.
Time to Shine We can use our ideas and our imagination to do many wonderful things.	**I Wonder** We can make discoveries about the wonders of nature in our own backyard.	**Let's Work It Out** Working as part of a team can help me find a way to solve problems.	**Choices** We can make many good choices and decisions every day.
Great Ideas	**In My Backyard**	**Try and Try Again**	**Good Choices**
Let's Pretend	**Wonders of Nature**	**Teamwork**	**Let's Decide**
Stories to Tell Each one of us has a different story to tell.	**Let's Find Out!** Looking for answers is an adventure.	**Think About It!** It takes time to solve problems.	**Many Paths** Each decision opens the door to a new path.
Express Yourself We share our ideas in many ways.	**Look Around** There are surprises all around us.	**Figure It Out** We can solve problems by working together.	**Starting Now** Unexpected events can lead to new decisions.
Be Creative! We can all express ourselves in creative, wonderful ways.	**Tell Me More** Looking and listening closely will help us find out the facts.	**Think It Through** Solutions come in many shapes and sizes.	**Turning Points** We make new judgments based on our experiences.
Our Voices We can each use our talents to communicate ideas.	**Just Curious** We can find answers in surprising places.	**Make a Plan** Often we have to think carefully about a problem in order to solve it.	**Sorting It Out** We make decisions that can lead to new ideas and discoveries.
Imagine That The way we express our thoughts and feelings can take different forms.	**Investigate!** We never know where the search for answers might lead us.	**Bright Ideas** Some problems require unusual approaches.	**Crossroads** Decisions cause changes that can enrich our lives.
With Flying Colors Creative people help us see the world from different perspectives.	**Seek and Discover** To make new discoveries, we must observe and explore.	**Brainstorms** We can meet any challenge with determination and ingenuity.	**All Things Considered** Encountering new places and people can help us make decisions.

All Kinds of Friends

*When we work and play together,
we learn more about ourselves.*

"Wait for Me" a poem by *Sarah Wilson*

SubTheme: Working Together

Dan and Dad

SKILLS			
Phonics	**Comprehension**	**Vocabulary**	**Beginning Reading Concepts**
• **Introduce** Initial /d/*d* • **Introduce** Final /d/*d* • **Review** /d/*d*; Blending with Short *a*	• **Introduce** Story Details • **Review** Story Details	• **Introduce** High-Frequency Words: *and* • **Review** *and, my, a*	• **Introduce** Numbers

Dad, Dan, and I

SKILLS			
Phonics	**Comprehension**	**Vocabulary**	**Beginning Reading Concepts**
• **Introduce** Initial /s/*s* • **Review** Initial /s/*s*; /d/*d*; Blending with Short *a*	• **Introduce** Classify and Categorize • **Review** Classify and Categorize	• **Introduce** High-Frequency Words: *I* • **Review** *I, and, my*	• **Review** Numbers

S K I L L S			
Phonics	**Comprehension**	**Vocabulary**	**Beginning Reading Concepts**
• **Introduce** Initial /m/*m*	• **Review** Story Details	• **Introduce** High-Frequency Words: *is*	• **Introduce** Shapes: Circle, Triangle
• **Introduce** Final /m/*m*		• **Review** *is, I, and, that*	
• **Review** /m/*m*; Blending with Short *a*			

S K I L L S			
Phonics	**Comprehension**	**Vocabulary**	**Beginning Reading Concepts**
• **Introduce** Initial /i/*i*	• **Review** Classify and Categorize	• **Introduce** High-Frequency Words: *said*	• **Review** Shapes: Square, Rectangle
• **Introduce** Medial /i/*i*		• **Review** *said, I, is*	
• **Introduce** Blending with Short *i, a*			
• **Review** /i/*i*; Blending with Short *i, a*			

S K I L L S			
Phonics	**Comprehension**	**Vocabulary**	**Beginning Reading Concepts**
• **Review** /d/*d*, /m/*m*, /s/*s*; Blending with Short *i, a*	• **Review** Story Details	• **Review** *I, and, is, said*	• **Review** Shapes and Numbers
	• **Review** Classify and Categorize		

Unit Planner

Dan and Dad

Dad, Dan, and I

	WEEK 1 Dan and Dad	**WEEK 2** Dad, Dan, and I
📖 **Leveled Books**	Patterned Book: *Building*	Patterned Book: *Sid and I*
☑ **Tested Skills**	☑ **Phonics and Decoding** Initial /d/d, 66W–66, 70C–70 Final /d/d, 68C–68, 70C–70 Blending with Short *a*, 72C–72, 76C–76 ☑ **Comprehension** Story Details, 69C–69, 75A–75 ☑ **Vocabulary** High-Frequency Word: *and*, 71C–71 *and*, *my*, *a*, 77C–77 ☑ **Beginning Reading Concepts** Numbers, 79C–79	☑ **Phonics and Decoding** Initial /s/s, 78I–78, 80C–80, 82C–82 Initial /d/d, 82C–82 Blending with Short *a*, 84C–84, 88C–88 ☑ **Comprehension** Classify and Categorize 81C–81, 87A–87 ☑ **Vocabulary** High-Frequency Word: *I*, 83C–83 *I*, *and*, *my*, 89C–89 ☑ **Beginning Reading Concepts** Numbers, 91C–91
Language Arts	✏ **Writing:** Letter Formation, 66W–66, 68C–68 Interactive Writing, 78A–78B	✏ **Writing:** Letter Formation, 78I–78, Interactive Writing, 90A–90B

CENTER Activities

Curriculum Connections		
Social Studies	Language Arts: 67B	Math: Pumpkin Patch, 85/86D
Mathematics	Math: 69B	Science: Float or Sink, 89B
Science	Art: 71A	
Music	Math: Sorting Leaves, 73/74D	
Art	Social Studies: Building Together, 77B	
Drama		
Language Arts		
🤝 CULTURAL PERSPECTIVES		Street Fairs, 79B; Cupcakes, 81B; Teepees, 83A

I Am Sam!

Sid Said

Is Sam Mad?

WEEK 3 — I Am Sam!

Patterned Book: *Our Mobile*

☑ **Phonics and Decoding**
Initial /m/m, 90I–90, 94C–94
Final /m/m, 92C–92, 94C–94
Blending with Short *a*, 96C–96, 100C–100

☑ **Comprehension**
Story Details, 93C–93, 99A–99

☑ **Vocabulary**
High-Frequency Word: *is*, 95C–95
is, I, and, that, 101C–101

☑ **Beginning Reading Concepts**
Shapes: Circle, Triangle, 91C–91

✎ **Writing:** Letter Formation, 90I–90, 92C–92
Interactive Writing, 102A–102B

Language Arts: ABC Quilt, 91B

Math: Counting Time, 93B

Art: Mask Making, 97/98D

Art: Animal Mobiles, 101B

Shadow Puppets, 95A

WEEK 4 — Sid Said

Patterned Book: *Come In!*

☑ **Phonics and Decoding**
Initial /i/i, 102I–102, 106C–106
Medial /i/ i, 104C–104, 106C–106
Blending with Short *i, a*, 108C–108, 112C–112

☑ **Comprehension**
Classify and Categorize, 105C–105, 111A–111

☑ **Vocabulary**
High-Frequency Word: *said*, 107C–107
said, I, is, 113C–113

☑ **Beginning Reading Concepts**
Shapes: Square, Rectangle, 103C–103

✎ **Writing:** Letter Formation, 102I–102, 104C–104
Interactive Writing, 114A–114B

Language Arts: Name That Letter, 103B

Science: Where Does It Belong? 105B

Science: 107B

Art: Class Mural, 109/110D

Math: Who's First? 113B

WEEK 5 — Is Sam Mad?

Self-Selected Reading of Patterned Books

☑ **Phonics and Decoding**
Initial /d/d, /s/s, /m/m, 114I–114, 118C–118
Final /d/d, /m/m, 116C–116, 118C–118
Blending with Short *i, a*, 120C–120, 124C–124

☑ **Comprehension**
Story Details, 117C–117
Classify and Categorize, 123A–123

☑ **Vocabulary**
High-Frequency Words: *I, and, is, said*, 119C–119, 125C–125

☑ **Beginning Reading Concepts**
Shapes and Numbers, 115C–115

✎ **Writing:** Interactive Writing, 126A–126

Language Arts: Food Order, 115B

Math: How Much, 117B

Art: Trains, 119B

Math: Block Sorting, 121/122D

Social Studies: Build a City, 125B

WEEK 6 — Review, Assessment

Self-Selected Reading

☑ **Assess Skills**

Phonics and Decoding
Initial /d/d, /s/s, /m/m, /i/i
Final /d/d, /m/m
Medial /i/i
Blending with Short *i, a*

Comprehension
Story Details
Classify and Categorize

Vocabulary
High-Frequency Words: *and, I, is, said, my, that*

Beginning Reading Concepts
Numbers
Shapes: Circle, Triangle, Square, Rectangle

☑ **Unit 2 Assessment**

☑ **Standardized Test Preparation**

Unit Resources

LITERATURE

DECODABLE STORIES These four-color stories in the Pupil Edition consist of words containing the phonetic elements that have been taught, as well as the high-frequency words. The stories reinforce the comprehension and concepts of print skills.

LEVELED BOOKS These engaging stories include the high-frequency words and words with the phonetic elements that are being taught. They reinforce the comprehension skills and correlate to the unit themes.

📖 **Patterned**

- *Building*
- *Sid and I*
- *Our Mobile*
- *Come In!*

ABC BIG BOOK Children build alphabetic knowledge and letter identification as they enjoy a shared reading of this story that correlates to the theme.

- *The ABC Street Fair*

LITERATURE BIG BOOKS Shared readings of the highest-quality literature reinforce comprehension skills and introduce children to a variety of genres.

- *Warthogs in the Kitchen*
- *The Chick and the Duckling*

READ ALOUDS Traditional folk tales, fables, fairy tales, and stories from around the world can be shared with children as they develop their oral comprehension skills and learn about other cultures.

- *Tweedy's Toys*
- *The Legend of Bluebonnet*
- *The Town Mouse and the Country Mouse*
- *Mary Had a Little Lamb*

💾 **STUDENT LISTENING LIBRARY**
Recordings of the Big Books, Patterned Books, and Unit Opener and Closer Poetry.

SKILLS

PUPIL EDITION Colorful practice pages help you to assess children's progress as they learn and review each skill, including phonics, high-frequency words, readiness, comprehension, and letter formation.

PRACTICE BOOK Practice pages in alternative formats provide additional reinforcement of each skill as well as extra handwriting practice.

BIG BOOK OF PHONICS RHYMES AND POEMS Traditional and contemporary poems emphasize phonics and rhyme and allow children to develop oral comprehension skills.

BIG BOOK OF REAL-LIFE READING This lively big book, which introduces children to important study skills, focuses on simple diagrams in this unit. The context for the teaching is the Read Aloud selection children have just heard.

WORD BUILDING BOOK

a b c Letter and word cards to utilize phonics and build children's vocabulary. Includes high-frequency word cards.

LANGUAGE SUPPORT BOOK

ESL Parallel teaching and practice activities for children needing language support.

McGraw-Hill School TECHNOLOGY

Phonics CD-ROM Provides interactive lessons for additional phonics support.

interNET CONNECTION Extend lessons through Research and Inquiry Ideas.

Visit www.mhschool.com

Resources for Meeting Individual Needs

	EASY	ON-LEVEL	CHALLENGE	LANGUAGE SUPPORT

UNIT 2

Dan and Dad

	EASY	ON-LEVEL	CHALLENGE	LANGUAGE SUPPORT
Dan and Dad	**Dan and Dad** Teaching Strategies 66, 67, 68, 69, 70, 71, 72, 75, 76, 77 Alternate Teaching Strategy T24–T27 Writing 78B Phonics CD-ROM	**Dan and Dad** Teaching Strategies 66–72, 75–77 Alternate Teaching Strategy T24–T27 Writing 78B Patterned Book *Building* Phonics CD-ROM	Patterned Book *Building* Teaching Strategies 66, 67, 68, 69, 70, 71, 72, 75, 76, 77 Writing 78B Phonics CD-ROM	Teaching Strategies 66, 67, 68, 69, 70, 71, 72, 75, 76, 77 Alternate Teaching Strategy T24–T27 Writing 78B Phonics CD-ROM
Dad, Dan, and I	**Dad, Dan, and I** Teaching Strategies 78, 79, 80, 81, 82, 83, 84, 87, 88, 89 Alternate Teaching Strategy T24, T25, T27–T29 Writing 90B Phonics CD-ROM	**Dad, Dan, and I** Teaching Strategies 78–84, 87–89 Alternate Teaching Strategy T24, T25, T27–T29 Writing 90B Patterned Book *Sid and I* Phonics CD-ROM	Patterned Book *Sid and I* Teaching Strategies 78, 79, 80, 81, 82, 83, 84, 87, 88, 89 Writing 90B Phonics CD-ROM	Teaching Strategies 78, 79, 80, 81, 82, 83, 84, 87, 88, 89 Alternate Teaching Strategy T24, T25, T27–T29 Writing 90B Phonics CD-ROM
I Am Sam!	**I Am Sam!** Teaching Strategies 90, 91, 92, 93, 94, 95, 96, 99, 100, 101 Alternate Teaching Strategy T26, T27, T30, T31 Writing 102B Phonics CD-ROM	**I Am Sam!** Teaching Strategies 90–96, 99–101 Alternate Teaching Strategy T26, T27, T30, T31 Writing 102B Patterned Book *Our Mobile* Phonics CD-ROM	Patterned Book *Our Mobile* Teaching Strategies 90, 91, 92, 93, 94, 95, 96, 99, 100, 101 Writing 102B Phonics CD-ROM	Teaching Strategies 90, 91, 92, 93, 94, 95, 96, 99, 100, 101 Alternate Teaching Strategy T26, T27, T30, T31 Writing 102B Phonics CD-ROM
Sid Said	**Sid Said** Teaching Strategies 102, 103, 104, 105, 106, 107, 108, 111, 112, 113 Alternate Teaching Strategy T27, T29, T31, T32 Writing 114B Phonics CD-ROM	**Sid Said** Teaching Strategies 102–108, 111–113 Alternate Teaching Strategy T27, T29, T31, T32 Writing 114B Patterned Book *Come In!* Phonics CD-ROM	Patterned Book *Come In!* Teaching Strategies 102, 103, 104, 105, 106, 107, 108, 111, 112, 113 Writing 114B Phonics CD-ROM	Teaching Strategies 102, 103, 104, 105, 106, 107, 108, 111, 112, 113 Alternate Teaching Strategy T27, T29, T31, T32 Writing 114B Phonics CD-ROM
Is Sam Mad?	**Is Sam Mad?** Teaching Strategies 114, 115, 116, 117, 118, 119, 120, 123, 124, 125 Alternate Teaching Strategy T24–T32 Writing 126B Phonics CD-ROM	**Is Sam Mad?** Teaching Strategies 114–120, 123–125 Alternate Teaching Strategy T24–T32 Writing 126B Patterned Book *Patterned Book Choice* Phonics CD-ROM	Patterned Book *Patterned Book Choice* Teaching Strategies 114, 115, 116, 117, 118, 119, 120, 123, 124, 125 Writing 126B Phonics CD-ROM	Teaching Strategies 114, 115, 116, 117, 118, 119, 120, 123, 124, 125 Alternate Teaching Strategy T24–T32 Writing 126B Phonics CD-ROM

INFORMAL

Informal Assessment

- Phonics and Decoding, 66W, 68C, 70C, 72C, 76C; 78I, 80C, 82C, 84C, 88C; 90I, 92C, 94C, 96C, 100C; 102I, 104C, 106C, 108C, 112C; 114I, 116C, 118C, 120C, 124C

- Comprehension, 67B, 69B–69C, 75A, 77A; 79B, 81B–81C, 87A, 89A; 91B, 93B, 93C, 99A, 101A; 103B, 105B, 105C, 111A, 113A; 115A, 115B, 117B, 117C, 123A, 125A

- High-Frequency Words, 71C, 77C; 83C, 89C; 95C, 101C; 107C, 113C; 119C, 125C

- Beginning Reading Concepts, 67C, 79C, 91C, 103C, 115C

Performance Assessment

- Research and Inquiry Project, 66O, 126C

- Interactive Writing, 78A; 90A; 102A; 114A; 126A

- Listening, Speaking, Viewing Activities, 66U, 68A, 70A, 72A, 76A; 78G, 80A, 82A, 84A, 88A; 90G, 92A, 94A, 96A, 100A; 102G, 104A, 106A, 108A, 112A; 114G, 116A, 118A, 120A, 124A

- Portfolio

  Writing, 78A; 90A; 102A; 114A; 126A

  Cross-Curricular Activities, 67B, 69B, 71B, 73/74D, 77B; 79B, 81B, 83B, 85/86D, 89B; 91B, 93B, 95B, 97/98D, 101B; 103B, 105B, 107B, 109/110D, 113B; 115B, 117B, 119B, 121/122D, 125B

Practice

- **Phonics and Decoding**

  /d/d, 66, 68, 70, 82, 118

  /m/m, 90, 92, 94, 116, 118

  /s/s, 78, 80, 82, 118

  Blending with Short i, a, 72, 76, 84, 88, 96, 100, 108, 112, 114, 120, 124

- **Comprehension**

  Story Details, 89, 75, 93, 99, 117

  Classify and Categorize, 81, 87, 105, 111, 123

- **High-Frequency Words**

  and, I, is, said, 71, 77; 83, 89; 95, 101; 107, 113; 119, 125

- **Beginning Reading Concepts**

  67C, 79C, 91C, 103C, 115C

FORMAL

Unit 2 Assessment

- **Phonics and Decoding**

  Initial and Final /d/d

  Initial and Final /m/m

  Initial /s/s

  Blending with Short i, a

- **Comprehension**

  Story Details

  Classify and Categorize

- **High-Frequency Words**

  and, I, is, said

- **Beginning Reading Concepts**

Diagnostic/Placement Evaluation

- Individual Reading Inventory
- Running Record
- Phonics and Decoding Inventory
- Grade K Diagnostic/Evaluation
- Grade 1 Diagnostic/Evaluation
- Grade 2 Diagnostic/Evaluation
- Grade 3 Diagnostic/Evaluation

Test Preparation

- Standardized Test Preparation Practice Book

Assessment Checklist

Student .... Grade ....

Teacher ....

	Dan and Dad	Dad, Dan, And I	I Am Sam!	Sid Said	Is Sam Mad?	Assessment Summary
LISTENING/SPEAKING						
Participates in oral language experiences						
Listens and speaks to gain knowledge of culture						
Speaks appropriately to audiences for different purposes						
Communicates clearly (gains increasing control of grammar)						
READING						
Demonstrates knowledge of concepts of print						
Uses phonological awareness strategies, including						
• Identifying, segmenting, and combining syllables						
• Producing rhyming words						
• Identifying and isolating initial and final sounds						
Uses letter/sound knowledge, including						
• Applying letter-sound correspondences to begin to read						
• Phonics and Decoding: initial, final /d/ *D,d*						
• Phonics and Decoding: initial, /s/ *S,s*						
• Phonics and Decoding: initial, final /m/ *M,m*						
• Phonics and Decoding: initial, medial /i/ *I,i*						
• Blending with a, *i*						
Develops an extensive vocabulary, including						
• High-frequency words: *and, I, is, said*						
Uses a variety of strategies to comprehend selections						
• Story Details						
• Classify and Categorize						
Responds to various texts						
Recognizes characteristics of various types of texts						
Conducts research using various sources						
Reads to increase knowledge						
WRITING						
Writes his/her own name						
Writes each letter of the alphabet						
Uses phonological knowledge to write messages						
Gains increasing control of penmanship						
Composes original texts						
Uses writing as a tool for learning and research						

+ Observed   − Not Observed

Introducing
the Theme

All Kinds of Friends
When we work and play together, we learn more about ourselves.

PRESENT THE THEME Read the theme statement to children. Share one thing you have learned about yourself while spending time with friends, such as, I like to dance. Invite volunteers to tell something they know about themselves.

READ THE POEM Read the poem aloud and ask children why they think the children in the poem like to walk home together.

> Wait for me
> and I'll be there
> and we'll walk home
>   together,
> if it's raining
> puddle pails
> or if it's sunny
>   weather.
>
> Wait for me
> and I'll be there
> and we'll walk home
>   together.
> You wear red
> and I'll wear blue,
> and we'll be friends
>   forever.
>
> *Sarah Wilson*

Student Listening Library

DISCUSS THE POEM As you read the poem, have children picture friends walking home together from school. Ask how walking in rainy weather is different from walking in sunny weather.

THEME SUMMARY Each lesson relates to the unit theme *All Kinds of Friends* as well as to the global theme *Connection*. These thematic links will help children to make connections from their experiences with working and playing with friends as they read and listen to the literature of the unit.

Literature selections presented within the first two lessons are also related to the subtheme *Working Together*. Lead children to see that we get a good feeling from working with our friends.

Selections for the third and fourth lessons are more closely tied to the subtheme *Playing Together*. Discuss ways in which children learn about themselves through playing with friends.

The fifth lesson gives children the opportunity to reread their favorite literature selections and discuss the main theme of *All Kinds of Friends*.

Research *and* Inquiry

Theme Project: Wild Animal Murals

 Read the Literature Big Book *Warthogs in the Kitchen,* then lead children in a discussion about the different types of wild animals in Africa. Tell children they will work in groups to find out more information about these animals.

List What They Know Help each group create a list of words or pictures that tells about their animal.

Ask Questions and Identify Resources Cite different ways of finding out more information about these animals. (books, computers, etc.)

Create a Presentation Using information they found, have each group paint and label an Animal Mural for their animal.

inter NET CONNECTION To help children learn more about wild animals, visit **www.mhschool.com/reading**.

CENTER Activities

Setting Up the Centers

Independent Learning Centers will help to reinforce children's skills across all areas of the curriculum. Here's what you will need to help you set up the centers in this unit.

Reading/Language Arts Center

- paper, tagboard, index cards
- markers, crayons
- counters
- quilt or picture of quilt
- food pictures
- audiocassette player
- Student Listening Library Audiocassette

For suggested activities, see pages 67B, 91B, 103B, 115B.

Math Center

- rice, sand, dry cereal
- empty bowls, measuring cups and spoons
- paper cups
- index cards, craft sticks
- markers, counters
- pumpkin cut-outs, blocks

For suggested activities, see pages 69B, 73/74D, 85/86D, 93B, 113B, 117B, 121/122D.

Science Center

- bowl, water
- animal cards, word cards, pet pictures
- stick-on notes, counters

For activities, see pages 89B, 105B, 107B.

Social Studies/ Cultural Perspectives Center

- recycled boxes, cans, trays, egg cartons
- pictures of buildings
- butter, sugar, eggs, flour, baking powder
- spoons, cupcake liners, cupcake pan
- paper, cardboard, craft sticks
- markers, clay, paste, scissors
- basket, lamp

For activities, see pages 77B, 79B, 81B, 83B, 95B.

Art/Music/Drama Center

- construction paper, mural paper
- paper bags, paper cups
- markers, paint, paintbrushes
- coat hangers, string, scissors, craft materials

For activities, see pages 71B, 97/98D, 101B, 109/110D.

Managing the Centers

MANAGEMENT TIP Place activities that are changed frequently in heavy-duty containers that are color-coded to match the centers where they are used.

INSTRUCTIONAL TIP If children have difficulty getting started on a creative project, give them some ideas of how you would begin and give them permission to use your ideas as a springboard.

ASSESSMENT TIP Whenever possible, try to assess children at a mid-point of their activity. This way you will be able to redirect them if they are having difficulty with the activity.

CLEAN-UP TIP Obtain several large cans from the cafeteria. Clean them, cover in decorative paper, and remove all sharp edges. Place these cans in centers to use as trash receptacles. This will reduce movement throughout the room and keep litter off the floor.

Dan and Dad

Children will read and listen to a variety of stories about friends who achieve great results by working together cooperatively and sharing ideas.

Decodable Story,
pages 73–74 of the
Pupil Edition

Listening
Library
Audiocassette

Patterned Book,
page 77B

Teacher Read Aloud,
page 71A

Listening
Library
Audiocassette

ABC Big Book,
pages 67A–67B

Listening
Library
Audiocassette

Literature Big Book,
pages 69A–69B

Pupil Edition,
pages 68–77

Big Book of Real-Life Reading,
page 8

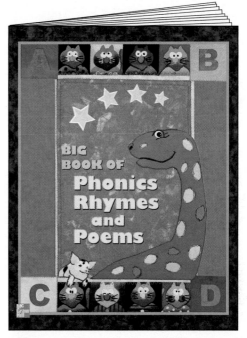

Big Book of Phonics Rhymes and
Poems, pages 14–15, 16

 **Listening**
Library
Audiocassette

ADDITIONAL RESOURCES

Practice Book,
pages 68–77

- **Phonics Kit**
- **Language Support Book**
- **Alternate Teaching Strategies,**
  pages T24–T27

McGraw-Hill School
TECHNOLOGY

Phonics CD-ROM Provides
extra phonics support.

interNET CONNECTION Research & Inquiry Ideas.

Visit www.mhschool.com

Dan and Dad

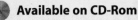
READING AND LANGUAGE ARTS

- **Phonological Awareness**

- **Phonics** initial and final /d/*d*

- **Comprehension**

- **Vocabulary**

- **Beginning Reading Concepts**

- **Listening, Speaking, Viewing, Representing**

DAY 1

Focus on Reading Skills

Develop Phonological Awareness, 66U–66V
"Dinosaurs for Dinner" *Big Book of Phonics Rhymes and Poems*, 14–15

 **Introduce Initial /d/*d*,** 66W–66
Practice Book, 66
Phonics/Phonemic Awareness
Practice Book

 CD-ROM

Read the Literature

Read *The ABC Street Fair* Big Book, 67A–67B
Shared Reading

Build Skills

☑ Numbers, 67C–67
Practice Book, 67

DAY 2

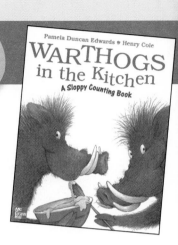

Focus on Reading Skills

Develop Phonological Awareness, 68A–68B
"The Red Balloon" *Big Book of Phonics Rhymes and Poems,* 16

 **Introduce Final /d/*d*,** 68C–68
Practice Book, 68
Phonics/Phonemic Awareness
Practice Book

 CD-ROM

Read the Literature

Read *Warthogs in the Kitchen* Big Book, 69A–69B
Shared Reading

Build Skills

☑ Story Details, 69C–69
Practice Book, 69

- **Cross Curriculum**

 Language Arts, 67B

 Math, 69B

- **Writing**

 Writing Prompt: What booth would you have visited at the street fair?

 Journal Writing, 67B
Letter Formation, 66W

 Writing Prompt: What was the funniest part of the story? Write about it.

 Journal Writing, 69B
Letter Formation, 68C

 = **Skill Assessed in Unit Test**

DAY 3

Tweedy's Toys

Focus on Reading Skills

Develop Phonological Awareness, 70A–70B
"Dinosaurs for Dinner" and "The Red Balloon" *Big Book of Phonics Rhymes and Poems,* 14–16

 **Review /d/d,** 70C–70
Practice Book, 70
Phonics/Phonemic Awareness
Practice Book

 **CD-ROM**

Read the Literature

Read "Tweedy's Toys" Teacher Read Aloud, 71A–71B
Shared Reading

Read the Big Book of Real-Life Reading, 8–9
 Diagram

Build Skills

 High-Frequency Word: *and,*
71C–71
Practice Book, 71

 **Art,** 71B

 Writing Prompt: Think about a favorite toy. Draw a picture and write about it.

DAY 4

Dan and Dad

Focus on Reading Skills

Develop Phonological Awareness, 72A–72B
"Apples"

Review Blending with Short *a* 72C–72
Practice Book, 72
Phonics/Phonemic Awareness
Practice Book

 **CD-ROM**

Read the Literature

Read "Dan and Dad" Decodable Story, 73/74A–73/74D

 Initial and Final /d/d; Blending
 Story Details
 High-Frequency Words: *and*
 Concepts of Print

Build Skills

 Story Details, 75A–75
Practice Book, 75

 Math, 73/74D

 Writing Prompt: Have you ever helped someone at home? Write about it.

Letter Formation
Practice Book, 73–74

DAY 5

by Ton Paul
illustrated by Susan Lexa

Dan and Dad

Focus on Reading Skills

Develop Phonological Awareness, 76A–76B
"Apples"

Review Blending with Short *a*, 76C–76
Practice Book, 76
Phonics/Phonemic Awareness
Practice Book

 **CD-ROM**

Read the Literature

Reread "Dan and Dad" Decodable Story, 77A

Read "Building" Patterned Book, 77B
Guided Reading
 Initial and Final /d/d; Blending
 Story Details
 High-Frequency Words: *and*
 Concepts of Print

Build Skills

 High-Frequency Words: *and, my, a,* 77C–77
Practice Book, 77

 Social Studies, 77B

Writing Prompt: What season is your favorite? Draw a picture and write a few sentences that tell why.

Interactive Writing, 78A–78B

Develop Phonological Awareness

Listen

Dinosaurs for Dinner

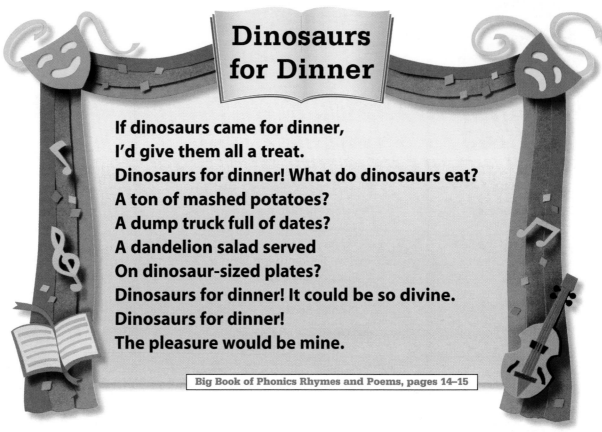

If dinosaurs came for dinner,
I'd give them all a treat.
Dinosaurs for dinner! What do dinosaurs eat?
A ton of mashed potatoes?
A dump truck full of dates?
A dandelion salad served
On dinosaur-sized plates?
Dinosaurs for dinner! It could be so divine.
Dinosaurs for dinner!
The pleasure would be mine.

Big Book of Phonics Rhymes and Poems, pages 14–15

Objective: Develop Listening Skills

LISTEN FOR SYLLABLES

• Read the poem "Dinosaurs for Dinner" aloud. Then say the word *di-no-saur* slowly. Pause between syllables of the word. Ask children to clap and count the syllables as you repeat the word. Identify that there are three syllables.

LISTEN FOR THE NUMBER OF SYLLABLES

• Continue the game, using other words from the poem.

> dinner   potatoes   mine   dandelion

Objective: Listen for Initial /d/

LISTEN TO WORDS IN THE POEM

- Read the title of the poem "Dinosaurs for Dinner." Make the /d/ sound and have children repeat it after you. Say the words in the title that begin with this sound. Have children repeat the words.

- Read the poem line by line. Stop and have children repeat words that begin with /d/.

REPEAT THE WORDS

- Point to objects in your classroom whose names begin with /d/. Have children repeat the word, emphasizing the /d/ sound.

- Invite children to find other objects whose names begin with /d/.

> desk   dish   dime

From Phonemic Awareness to Phonics

Objective: Identify /d/D, d

IDENTIFY THE LETTER FOR THE SOUND

- Explain to children that the letter *d* stands for the sound /d/. Have children repeat the sound after you.

- Display pages 14–15 in the Big Book of Phonics Rhymes and Poems. Point to the letters in the corner and identify them. Have children repeat the sound after you.

REREAD THE POEM

- Read the poem again as you point to each word. Emphasize words with the initial /d/ sound.

- Invite children to repeat the words that begin with /d/ after you.

LOOK FOR WORDS WITH D, d

- Have children look for words that begin with D or d in the poem. Give them self-stick dots to place under the letters.

Dd

Dinosaurs for Dinner

If dinosaurs came for dinner,
I'd give them all a treat.

Dinosaurs for dinner!
What do dinosaurs eat?

A ton of mashed potatoes?
A dump truck full of dates?

Big Book of Phonics Rhymes and Poems, pages 14–15

OBJECTIVES

Children will:

- **identify the letters** *D, d*
- **identify /d/** *D, d*
- **form the letters** *D, d*

MATERIALS

- **letter cards from the Word Play Book**

TEACHING TIP

MANAGEMENT Be aware during the year that children will be at different stages of fine motor development. Keep dashed-line tracing letter charts available during the year for children who are not ready to write independently. Children need ample experiences to gain confidence and strengthen fine motor skills.

ALTERNATE TEACHING STRATEGY

INITIAL /d/*d*

For a different approach to teaching this skill, see page T24.

▶ **Visual/Auditory/ Kinesthetic**

Introduce Initial /d/d

TEACH

Identify /d/ D, d   Tell children they will learn to write the letter that stands for the sound /d/. Write the letters *D, d* on the chalkboard and identify the letters as capital and lowercase. Then write this sentence on the chalkboard, and read it aloud: *Does the dog dig?* Repeat the sentence, emphasizing initial /d/. Invite volunteers to underline words that begin with *d*. Have children say the sound as they hold up their *d* letter cards.

Form D, d   Display letter *D, d* and trace them with your finger. Demonstrate how to write the letters, and describe each motion. With your back to the children, trace large letters *D, d* in the air. Ask children to do the same. Then have them fold a sheet of paper in fourths and write four *D*s on one side and four *d*s on the reverse side. Invite them to fold the paper so that their best letter *d* is on top.

PRACTICE

Complete the Pupil Edition Page   Read the directions on page 66 of the Pupil Edition, and make sure children clearly understand what they are being asked to do. Identify each picture, and complete the first item together. Then work through the paper with the children or have them complete the page independently.

ASSESS/CLOSE

Identify and Use D, d   Say the following list of words, and have children clap when they hear a word that begins with the sound /d/d: *do, tap, den, dog, cat, dip.* Each time they clap, hold up one more finger. Ask children to write *D, d* for each finger you are holding up. Observe children's letter formations.

Dd

Name_____

dog   fish   doctor

jumprope   desk   doll

door   dinosaur   window

deer   lion   dolphin

Write the letters *Dd*. • Say the word that names each picture. • Listen for the sound at the beginning of each word. • Draw a circle around each picture whose name begins with the same sound as *dog*.

McGraw-Hill School Division

66   Unit 2   Introduce Initial /d/*d*

Pupil Edition, page 66

ADDITIONAL PHONICS RESOURCES

Practice Book, *page 66*
Phonics Workbook

McGraw-Hill School
TECHNOLOGY

Phonics CD-ROM
Activities for practice with Initial Letters

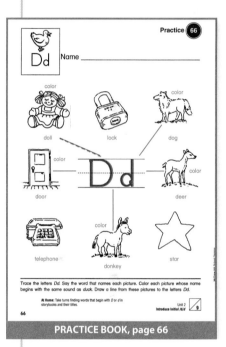

PRACTICE BOOK, page 66

Meeting Individual Needs for Phonics

EASY	ON-LEVEL	CHALLENGE	LANGUAGE SUPPORT
Give children clay, and show them how to roll it into coils. Invite them to use large, laminated *D* and *d* letter cards as guides, on top of which they shape the clay letters. Children say the sound as they shape the capital and lowercase clay letters.	**Give** children pictures of objects that do and do not begin with *d,* for example: *door, dog, bird, cat, doll.* Ask them to identify the pictures of things that begin with *d.* They then write the letter *d* for each picture.	**Have** children write *D* on a sheet of paper, as large or as small as they would like. Then they draw a picture or design that incorporates that letter. They may wish to draw another picture that includes lowercase *d.* Display pictures and invite children to find the letters.	**Have** children make the sound /d/ and use a hand mirror to watch their tongue position. Point out that they should place their tongues behind their teeth as they make the sound. Have them repeat short words: *do, dig, dot, Dan, dip.*

OBJECTIVES

OBJECTIVES

Children will:

- recognize words with initial *D,d*
- recognize the order of letters in the alphabet

CONSTANCE ANDREA KEREMES lives in Arizona. She is the author of children's stories and poems, and is also a children's librarian.

LINDY BURNETT lives in Atlanta, Georgia. Her drawings appear in magazines, advertising, and children's books.

TEACHING TIP

Help children to become familiar with the phrase *ABC order* during the day. Use ABC order to arrange cubbies, books, supplies, and so on. Have children line up in ABC order when it is appropriate. Make sure you use the phrase *ABC order* in these situations.

Read the Big Book

Before Reading

Build Background

EVALUATE PRIOR KNOWLEDGE Ask children to describe different types of fairs that they have been to. Ask children to talk about things they saw. Explain that they will read a book about a street fair that also includes the alphabet.

WHAT DO YOU SEE AT A FAIR? Make a picture chart of things that children have done and seen at fairs. If appropriate, focus on street fairs.

Preview and Predict

DISCUSS AUTHOR AND ILLUSTRATOR Display the Big Book cover and read the title. Then read the author's name and the illustrator's name, and share some background information. Explain that the author writes the words, and the illustrator draws the pictures.

TAKE A PICTURE WALK Take a picture walk through the first four spreads of the book. Talk about what children see, and how the alphabet is a part of the story. See if any of the events at the fair match the events on the class picture chart.

MAKE PREDICTIONS Ask children to predict what the story might be about.

Set Purposes

Tell children you will read to find out what the children do at the street fair.

The ABC Street Fair, pages 4–5

During Reading

Read Together

• Point to the capital and lowercase letters at the top of each page as you say the name of the letter. Run your finger under each word as you read it. Have children repeat the word after you, connecting the initial sound with the letter. *Concepts of Print.*

• Make the /d/ sound and have children say the sound with you. After you read page 6, focus on the initial /d/ sound in each word. Ask if children can think of other words that begin with /d/ to describe desserts. *Phonics*

• As you read the story, have children discuss the illustrations. Ask questions that will help them focus. *Use Illustrations*

• After you read page 26, ask a volunteer to tell you when an umbrella is needed. Ask, "Do the children need an umbrella on the day of the street fair?" Direct the children's attention out the window. Ask, "Do we need an umbrella today?" *Make Inferences*

Beautiful **b**alloons **Bb**

The ABC Street Fair, page 3

After Reading

Return to Predictions and Purposes

• Ask children if they found out what they wanted to learn about the street fair. See if any events at the fair match the class picture chart.

Literary Response

JOURNAL WRITING Ask children to draw something at the street fair that they would like to see or do. Have them write about it in their journals.

ORAL RESPONSE Ask questions such as:

• *Have you ever been to a street fair? What was it like?*

ABC Activity

Use the story to provide additional writing practice. Turn to pages 2 and 19 and have children identify and write the letters.

CENTER Activity

Cross Curricular: Language Arts

NAME GAME Have children create alliterations for their names, using the first initial of their first names. Give examples to show descriptive words (Bouncing Bobby) and possessive words (Katie's Kites). Invite children to draw a picture to match their alliterative phrase.

▶ **Linguistic/Spatial**

OBJECTIVES

Children will:

• identify numbers 1–6

....

MATERIALS

• *The ABC Street Fair*
• number cards

TEACHING **TIP**

MANAGEMENT To help children with the order of numbers 1–10, provide a number line for each child. Fold back the numbers 7–10 so that children can focus on the numbers in this lesson.

Introduce Numbers

PREPARE

Warm up: Say a Number You Know
Ask each child to tell his or her age. Ask: *How many candles were on your last birthday cake? Hold up that many fingers.*

TEACH

Count and Recognize Numbers
Arrange the number cards 1–6 in order. Have children count aloud with you as you point to the cards. Then open to page 2 of the Big Book *The ABC Street Fair* and ask how many apples the helper is holding. Point to each as children count aloud with you. Then ask a volunteer to point to the matching number card. Have children search the classroom for a group that has the same number.

PRACTICE

Match Numbers and Groups
Read the directions on page 67 to the children, and make sure they clearly understand what they are asked to do. Identify each picture, and complete the first item together. Then work through the page with children, or have them complete the page independently.

ASSESS/CLOSE

Review the Page
Check children's work on the Pupil Edition page. Note areas where children need extra help.

Name_____

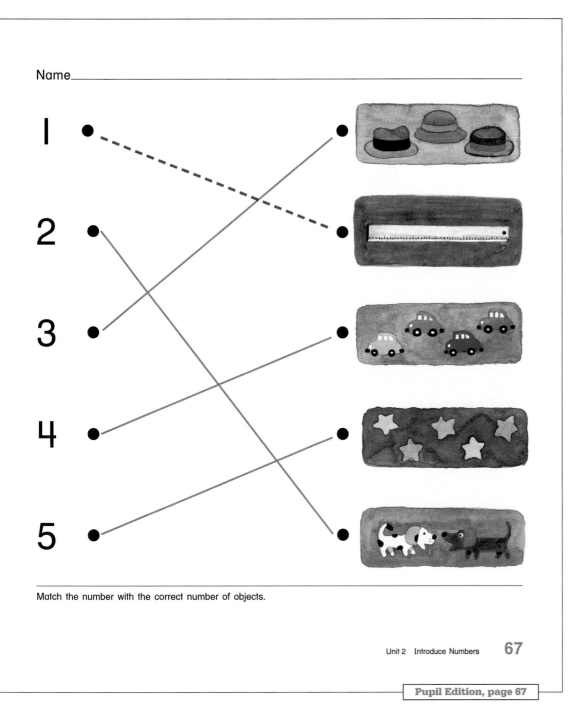

1

2

3

4

5

Match the number with the correct number of objects.

Pupil Edition, page 67

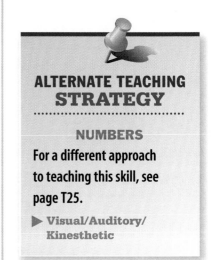

ALTERNATE TEACHING
STRATEGY
·······································
NUMBERS
For a different approach
to teaching this skill, see
page T25.

▶ **Visual/Auditory/
Kinesthetic**

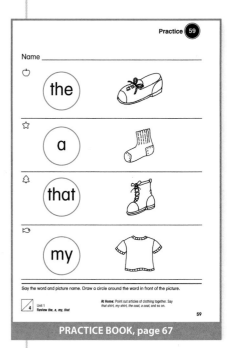

Practice 59

Name_____

the

a

that

my

Say the word and picture name. Draw a circle around the word in front of the picture.

Unit 1
Review *the, a, my, that*

At Home: Point out articles of clothing together. Say
that shirt, my shirt, the coat, a coat, and so on.

59

PRACTICE BOOK, page 67

Meeting Individual Needs for Beginning Reading Concepts

EASY	ON-LEVEL	CHALLENGE	LANGUAGE SUPPORT
Provide 21 counters. Show a number card for 1 and say the number. Ask a child to show 1 counter and say the number. Continue with numbers to 6.	**Provide** 21 counters and number cards 1–6. Ask a child to put the number cards in order. Then have the child put the corresponding number of counters with each number card.	**Ask** pairs of children to take turns tossing a dot cube for 1–6. The first child counts the dots and says the number. The partner shows that number of counters and the corresponding number card. Children take turns.	**Help** children with number recognition by using sandpaper or other tactile numbers. Have children trace the number with their fingers as they say the number name.

Develop Phonological Awareness

Listen

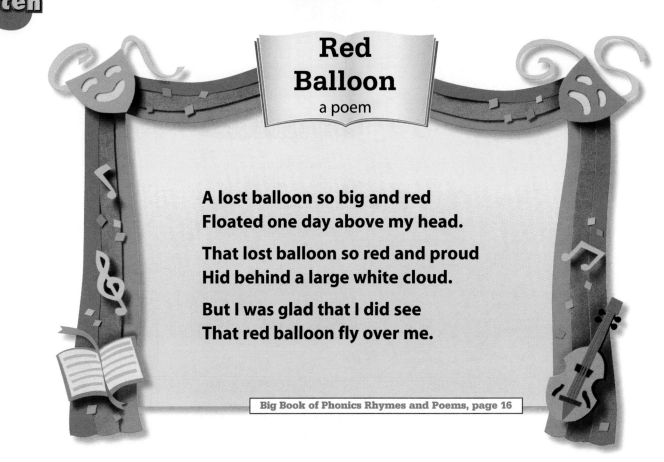

Red Balloon
a poem

A lost balloon so big and red
Floated one day above my head.

That lost balloon so red and proud
Hid behind a large white cloud.

But I was glad that I did see
That red balloon fly over me.

Big Book of Phonics Rhymes and Poems, page 16

Objective: Listen for Action Words

READ THE POEM Read the poem "Red Balloon." Have children retell the story of the poem. Read the first stanza again. Ask children to describe what happened to the balloon. Invite volunteers to role-play the word *floated*. Continue with the words *hid* and *fly*.

PANTOMIME THE ACTION WORDS Read the poem again. Ask children to listen for the words *float, hid*, and *fly*. Have them act out the actions when they hear the words.

> float   hid   fly

SUBSTITUTE ACTION WORDS Reread the first stanza, substituting the word *blew* for *floated*. Have

children pantomime the action as you reread the stanza. Do the same for the second and third stanzas, substituting the following words.

> ran→hid
> glide→fly

Objective: Listen for Final /d/

LISTEN TO WORDS Say the word *red*. Emphasize the final /d/ sound and have children say the sound with you. Then say the word *head* and have children repeat it. Explain that both words have the final /d/ sound.

NOD FOR FINAL /d/ Say the following words. Children *nod* when they hear final /d/.

> hid   proud   cloud
> dog   glad   man
> bed   get   black

PLAY A RHYMING GAME Have children sit in a circle. Hold up a red block and tell children the way to play the game is to say a word that rhymes with *red*. Then say the words *red* and *head* and pass the block to the child sitting to your right. Then have that child say the word *red* and a rhyming word. Continue until everyone has had a turn.

> red-bed   red-sled   red-fed   red-Ted

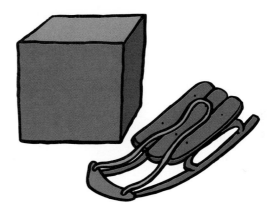

Read Together

From Phonemic Awareness to Phonics

Objective: Identify Final /d/

Explain to children that the letter *d* stands for the /d/ sound. Ask children to say the sound with you. Display the Big Book of Phonics Rhymes and Poems, page 16. Point to the letters in the corner and identify them. Point out the lower-case *d*. Have children say the sound with you.

REREAD THE POEM Reread the poem. Frame each word with final *d*, and have children say the words.

MATCH WORDS WITH FINAL *d* Make word cards to match words in the poem with

final *d*. Invite volunteers to match the cards with words in the poem. Read them together.

> red   floated   head   proud
> hid   cloud   glad   did

DIFFERENTIATE FINAL SOUNDS Say the following words: *red, can, bed*. Ask children to say the words that have final /d/. Repeat with the following groups of words:

> mad, glad, yes; Sid, him, kid;
> car, mud, bud; Ted, Fred, Ken;

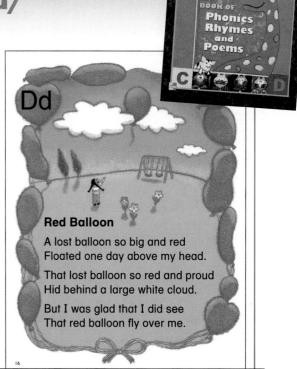

Dd

Red Balloon

A lost balloon so big and red
Floated one day above my head.

That lost balloon so red and proud
Hid behind a large white cloud.

But I was glad that I did see
That red balloon fly over me.

16

Big Book of Phonics Rhymes and Poems, page 16

68B

OBJECTIVES

Children will:

- identify the letter *d*
- identify /d/*d*
- form the letter *d*

....

MATERIALS

- letter cards from the Word Play Book

TEACHING TIP

INSTRUCTIONAL For children who are having difficulty writing letters, break down the process of writing the letter into small steps. Then have them practice the first step and continue with other steps when they are ready.

ALTERNATE TEACHING STRATEGY
....

FINAL /d/*d*

For a different approach to teaching this skill, see page T24.

▶ **Visual/Auditory/ Kinesthetic**

Introduce Final /d/ *d*

TEACH

Identify /d/ *d* Tell children they will learn to write the sound /d/ with the letter *d*. Have children repeat the /d/ sound after you. Provide pictures of objects that end with /d/*d* as well as pictures of objects that end with other sounds. Ask children to identify those pictures whose names end with /d/ by holding up their *d* letter cards.

Form D, d Display the letter *d* and trace it in the air with your back to the children. Ask children to do the same. Then have them write *d* on three squares of paper. Read the following sentence: *Ed is in bed and feels bad.* Each time they hear a word that ends in *d,* they turn over one square.

PRACTICE

Complete the Pupil Edition Page Read the directions on page 68 of the Pupil Edition, and make sure the children clearly understand what they are being asked to do. Identify each picture, and complete the first item together. Then work through the page with the children or have them complete the page independently.

ASSESS/CLOSE

Identify and Use *d* Say the following list of words, and have the children hold up their *d* squares when they hear a word that ends with the letter *d*: *had, big, bed, the, mad.* Ask them to write a *d* on the reverse side of each square for every word they heard that ends in *d*. Collect children's work to check the letter formation.

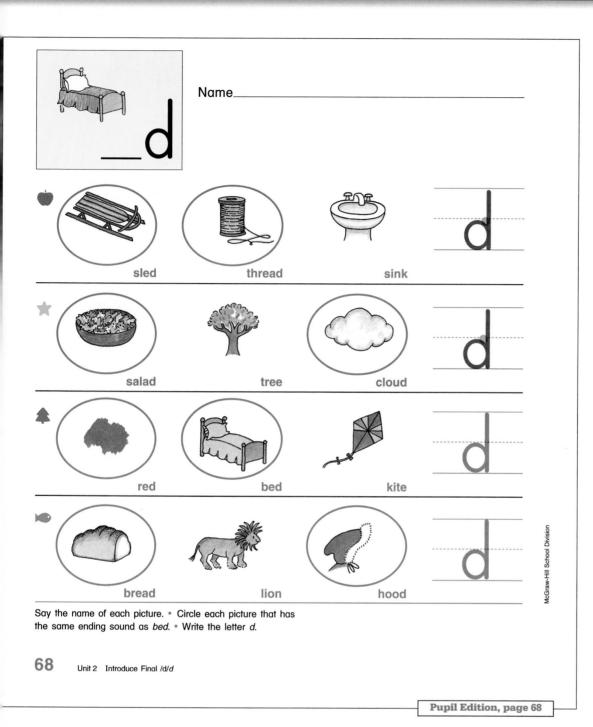

Name _____

sled	thread	sink	d
salad	tree	cloud	d
red	bed	kite	d
bread	lion	hood	d

Say the name of each picture. • Circle each picture that has the same ending sound as *bed*. • Write the letter *d*.

McGraw-Hill School Division

68   Unit 2   Introduce Final /d/d

Pupil Edition, page 68

ADDITIONAL PHONICS RESOURCES

Practice Book, *page 68*
Phonics Workbooks

McGraw-Hill School
TECHNOLOGY

Phonics CD-ROM
Activities for practice with Final Letters

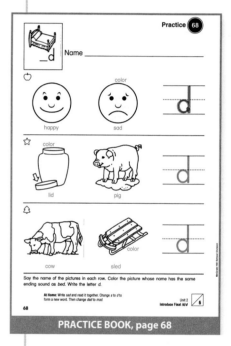

PRACTICE BOOK, page 68

Meeting Individual Needs for Phonics

EASY	ON-LEVEL	CHALLENGE	LANGUAGE SUPPORT
Write the word *red* on the chalkboard and identify it. Ask the children to say the sound at the end of the word. Give children foil trays filled with sand and ask them to write *d* in the sand each time they hear a word that ends with *d*. Say: *sad, in, lid, had, big, bed.*	**Give** children word cards that do and do not end in *d*, for example, *sat, sad, bet, bed, pig, hid.* Have children sort them for final *d* and draw a picture for one of the final *d* words. Ask children to label the picture with the word or with the letter *d*.	**Tell** riddles and have children guess the answers using words that end in *d*, for example: *What is the color of a fire engine?* (red) *This word means the same as unhappy.* (sad) *This is something you sleep on.* (bed)	**Provide** opportunities for children to listen to tape recordings of words and phrases that end in the sound /d/. Then have them practice repeating the words on the tape recorder and listen to their recordings.

- recognize words with final *d*
- look for story details

PAMELA DUNCAN EDWARDS AND HENRY COLE both work at the same school in Virginia. Ms. Edwards is a librarian, and Mr. Cole is a science teacher. They have worked together on several books, including *Some Smug Slug* and *Livingstone Mouse*. Ms. Edwards loves to cook, and Mr. Cole loves to eat!

TEACHING TIP

You may wish to explain that a warthog is a type of wild pig. This African mammal has tusks and lumps on its face. Like other pigs, warthogs eat a wide variety of foods.

Read the Big Book

Before Reading

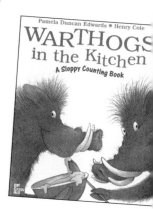

Build Background

EVALUATE PRIOR KNOWLEDGE Display measuring spoons and cups and a baking pan. Ask when people use these tools. Invite children to share their experiences.

WHAT MAKES UP A MUFFIN? Share a simple recipe for muffins. Talk about the ingredients. Invite children to draw a picture that shows the ingredients for muffins.

Preview and Predict

DISCUSS AUTHOR AND ILLUSTRATOR Read the title of the book, and name the author and the illustrator. Share background information about them.

TAKE A PICTURE WALK Then take a picture walk through about half of the book. Point out the numbers on certain pages, and ask children how the numbers might relate to the story.

MAKE PREDICTIONS Ask children to make predictions about what will happen in the story.

Set Purposes

Tell children you will read to find out what the warthogs are going to make.

3

Three cake makers read the book to check how.

8

4

Four scoops of sugar should go in now.

Warthogs in the Kitchen, pages 8–9

9

During Reading

Read Together

• Before you begin to read, point to the first word in the first sentence. Explain that this is where you will begin to read. Continue to track print as you read the story. *Tracking Print*

• After you read page 5, ask children what the warthog is doing and how they know. Point out that even though the warthog is not facing the readers, they can use words and pictures to understand. *Use Story Details*

• After you read page 8, ask children to name the number on the page. Then ask how that number relates to that page of the story. (There are three cake makers.) Ask what type of book the warthogs are reading. (recipe book) *Use Story Details*

• Ask children to make the /d/ sound. Then reread page 14, and ask what word ends with that sound. (should) *Phonics and Decoding*

"I've found a jar of pickles! Should pickles go in, too?"

14

Warthogs in the Kitchen, page 14

After Reading

Return to Predictions and Purposes

Ask children if their predictions about the story were correct. Encourage them to give reasons that explain why the book is a fantasy.

Literary Response

JOURNAL WRITING Ask children to draw a picture that shows one of their favorite parts of the story. Have them write about the picture.

ORAL RESPONSE Engage children in a discussion of a book by asking questions such as:

• *Which part of the story did you think was funny? Why?*
• *Would you like to have a warthog in your kitchen? Why or why not?*

Cross Curricular: Math Center

Set up a container of rice or sand, empty bowls, and a set of measuring cups. Provide simple rebus picture measuring cards for children to follow. Also include direction cards that show children how much sand or rice to measure into each bowl. Have children place the card in front of each bowl as a label.

Children will:

- use story details to understand a story

MATERIALS

- *Warthogs in the Kitchen* Big Book

TEACHING TIP

INSTRUCTIONAL Use self-stick notes and cover the numbers in the Big Book. Have children match the numbers with the words, using picture clues to help.

Review Story Details

PREPARE

Describe the Characters Ask children to recall the story *Warthogs in the Kitchen*. Ask them to describe what a warthog looks like, using as many details as possible.

TEACH

Identify Story Details Turn to page 3 and read the text. Ask how the number relates to that page of the story, and ask what type of book the warthogs are reading. Explain how pictures and text add details that help us to understand the story. Choose other spreads in the book and have children describe what is happening, using text and illustrations to focus on story details.

PRACTICE

Complete the Pupil Edition Page Read the directions on page 69 to the children, and make sure they clearly understand what they are asked to do. Identify each picture, and complete the first item together. Then work through the page with children or have them complete the page independently.

ASSESS/CLOSE

Review the Page Review children's work, and note children who are experiencing difficulty.

Name _____

  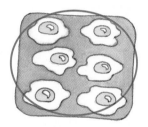

Think about the story "Warthogs in the Kitchen." • In each row, circle the pictures that show something from the story.

Pupil Edition, page 69

ALTERNATE TEACHING STRATEGY

· ·

STORY DETAILS

For a different approach to teaching this skill, see page T26.

▶ **Visual/Auditory/ Kinesthetic**

PRACTICE BOOK, page 69

Meeting Individual Needs for Comprehension

EASY	ON-LEVEL	CHALLENGE	LANGUAGE SUPPORT
Hold up a measuring cup, and have children describe it, using as many details as possible. Then hold up a measuring spoon and do the same. Talk about how the tools are alike and different.	**Work** together to have children describe your classroom. Begin by focusing on one area, and write down descriptions that children dictate. Ask questions that help them focus on details. Continue with other areas.	**Provide** books with pictures or photographs of unusual animals. Ask children to describe the animals, using as many details as possible. Then read about the animal, sharing facts of interest.	**Ask** children to describe something they are wearing. Focus on color, material, patterns, and so on. Explain that children are using details in their descriptions.

Develop Phonological Awareness

Listen

Dinosaurs for Dinner
a poem

The Red Balloon
a poem

If dinosaurs came for dinner,
I'd give them all a treat.
Dinosaurs for dinner!
What do dinosaurs eat?
A ton of mashed potatoes?
A dump truck full of dates?
A dandelion salad served on
    dinosaur-sized plates?
Dinosaurs for dinner!
    It could be so divine.
Dinosaurs for dinner!
    The pleasure would be mine.

A lost balloon so big and red
Floated one day above my
    head.
That lost balloon so red and
    proud
Hid behind a large white cloud.
But I was glad that I did see
That red balloon fly over me.

Big Book of Phonics Rhymes and Poems, pages 14–15, 16

Objective: Focus on Syllables

READ THE POEM Read the poem "Dinosaurs for Dinner." Invite children to join in on the repeating line.

CLAP FOR SYLLABLES Ask: *Do dinosaurs eat potatoes?* Have children say *potatoes* and clap the syllables with you. Repeat the question, substituting *dates* and *salad* for *potatoes*. Have children clap for each syllable.

> potatoes   dates   salad

PLAY A GAME Collect pictures of food and place them in a box. Invite a volunteer to choose a picture. The child asks *Do dinosaurs eat...?*, adding the food name and clapping the syllables.

Objective: Listen for /d/

LISTEN FOR INITIAL /D/ Read the title "Dinosaurs for Dinner." Emphasize the initial /d/ sound. Have children say the /d/ sound. Say the word *dance* and ask if *dance* begins like *dinosaur*. Invite children to dance in place. Reread the poem, having children dance when they hear /d/ at the beginning of a word.

LISTEN FOR FINAL /D/ Read the poem "The Red Balloon," stressing the words with final /d/. Have children say the /d/ sound. Distribute red paper and point out that the word *red* ends with the /d/ sound. Say words from the poem. Have children hold up their paper if they hear a word that ends with /d/.

> lost   red   proud   hid   see

IDENTIFY WORDS WITH /D/ Say the following word pairs. Ask volunteers to identify the word with the /d/ sound.

dog/can	good/kite	book/sad
duck/mat	you/road	dig/car
pot/bed	bread/man	dip/let

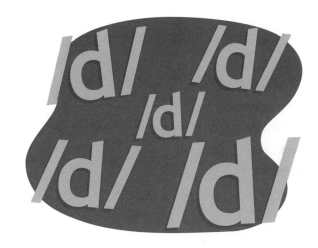

Read Together

From Phonemic Awareness to Phonics

Objective: Identify /d/D,d

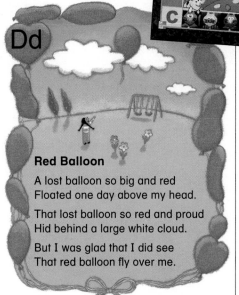

IDENTIFY THE LETTER Display the Big Book of Phonics Rhymes and Poems, pages 14–15 and 16. Point to the letters and identify them. Say the sound the letters stand for.

REREAD THE POEM Reread the poem. Frame each word that has the letter *d* and emphasize the /d/ sound.

FIND WORDS WITH D, d Write the letters *D, d* on an index card. Have a volunteer use the card to point to a word in the poem with *D* or *d*. Say the word.

Dd

Dinosaurs for Dinner

If dinosaurs came for dinner,
I'd give them all a treat.

Dinosaurs for dinner!
What do dinosaurs eat?

A ton of mashed potatoes?
A dump truck full of dates?

Dd

Red Balloon

A lost balloon so big and red
Floated one day above my head.

That lost balloon so red and proud
Hid behind a large white cloud.

But I was glad that I did see
That red balloon fly over me.

Big Book of Phonics Rhymes and Poems, 14–15   Big Book of Phonics Rhymes and Poems, 16

OBJECTIVES

Children will:

- identify and use the letter /d/D, d
- write the letters D, d

....

MATERIALS

- letter cards from the Word Play Book

TEACHING TIP

INSTRUCTIONAL As re-inforcement for letter formation, have children form a *d* using their fingers. First have them form a circle with the thumb and forefinger of their left hand. Then tell them to use the forefinger of the right hand to form the straight line of the *d*.

ALTERNATE TEACHING STRATEGY

....

LETTER /d/d

For a different approach to teaching this skill, see page T24.

▶ **Visual/Auditory/ Kinesthetic**

Review /d/d

TEACH

Identify and use /d/ D, d

Remind children that some people have names that begin with *D*. Ask if anyone in the class has a name that begins with *D*. Also ask children if any members of their family or any of their pets have names that begin with *D*. Repeat the names aloud, emphasizing the initial /d/ sound. Have the children say the sound as they trace capital letter *D* in the air.

Tell children they will find and write the letter *d* at the beginning and at the end of words. Write *Dad* on the chalkboard. Have children repeat the /d/ sound after you. Form a circle and tell the following story. Ask children to sit *down* when they hear a word that begins with a *d* and to stand when they hear a word that ends in a *d*. Say: *Dan's dog was sick and felt bad. Dan said "Go to bed." The dog was glad he did.* Point out that on the word *did*, children should start out sitting and end up standing.

Write and use D, d

Write the story you told in the circle on the chalkboard. Read it aloud, pointing to each word. Ask children to locate all words that begin with *d*, and have them write a *D* or *d* to match each word. Then repeat the activity for words that end with *d*. Talk about the forms and positions that are used more or less in the story.

PRACTICE

Complete the Pupil Edition Page

Read the directions on page 70 of the Pupil Edition, and make sure children clearly understand what they are being asked to do. Identify each picture and complete the first item together. Then work through the page with the children, or have them complete the page independently.

ASSESS/CLOSE

Identify and Use D, d

Write *d____* and *____d* on the chalkboard. Make the following word cards and show them one at a time: *pad, dip, red, mad, do, dot*. Read the word, and have the children point to the *d* position in the headings. Place the cards on the chalkboard ledge below their heading.

Name_____

Say the name of the picture. • Where do you hear the sound /d/d? • Write *d* in the correct position to show if it is the beginning sound (as in *dog*), or the ending sound (as in *cloud*).

McGraw-Hill School Division

Pupil Edition, page 70

ADDITIONAL PHONICS RESOURCES

Practice Book, *page 70*
Phonics Workbook

McGraw-Hill School
TECHNOLOGY

Phonics CD-ROM
Activities for practice with Initial and Final Letters

PRACTICE BOOK, page 70

Meeting Individual Needs for Phonics

EASY	ON-LEVEL	CHALLENGE	LANGUAGE SUPPORT
Form a circle. Ask one child, *Did you walk to school?* The child answers, *I did/did not.* Then he or she turns to the next child in the circle and asks a question that begins with *Did you?* Each time the answer is *I did,* have children trace a *d* in the air.	**Write** *D____* and *d____* to represent initial *d* and *____d* to represent final *d.* Place the following word cards on the chalkboard ledge, and have children match the card to the appropriate position: *Dan, mud, sad, dog, Deb, had, dip, bed.*	**Help** children recall words that begin and end in /d/, for example: *mad, dip, lid, dig, den, bed, bud, dot.* Ask children to use one of the words in a sentence. Then have them illustrate their sentence.	**To** reinforce initial and final /d/d, suggest names that begin or end with /d/ to fill in the blank as children chant *Dan and ___.* Invite children to suggest names, such as *Deb, Dave, Donna, Sid, Ted.*

70

Teacher Read Aloud

Tweedy's Toys

By Constance Andrea Keremes

Tucked away in a forgotten corner of a very big, very busy city was a tiny toy shop. Tweedy's Toys was the name of the shop. It was owned by a little old man named Mr. Tweedy.

Early each morning, Mr. Tweedy would shuffle down the stairs from the loft where he lived above the shop. Munching the last of his breakfast toast, he would set about opening up the shop for business. First he polished the long glass counter until it shone like a mirror. Mr. Tweedy always smiled at his reflection.

"Hello there, handsome," he chuckled.

Then Mr. Tweedy shook out his feather duster and dusted all the toys along the rows and rows of shelves in the shop. Boxed games and bouncing balls, baby dolls and bobbing boats—they all got a wipe and a wink from Mr. Tweedy, who loved and cared for his toys as if they were his own little children.

Of all his many toys, the one that Mr. Tweedy liked best was the model train that he kept in his shop window.

Continued on page T2

Oral Comprehension

LISTENING AND SPEAKING Ask children if they have a favorite toy. Explain that you will read a story about a toy store that had some very special toys. Encourage them to think of pictures in their minds as you read.

When you are finished, focus on the story's plot by asking: *Why was Mr. Tweedy sad? What did the little train do? Who visited Mr. Tweedy's store at the end of the story?*

Activity Have children draw a picture of the train in the story. Then have small groups act out a favorite part of the story. Encourage them to use facial expressions, movements, gestures, and appropriate voices to add to their characterizations.

▶ **Kinesthetic/Interpersonal**

Real-Life Reading

Funnel

Engine

Wheels

Can you name the pa
of the train?

Door

Car

Big Book of Real-Life Reading, pages 8–9

Objective: Use a Diagram

READ THE PAGE Discuss model trains and actual trains that children have seen or ridden. Remind them of the story "Tweedy's Toys." Ask children to name parts of a train. Then explain that you will show them a diagram of a train. A diagram is a picture that shows how something looks or works. Then read the page and discuss the diagram.

ANSWER THE QUESTION Read the sentence. Read the words, and invite volunteers to point to each part of the train as its label is read. Ask: *What does the engine do? What other vehicles have engines?*

Cross Curricular: Art

CHOO-CHOO! Provide construction paper, scissors, and markers. Ask each child to draw a picture of a train car. Encourage them to fill their train car with their favorite things. Then have them cut out the cars and make a train display on your wall. Have volunteers describe some of the things they chose to include in their train car. Ask the class to name the parts of the train, as labels are attached to the train display.

▶ **Linguistic/Spatial**

OBJECTIVES

Children will:

- identify and read the high-frequency word *and*

....

MATERIALS

- word cards from the Word Play Book

TEACHING TIP

INSTRUCTIONAL Ask children to make the /d/ sound at the end of the word. Then say the word: *sad*. Invite them to say other rhyming words that end with /ad/.

Introduce High-Frequency Words: *and*

PREPARE

Listen to Words   Explain to children that they will be learning a new word: *and*. Say the following sentence: "I like Nan and Dan." Say the sentence again, and ask children to raise their hands when they hear the word *and*. Repeat with the sentence: *I see red and green flowers.*

TEACH

Model Reading the Word in Context   Give a word card to each child, and read the word. Reread the sentence, and have children raise their hands when they hear the word.

Identify the Word   Write the sentence above on the chalkboard. Track print and read each sentence. Children hold up their word card when they hear the word *and*. Then ask volunteers to point to and underline the word *and* in the sentence.

Write the Word   Review how to write the letters *a, n,* and *d*. Have children practice writing the letters in the air, as you stand with your back to the class. Then children practice writing and tracing the word.

PRACTICE

Complete the Pupil Edition Page   Read the directions on page 71 to the children, and make sure they clearly understand what they are asked to do. Complete the first item together. Then work through the page with children, or have them complete the page independently.

ASSESS/CLOSE

Review the Page   Review children's work, and note children who are experiencing difficulty or need additional practice.

Name _____

and

Nan   <u>and</u>   Dan

Dan   and   Dad

Dad   and   Nan

Read the words under the pictures. • Draw a line under the word *and*.

Unit 2   Introduce High-Frequency Words: *and*   **71**

Pupil Edition, page 71

ALTERNATE TEACHING STRATEGY

HIGH-FREQUENCY WORDS

For a different approach to teaching this skill, see page T27.

▶ **Visual/Auditory/ Kinesthetic**

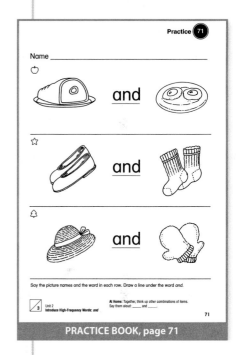

PRACTICE BOOK, page 71

Meeting Individual Needs for Vocabulary

EASY	ON-LEVEL	CHALLENGE	LANGUAGE SUPPORT
Write the word *and* on tagboard with writing lines. Use large letters and laminate. Children trace the letters as they use the word *and* in sentences.	**Have** children write their names on index cards. Then put the cards in a bag, and have a volunteer pick out two cards. Read the names: *Jake and Mary*. These children stand up. Continue with other volunteers.	**Have** children write or dictate sentences about their preferences, such as: *I like apples and grapes. I like books about dogs and cats.* Have them highlight the word *and*.	**Put** crayons in a box, and invite a child to pick out two. He or she completes the sentence, *I have a (red) and a (blue) crayon.* Other children trace the word *and* on their word cards.

71

Develop Phonological Awareness

Listen

Apples
a poem

Pick an apple, Nan.
Pick an apple, Dan.
One for Mom and one for Dad.
Apples, apples make us glad!

Objective: Focus on Context

READ THE POEM Read the poem "Apples." Repeat it several times until children are familiar with the words.

PICTURE THE SCENE Read the poem again. This time ask children to close their eyes and picture what is happening. Then ask questions about the poem.

> Who is picking apples?
> Who are the apples for?
> How do the apples make them feel?

SUBSTITUTE WORDS Tell children that you will read the first line of the poem and change one word. Then say: *Pick an orange, Nan.* Help children determine that *orange* is the new word. Continue reading each line and changing one word.

> Eat an apple, Dan.
> One for Mom and two for Dad.
> Apples, apples make us sad.

72A *Dan and Dad*

Objective: Blending Short *a* with /d/

LISTEN FOR THE SEGMENTED WORD Invite children to listen as you read the poem "Apples." Explain that you will read one word in a funny way. Then read the poem, segmenting each sound in *Dad*. Help children determine that *Dad* was read differently.

> /d/   /a/   /d/

MODEL BLENDING WITH BLOCKS Get two red blocks and one blue block. Say /d/, and set a red block on one end of a table. Say /a/, setting the blue block in the middle of the table. Say /d/, and place the last red block on the opposite end of the table. Starting from the left, point to each block, and say the sounds—/d/ /a/ /d/. Repeat, inviting children to join in. Push the blocks closer, and increase the speed with which you point to the sounds. Continue the activity until the blocks are sandwiched together and the word *dad* blends smoothly.

MORE BLENDING WITH BLOCKS Pass out two red blocks and one blue block to each child. Have them practice blending the word *dad* on their own.

From Phonemic Awareness to Phonics

Read Together

Objective: Identify Word Endings

LISTEN FOR RHYMING WORDS Read the last two lines of the poem "Apples," stressing the rhyming words. Ask children to name the words that rhyme, and then write them on the board.

> **Dad   glad**

IDENTIFY THE LETTERS Invite a volunteer to circle the letters in the words that are the same. Then identify the letters. Ask children to say the sounds these letters stand for.

NAME OTHER RHYMING WORDS Invite children to name other words that rhyme with *Dad* and *glad*. Write their suggestions on the board, circling the letters *ad* to show that these words also have the same ending letters.

> **sad   mad   pad   bad**

FIND WORDS Write the following words on index cards: *Dad, glad, mad, pad, lid, net, boy, bag.* Display four cards—two with

words that end with the letters *ad* and two with words that do not. Ask children to find the words that have the same ending letters. Say the words as they are identified, and have children repeat them after you.

OBJECTIVES

Children will:

- identify /a/ *a*
- blend and read short *a* words
- write short *a* words
- review /d/

....

MATERIALS

- letter cards from the Word Building Book

TEACHING TIP

INSTRUCTIONAL Write the word *Dad* on the chalkboard, and read it aloud. Pass around pictures of your dad or a dad you know. Talk about this person, using the word *dad* as you tell the children about him.

ALTERNATE TEACHING STRATEGY

....

BLENDING SHORT *a*

For a different approach to teaching this skill, see Unit 1, page T32.

▶ **Visual/Auditory/ Kinesthetic**

Review Blending with short a

TEACH

Identify *a* as the symbol for /a/

Tell children that today they will be reading and writing two new words with the letter *a* that stands for the sound /a/.

- Display the *a* letter card and say /a/. Have children repeat the sound.

BLENDING Model and Guide Practice

- Display a newspaper advertisement and discuss it. Explain that the word *ad* is short for *advertisement*. Place a *d* letter card to the right of the *a*. Blend the sounds together and have children repeat after you: *ad*.

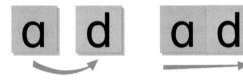

- Read aloud the poem "Apples" on page T72A. Point out the word *Dad*. Place a *D* letter card to the left of the *a*. Blend the sounds together and have children repeat the word *Dad*.

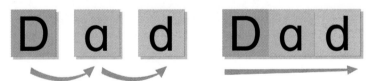

Use the Word in Context

- Have children imagine they are apple farmers who want to place a newspaper ad. Have children tell what their ads would say.

Repeat the Procedure

- Have children tell what they might say as they give an apple to Dad. Ask them to use the word *Dad* in at least one sentence.

PRACTICE

Complete the Pupil Edition Page

Read the directions on page 72 of the Pupil Edition, and make sure children clearly understand what they are being asked to do. Identify each picture, and complete the first item together. Work through the page with children, or have them complete it independently.

ASSESS/CLOSE

Write Short *a* Words

Observe children as they complete page 72. Then have them use letter cards to build the words *ad* and *Dad*.

Name_____

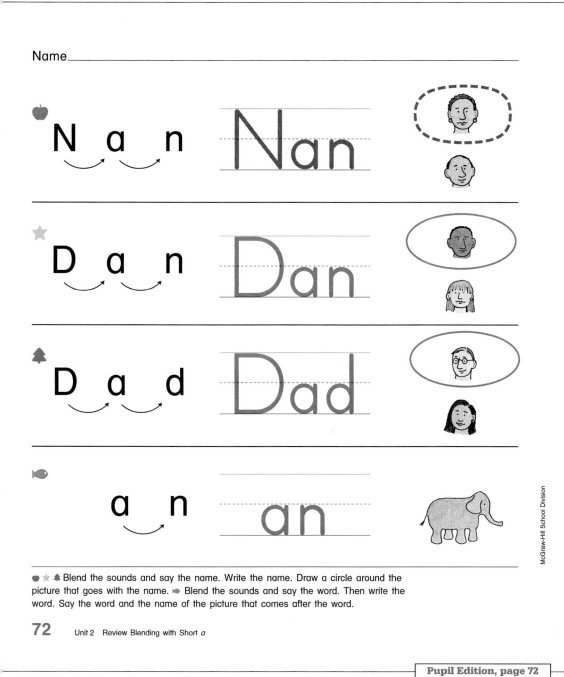

Blend the sounds and say the name. Write the name. Draw a circle around the picture that goes with the name. ➤ Blend the sounds and say the word. Then write the word. Say the word and the name of the picture that comes after the word.

72   Unit 2 • Review Blending with Short *a*

McGraw-Hill School Division

Pupil Edition, page 72

ADDITIONAL PHONICS RESOURCES

Practice Book, *page 72*
Phonics Workbook

McGraw-Hill School
TECHNOLOGY

Phonics CD-ROM
Activities for practice with Blending and Segmenting

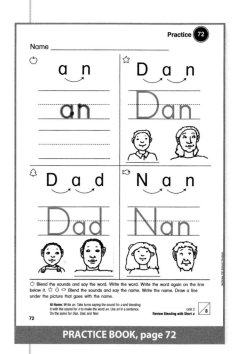

PRACTICE BOOK, page 72

Meeting Individual Needs for Phonics

EASY	ON-LEVEL	CHALLENGE	LANGUAGE SUPPORT
Have children cut out magazine pictures of people who look like dads. Ask children to glue the pictures to construction paper to make a "dad collage." Help children label their collages with the word *Dad*. Ask each child to blend and say the word *Dad* after it is written.	**Make** a "flip book." Write the word *ad* on the right side of a sentence strip. Write the letter *D* on an index card and staple it on the strip to the left of *ad*. Blend and read the word *Dad*, flip up the *D* card, and blend and read the word *ad*. For extra fun, flip faster and faster.	**Hold** up an *ad* word card, blend the sounds, and say the word. Have children brainstorm and write other words that rhyme with *ad* (*Dad, sad, fad, pad*). Invite children to read their word lists and use at least one word in a sentence.	**Write** the name *Dad* on the chalkboard, and have children blend sounds to say the word. Explain that *Dad* is another way to say *father*, and when it is used as a name, it is spelled with a capital *D*. Ask children to talk about their dads or dads they know.

72

Guided Instruction

BEFORE READING

PREVIEW AND PREDICT Take a brief **picture walk** through the book, focusing on the illustrations.

• Who is this story about? Where does it take place?

• Do you think the story is realistic or make-believe? Why?

SET PURPOSES As children look through the book, ask them what they would like to find out about as they read the story. Ask them questions, such as *Who is Dan?* or *Who is Dad?*

TEACHING TIP

To put book together:

1. Tear out the story page.

2. Cut along dotted line.

3. Fold each section on fold line.

4. Assemble book.

MANAGEMENT Be aware that some children will have difficulty focusing their attention when they are in a large group. Sitting these children near you will help you keep eye contact with them.

Dan and Dad

Dan

3

Nan

2

Dad

4

Guided Instruction

DURING READING

☑ **Letter Identification:** *D, d*

☑ **Story Details**

☑ **Concepts of Print**

☑ **High-Frequency Word:** *and*

(1) CONCEPTS OF PRINT Ask children to look at the title page. Model how to run your finger from left to right under each word. Then have children repeat the words as they track print.

(2) USE ILLUSTRATIONS Have children look at the picture on page 2. Ask children where they think Nan is. (in her backyard) Ask children what picture clues helped them.

(3) PHONICS: LETTER *D, d* Ask children to identify the first letter of the word on page 3. Then blend each sound to read the word: *D-a-n Dan*

(4) PHONICS: LETTER *D, d* Have children frame the letters of the word on page 4 and identify *D* and *d*.

LANGUAGE SUPPORT

ESL As children read the story, point out the way in which Nan, Dan, and Dad are identifying themselves. (by pointing to themselves with their thumbs or index fingers) Then have children identify themselves this way.

Guided Instruction

DURING READING

(5) **STORY DETAILS** Have children look at the picture on page 5. Ask children to describe what they think the weather is like. Ask children what details from the story give them clues.

(6) **CONCEPTS OF PRINT** Ask children to look at the words on page 6. Have children count the letters in each word. Ask them how many letters the first word has. (2) the second. (3) Then ask them which word is longer. (Nan)

(7) **HIGH-FREQUENCY WORD:** *and* Point to the second word on page 7 and track print as you read it: *and*. Have children do the same.

(8) **STORY DETAILS** Have children look at the picture on page 8. Then ask them to describe the photograph, using details they know from reading the story.

PHONICS: LETTER D
HOW TO ASSESS Have children locate and count all the capital D's in the story. (6) Then ask them to locate and count all the lower case d's. (6)

FOLLOW-UP
Have children make capital and lowercase d's using fingerpaints or a sand table.

my dad

5

Dan and my dad

7

my Nan

6

Dan and my Nan

8

Guided Instruction

AFTER READING

RETURN TO PREDICTIONS AND PURPOSES
Ask children if their predictions about the story were correct. Ask children if they found out who Nan, Dad, and Dan are.

RETELL THE STORY Have children retell the story in their own words. Allow children to refer to their book as necessary. Invite children to use picture clues to help them with story details.

LITERARY RESPONSE To help children respond to the story, ask:

- Have you ever raked leaves? Who did you rake leaves with?

- Do you have a special friend?

Invite children to draw and write about something they can do with a special friend.

CENTER
Activity

Cross Curricular: Math

SORTING LEAVES Cut out leaves of different shapes and colors. Have children sort the leaves by color and shape. Have children solve simple number stories written on index cards:
2 [red leaves] 2 [brown leaves] ___leaves in all

▶ Logical/Mathematical

OBJECTIVES

Children will:

• use story details to understand a story

MATERIALS

• *Dan and Dad*

TEACHING TIP

INSTRUCTIONAL

Encourage children to reread books. Point out that they may notice different details and have a better understanding when they reread a story.

Introduce Story Details

PREPARE

Discuss Story Details
Ask children to recall the story *Dan and Dad*. Ask how the story begins and who the characters are. Ask children to recall details about what the characters were doing, what they were wearing, and where the story takes place. Make a list of details.

TEACH

Review Details in the Story
Reread the story, stopping after each spread and talking about the details. Compare the story details in the list to details in the story and in the illustrations. Explain that noting details in the story makes it more interesting.

PRACTICE

Complete the Pupil Edition Page
Read the directions on page 75 to the children, and make sure they clearly understand what they are asked to do. Identify each picture, and complete the first item together. Then work through the page with children or have them complete the page independently.

ASSESS/CLOSE

Review the Page
Review children's work, and note children who are experiencing difficulty.

Name _____

Think about the story "Dan and Dad." • In each row, circle the picture that shows something from the story.

Unit 2 Review Story Details **75**

Pupil Edition, page 75

ALTERNATE TEACHING STRATEGY

STORY DETAILS

For a different approach to teaching this skill, see page T26.

▶ **Visual/Auditory/Kinesthetic**

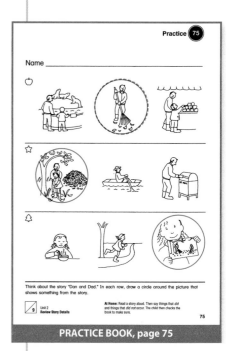

PRACTICE BOOK, page 75

Meeting Individual Needs for Comprehension

EASY	ON-LEVEL	CHALLENGE	LANGUAGE SUPPORT
Show children pictures from magazines and ask them to describe details that they see. Talk about what the people are doing, where they are, what they are wearing, and what might happen next.	**Have** partners work together. One child pretends to pose for a photograph. The partner draws the child, adding as many details as possible to the drawing. Then children switch roles.	**Have** children draw a picture by following your directions, such as: *Draw a small boy wearing a red shirt. He has brown curly hair. He is standing next to a tree.* Then have children compare their pictures and talk about the details.	**Invite** children to bring in a favorite photograph from home. Look at photographs together, pointing out details. Use descriptive words to talk about the photos. Invite children to repeat words after you.

Develop Phonological Awareness

Listen

Apples
a poem

Pick an apple, Nan.
Pick an apple, Dan.
One for Mom and one for Dad.
Apples, apples make us glad!

Objective: Determine Words in a Sentence

READ THE POEM Read the poem "Apples." Repeat it several times, inviting children to join in on the last line.

> Apples, apples make us glad!

COUNT WORDS Provide children with connecting cubes. Read the first line of the poem, pausing between words. Have children take one cube for each word. Have them connect and count the cubes. Help children determine there are four words in the first line. Then ask children to set the connected cubes aside.

COMPARE SENTENCES Repeat the activity with the second line of the poem. Have children compare the two lines of cubes to see that both sentences have four words. Then count and compare the number of words in lines three and four.

TRY A LONGER SENTENCE Say a longer sentence. Children join cubes and count the words.

> Nan and Dan pick apples to make a pie.

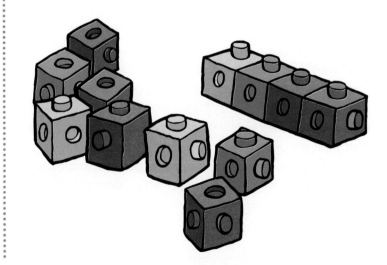

Objective: Blending Short *a* with /n/ and /d/

LISTEN AND BLEND SEGMENTED SOUNDS Say the name *Dan*, segmenting each sound. Repeat several times, increasing the speed until the sounds blend together. Have children identify the name. Repeat the blending activity and encourage children to join in.

BLEND A NAME Say the name *Dan* again, segmenting each sound. Have children determine the name has three sounds. Then divide children into three groups. Assign the first group the sound /d/, the second group /a/, and the last group /n/. Have each group practice saying their sound. Acting like a conductor, point to each group and have children sound out *Dan*. Repeat several times, gradually blending the sounds and saying the name *Dan*.

> **/d/-/a/-/n/—Dan**

BLEND OTHER NAMES Invite children to blend the sounds in other names. Repeat the above activity using the names *Nan* and *Dad*.

> **/n/-/a/-/n/ Nan**
> **/d/-/a/-/d/ Dad**

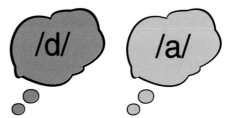

Read Together

From Phonemic Awareness to Phonics

Objective: Identify *an* and *ad* Rhymes

LISTEN FOR RHYMING WORDS Read the first two lines of the poem "Apples." Ask children to name the rhyming words and write them in a column on the board. Repeat with the last two lines of the poem, writing those rhyming words in a separate column.

> | Nan | Dad |
> |-----|------|
> | Dan | glad |

IDENTIFY THE LETTERS Say the words *Nan* and *Dan* and circle *an* in each name. Identify the let-ters and say the sounds. Repeat with the words *Dad* and *glad*. Help children determine that *Nan* and *Dan* do not rhyme with *Dad* and *glad*, because the ending letters are different.

NAME RHYMING WORDS Have children name words that rhyme with either *Nan* or *Dad*. Write each response on an index card. Give the card to the child, who places it on the chalk ledge under the appropriate group of rhyming words. Have the child

show that it matches by framing the ending letters and saying the sounds.

> **Nan Dan fan man pan**
> **Dad glad pad mad sad**

OBJECTIVES

Children will:

- blend and read short *a* words
- write short *a* words
- review /d/ and /n/

MATERIALS

- letter cards from the Word Play Book

TEACHING TIP

INSTRUCTIONAL Write the words *can* and *dad* on the chalkboard. Blend and say the words. Ask children how the words are alike and different in sound, in looks, and in meaning. Explain that the different ending letters make different sounds, so the words are different and have different meanings.

ALTERNATE TEACHING STRATEGY

BLENDING SHORT *a*

For a different approach to teaching this skill, see Unit 1, page T32.

▶ **Visual/Auditory/ Kinesthetic**

Review Blending with short *a*

TEACH

Blend /a/*a* with /n/*n* and /d/*d*

Tell children they will review the /a/, /n/, and /d/ sounds and the letters *a, n,* and *d*. Turn to page T72A and read aloud the poem "Apples." Write the words *an, Nan, Dan,* and *Dad* on the chalkboard, and identify the letters in each word. Ask children to identify how the words on the board are the same and different. Point out that *an, Nan,* and *Dan* all have the letters *an* whereas *Dad* has *ad* at the end.

Identify and Write Blended *an, ad, na,* and *da*

Say: *Dan and Nan picked an apple for Dad.* Write the sentence on the chalkboard in white chalk. Have volunteers underline the *an* in words with pink chalk and the *ad* in words with blue chalk. Have volunteers circle the *na* or *da* in words. Point out the words *Dan* and *Dad,* and have children write the words.

PRACTICE

Complete the Pupil Edition Page

Read aloud the directions on page 76, and make sure children clearly understand what they are being asked to do. Identify each picture, and complete the first item together. Then work through the page with children, or have them complete the page independently.

ASSESS/CLOSE

Identify and Use Short *a, d,* and *n*

Say the following sentence, and have children tap when they hear the word *Dan: I like Dan, and Dan likes me.* Repeat the activity with the following words: *Nan, Dad,* and *an.*

Name_____

Dad) Nan

Dad

Nan (Dan)

Dan

(Nan) Dan

Nan

(Dan) Dad

Dan

Look at each picture. • Read the names. Draw a circle around the name that goes with the picture. • Write the name.

McGraw-Hill School Division

76 Unit 2 Review Blending with Short *a*

Pupil Edition, page 76

ADDITIONAL PHONICS RESOURCES

Practice Book, *page 76*
Phonics Workbook

McGraw-Hill School
TECHNOLOGY

Phonics CD-ROM
Activities for practice with Blending and Segmenting

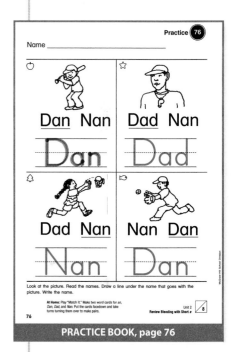

PRACTICE BOOK, page 76

Meeting Individual Needs for Phonics

EASY	ON-LEVEL	CHALLENGE	LANGUAGE SUPPORT
Give children the following word cards in random order: *an, Nan, Dan, Dad.* Have children blend and read the words to find the "odd man out"—the word that does not rhyme. When they come to the word *Dad,* have children say "odd man out"!	**Give** children the following word cards in random order: *an, Nan, Dan, Dad.* Ask children to arrange the cards so that *an* is first and each word after that has only one letter that is different from the previous word. Have children blend the sounds to read the words.	**Give** children the letter cards *a, d,* and *n.* Invite the children to arrange the cards to make as many words as possible, using as many or as few letters as they wish. Possible combinations include: *a, an, ad, Dan, Dad.*	**Write** the word *Dan* on the chalkboard. Explain that *Dan* is a person's name, and that one way to tell is by the capital *D* at the beginning. Write the following words on the board in random order: *Dad, Dan, Nan, an, ad.* Have children identify the names by the capital letters.

76

Reread the Decodable Story

Dan and Dad

Dan and Dad

☑ **Use Illustrations**
☑ **Concepts of Print**
☑ **Initial and Final *D,d***
☑ **High-Frequency Words: *and***

Guided Reading

SET PURPOSES Tell children that when they read the story again, they can find out more about what happened. Explain that you also want them to look for words with initial and final *D, d*. Remind children that they know the word *and* and will see it again in this story.

REREAD THE BOOK As you reread the story, keep in mind any problems children experienced during the first reading. Use the following prompts to guide reading.

• **CONCEPTS OF PRINT** Ask children to look for both the capital *D* and the lower-case *d* as they reread the story. Remind them of when the capital *D* is used. (name)

• **USE ILLUSTRATIONS** Talk about the photograph and how it is part of the illustration.

RETURN TO PURPOSES Ask children if they found out more about what they wanted to know about the story. Ask them if they can now easily identify the word *and*.

LITERARY RESPONSE

 Take photographs of pairs of children in your classroom. Have them write about the photos. You may wish to encourage them to include the word *and* in their writing.

Read the Patterned Book

Building

☑ **Initial and Final** *D,d*
☑ **Story Details**
☑ **High Frequency Word:** *and*
☑ **Concepts of Print**

Building
by Ian Paul
illustrated by Susan Lexa

Guided Reading

PREVIEW AND PREDICT Read the title and the author's and the illustrator's names. Take a **picture walk** through pages 2–4, noting what the boys are doing and what they are making. Have children make a prediction about what will happen in the story.

SET PURPOSES Have children decide what they want to find out from the story. Tell children you will read the story to find out what the boys are doing in the back area. Tell them that the story contains words with the letters *D, d*.

READ THE BOOK Use the following prompts while the children are reading or after they have read independently. Remind them to run their fingers under each word as they read.

Pages 2–3: On page 2, point to the word *and*. Let's read it together: *and*. Can you find the word *and* on page 3? *High-Frequency Words*

Pages 4–5: What capital letters do you see on these pages? (D, N, T) Why are they capitalized? (Because they are names.) *Concepts of Print*

Pages 6–7: What are the boys putting away? (the blocks) *Story Details*

Page 8: Can you find a word that begins with capital *D* on this page? (Dan) Can you find a word that begins with lowercase *d*? (done) *Phonics*

RETURN TO PREDICTIONS AND PURPOSES Ask children if they found out what they needed to know from the story. See if their predictions were correct.

LITERARY RESPONSE The following questions will help focus children's responses:

- What did the boys do together?

- What do you like to do with your friends?

Invite children to draw and write about something they like to do with their friends in their journals.

LANGUAGE SUPPORT

 Read the story again, and encourage children to talk about different things that people build. Look for pictures of different types of buildings and help children identify them (house, school, office buildings, store, etc.) Then have pairs of children reread the story and point out the buildings.

CENTER Activity

Cross Curricular: Social Studies

BUILDING TOGETHER Collect recyclable boxes, cans, meat trays, egg cartons, and so on to create a building center. Have children work in pairs to design and build buildings and sculptures. Display pictures of different types of buildings. Encourage cooperation, and have children clean up when they are finished.

▶ **Spatial/Kinesthetic**

OBJECTIVES

Children will:

- identify and read the high-frequency word *and*

....

MATERIALS

- word cards from the Word Play Book
- *Sid and I*

TEACHING TIP

INSTRUCTIONAL If children have difficulty recognizing letters, provide additional activities. Children can trace or make tactile letters by gluing beans or noodles onto index cards with letters on them.

Review *and, my, a*

PREPARE

Listen to Words   Explain to the children that they will be reviewing a word: *and*.

Say the word together. Then ask children to say rhyming words, such as *sand, band, hand, land,* and so on.

TEACH

Model Reading the Word in Context   Have children reread the decodable book. Ask children to listen for the word *and*.

Identify the Word   Have children look at their word cards, and ask them to look for the words in sentences. Have children read the sentences and track print. Have them put a self-stick note below the word: *and*. Have children move the stick-on note from page to page.

Review High-Frequency Words   Hold up word cards for the following words: *the, a, my, that, and.* Children say the words.

PRACTICE

Complete the Pupil Edition Page   Read the directions on page 77 to the children, and make sure they clearly understand what they are asked to do. Complete the first item together. Then work through the page with children or have them complete the page independently.

ASSESS/CLOSE

Review the Page   Review children's work, and note children who are experiencing difficulty or need additional practice.

Name _____

🍎

Dan (and) Nan

⭐

Nan (and) <u>my</u> Dad

🌲

Dan (and) <u>a</u>

🍎⭐🌲 Read the words. Draw a circle around the word *and*. Draw a line under the word *a*. Draw two lines under the word *my*. 🌲Draw a picture of a friend. Then read the words in this row again with the name of the picture.

Unit 2 Review *and, my, a*   **77**

Pupil Edition, page 77

ALTERNATE TEACHING
STRATEGY

HIGH-FREQUENCY WORDS

For a different approach to teaching this skill, see page T27.

▶ **Visual/Auditory/ Kinesthetic**

Practice 77

Name _____

○ my 🖌️ (and) 🎨

☆ a 🪑 (and) 🪑🪑

🔔 my (and)

○ ☆ Read each word and say the picture names. Draw a circle around the word *and*. Draw a line under the word *my*. Draw two lines under the word *a*. 🔔 Draw a circle around the word *and*. Draw a line under the word *my*. Draw a picture of two things that belong to you.

Unit 2
Review *and, my, a*

At Home: Play "Pair Up." You say *a ___.* The child says *and ___,* completing the pair.

77

PRACTICE BOOK, page 77

Meeting Individual Needs for Vocabulary

EASY	ON-LEVEL	CHALLENGE	LANGUAGE SUPPORT
Give a word card to partners. Have them tell a short story about themselves, using the word *and*. Give an example, such as: *Jan and Nate like to play together. They play with blocks and clay.* Children hold up the word card when they say *and*.	**Invite** children to think of rhymes using the word *and*. Give partners word cards, and give examples, such as: *house and mouse; dog and a log; cat and a mat.* Children can draw pictures of their rhyming words.	**Give** each child a word card. Then have them make a string of words based on a topic you give them, such as *Things in the Library: books and tapes and magazines and chairs and tables and computers.* Children hold up their word cards when they add a word.	**Have** children talk about people in their families, using the word *and*. Write the word on the chalkboard and point to it when children say the word.

Interactive Writing

Write a Recipe

GRAMMAR/SPELLING CONNECTIONS
Model subject-verb agreement, complete sentences, and correct tense so that students may gain increasing control of grammar when speaking and writing.

Prewrite

LOOK AT THE STORY PATTERN Reread the story *Warthogs in the Kitchen*. Talk about the sequence of events as the warthogs make the cupcakes. Explain that cooks need to follow steps in order. A recipe helps to show the order of the steps.

Draft

WRITE A CLASS RECIPE Explain that children are going to create phrases to tell the steps to make modelling clay.

- Begin by making a list of ingredients. Then invite children to help you write phrases that explain what to do. Help as necessary, and write the phrases on sentence strips. Leave space for children to write the word *I*.

- Read the sentence strips together and make sure they are in the correct order. Children may draw illustrations to show each step of the recipe.

Publish

CREATE A RECIPE Transcribe the sentence strips onto a chart. Include the illustrations.

MODELLING CLAY RECIPE

1 cup flour	1 tablespoon oil
1/2 cup salt	1 cup water
2 teaspoons cream of tartar	
food coloring	

1. I mix ingredients in a pan.
2. I cook over medium heat and stir.
3. I let the clay cool when it makes a lump.
4. I knead the clay.
5. I store the clay in a container.

Presentation Ideas

MAKE MODELLING CLAY Display the recipe chart and follow the steps to make modelling clay. Talk about the process and the results.

▶ **Representing/Speaking**

MAKE CUPCAKES Use the modelling clay to make cupcakes like the warthogs may have made. Provide some tools, such as craft sticks and plastic spoons for sculpting. Have children show their cupcakes and describe them.

▶ **Speaking/Listening**

Meeting Individual Needs for Writing

EASY	ON-LEVEL	CHALLENGE
Draw Pictures Have small groups draw pictures to show the steps to make modelling clay. Then they put the steps in order.	**Clay Words** Invite children to make a list of words that describe the modelling clay. Have them dictate their words. Then reread them together, and ask children how they could sort the words.	**Rewrite the Story** Create a tale of the warthogs making modelling clay. Ask children how the story might change. Have children dictate their ideas, and write as appropriate. Children then illustrate their stories.

Dad, Dan, and I

The variety of literature in this lesson will offer children opportunities to read and listen to stories about people working with friends toward a common goal.

Decodable Story, pages 85–86 of the Pupil Edition

Listening Library Audiocassette

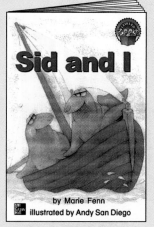

Patterned Book, page 89B

Legend of the Blue Bonnet
An old tale of Texas, retold and illustrated by Tomie dePaola

Teacher Read Aloud, page 83A

ABC Big Book, pages 79A–79B

Listening Library Audiocassette

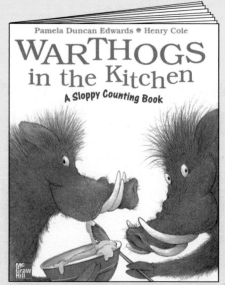

Literature Big Book, pages 81A–81B

Listening Library Audiocassette

Pupil Edition,
pages 78–89

Big Book of Real-Life Reading,
page 10

Big Book of Phonics Rhymes and
Poems, pages 46–47, 48

 **Listening**
Library
Audiocassette

ADDITIONAL RESOURCES

Practice Book,
pages 78–89

- **Phonics Kit**
- **Language Support Book**
- **Alternate Teaching Strategies,**
  pages T25, T27, T28, T29

McGraw-Hill School
TECHNOLOGY

Phonics CD-ROM Provides
extra phonics support.

inter**NET**
CONNECTION Research & Inquiry Ideas.

Visit www.mhschool.com

Dad, Dan, and I

READING AND LANGUAGE ARTS

- Phonological Awareness
- Phonics initial /s/s
- Comprehension
- Vocabulary
- Beginning Reading Concepts
- Listening, Speaking, Viewing, Representing

DAY 1

Focus on Reading Skills

Develop Phonological Awareness, 78G–78H
"Sing a Song of Sixpence" *Big Book of Phonics Rhymes and Poems,* 46–47

 **Introduce Initial /s/s,** 78I–78
Practice Book, 78
Phonics/Phonemic Awareness Practice Book

 **Phonics CD-ROM**

Read the Literature

Read *The ABC Street Fair* Big Book, 79A–79B
Shared Reading

Build Skills

☑ Numbers, 79C–79
Practice Book, 79

DAY 2

Focus on Reading Skills

Develop Phonological Awareness, 80A–80B
"Six Silly Seals" *Big Book of Phonics Rhymes and Poems,* 48

 **Review Initial /s/s,** 80C–80
Practice Book, 80
Phonics/Phonemic Awareness Practice Book

 **Phonics CD-ROM**

Read the Literature

Read *Warthogs in the Kitchen* Big Book, 81A–82B
Shared Reading

Build Skills

☑ Classify and Categorize, 81C–81
Practice Book, 81

- Cross Curriculum

 Cultural Perspective, 79B

 Cultural Perspective, 81B

- Writing

 Writing Prompt: Describe and draw something on sale at a street fair.

 Journal Writing, 79B
Letter Formation, 78I

 Writing Prompt: Write about something you have made in your kitchen.

 Journal Writing, 81B
Letter Formation, 80C

☑ = **Skill Assessed in Unit Test**

DAY 3

Legend of the Blue Bonnet

Focus on Reading Skills

Develop Phonological Awareness,
82A–82B
"Sing a Song of Sixpence" and "Six Silly Seals" *Big Book of Phonics Rhymes and Poems,* 46–48
Review /s/s, /d/d, 82C–82
Practice Book, 82
Phonics/Phonemic Awareness Practice Book

 **CD-ROM**

Read the Literature

Read **"Legend of the Blue Bonnet" Teacher Read Aloud,** 83A–83B
Shared Reading
Read the **Big Book of Real-Life Reading,** 10–11
☑ Diagram

Build Skills

☑ High-Frequency Words: *I*, 83C–83
Practice Book, 83

 Cultural Perspectives, 83B

✏ **Writing Prompt:** Write about your most favorite toy. Describe what makes it special.

DAY 4

Dad, Dan, and I

Focus on Reading Skills

Develop Phonological Awareness,
84A–84B
"A Pet for Nan and Dan"
Review Blending with Short *a*, 84C–84
Practice Book, 84
Phonics/Phonemic Awareness Practice Book

 **CD-ROM**

Read the Literature

Read **"Dad, Dan, and I" Decodable Story,** 85/86A–85/86D

☑ Initial /s/s; Blending
☑ Classify and Categorize
☑ High-Frequency Words: *I*
☑ Concepts of Print

Build Skills

☑ Classify and Categorize, 87A–87
Practice Book, 87

 Math, 85/86D

✏ **Writing Prompt:** What pumpkin face would you make? Draw and describe it.

Letter Formation
Practice Book, 85–86

DAY 5

Dad, Dan, and I / Sid and I
by Marie Fenn
illustrated by Andy San Diego

Focus on Reading Skills

Develop Phonological Awareness,
88A–88B
"A Pet for Nan and Dan"
Review Blending with Short *a*, 88C–88
Practice Book, 88
Phonics/Phonemic Awareness Practice Book

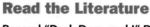 **CD-ROM**

Read the Literature

Reread **"Dad, Dan, and I" Decodable Story,** 89A

Read **"Sid and I" Patterned Book,** 89B
Guided Reading
☑ Initial /s/s; Blending
☑ Classify and Categorize
☑ High-Frequency Words: *I*
☑ Concepts of Print

Build Skills

☑ High-Frequency Words: *I, and, my,* 89C–89
Practice Book, 89

 Science, 89B

✏ **Writing Prompt:** Write about something you would like to make or build with a friend. Draw a picture of it.

Interactive Writing, 90A–90B

Develop Phonological Awareness

Listen

Sing a Song of Sixpence

Sing a song of sixpence
a pocket full of rye,
Four and twenty blackbirds
baked in a pie;
When the pie was opened,
the birds began to sing.
Wasn't that a dainty dish
to set before the King?

Big Book of Phonics Rhymes and Poems, pages 46–47

Objective: Listen for Differences

LISTEN TO THE POEM

- Read the poem several times, inviting children to join in on familiar words and phrases.
- Explain to children that you will now change a word in the poem. Encourage them to listen carefully.
- Say the first two lines of the poem, substituting the word *basket* for the word *pocket*. Ask children to identify the word that was changed.

CHANGE ANOTHER WORD

- Repeat the activity with the second two lines of the poem.

> **pie —> cake**

- Continue with other word substitutions in the poem.

Listen for Initial /s/

LISTEN FOR INITIAL SOUND

- Say the word *sing,* and emphasize the initial /s/ sound. Have children say the sound with you.
- Read the title of the poem. Ask how many words begin with the /s/ sound.

SEGMENTING Say the word *sing* and have children repeat it. Then ask them to say the word without the initial sound. Then repeat the word with the initial /s/.

ing   sing

- Repeat with the words *song, sixpence,* and *set.*

PLAY SIMPLE SIMON

- Point out that the words *simple* and *Simon* begin with the initial /s/ sound.

Tell children you will play the game. Have children listen to your directions. If you say "Simple Simon Says" before a direction, then children act out the action. If you do not say "Simple Simon Says" then they freeze.

> **Simple Simon says put your hands on your hips.**

Read Together

From Phonemic Awareness to Phonics

Identify Initial /s/S, s

IDENTIFY THE LETTER FOR THE SOUND

- Explain to children that the letter s stands for /s/. Say the sound and have children repeat it after you.
- Display pages 46–47 in the Big Book of Phonics Rhymes and Poems. Point to the letters in the corner, identify them, and repeat the sound. Have children make the sound.

REREAD THE POEM

- Reread the poem, tracking words as you read. Emphasize the words that begin with /s/.

SIT FOR WORDS WITH *s*

- Write the letter *s* on a large index card. Have children stand in a circle and give the card to a volunteer.
- Read the poem slowly. When you say a word that begins with /s/, the child holding the card sits down. He or she then passes the card to the next child.
- Read the poem several times, until all children are sitting.

Ss

Sing a Song of Sixpence

Sing a song of sixpence,
a pocket full of rye,
Four and twenty blackbirds
baked in a pie;

46

Big Book of Phonics Rhymes and Poems, pages 46–47

Introduce Initial /s/s

OBJECTIVES

Children will:

- identify the letters *S, s*
- identify /s/ *S, s*
- form the letters *S, s*

MATERIALS

- letter cards from the Word Play Book

TEACHING TIP

INSTRUCTIONAL As children identify the letter *s*, point out that the capital letter is the same form, but a different size. You may wish to keep a chart that shows other letters that follow this pattern.

ALTERNATE TEACHING STRATEGY

INITIAL /s/s

For a different approach to teaching this skill, see page T28.

▶ **Visual/Auditory/ Kinesthetic**

TEACH

Identify /s/ S, s   Tell children they will learn to write the sound /s/ with the letters *S, s*. Ask anyone whose name begins with *S* to say their name. Write *S, s* on the chalkboard, identify the letters, and have children make the sound with you. Ask children to hold up their *s* letter cards when they hear /s/ at the beginning of a word and say the following: *Sam said to sit here. Is Sam going to sing soon?*

Form S, s   Display letters *S, s* and trace them with your finger. With your back to the children, trace letters *S, s* in the air. Ask children to do the same. Then have them practice writing the letter on their palms.

PRACTICE

Complete the Pupil Edition Page   Read the directions on page 78 of the Pupil Edition, and make sure children clearly understand what they are being asked to do. Identify each picture, and complete the first item together. Then work through the page with children or have them complete the page independently.

ASSESS/CLOSE

Identify and Use S, s   Say the following list of words, and have children hiss *Ssss* and hold up their *s* letter cards when they hear a word that begins with the letter *s: set, sad, Sam, ran, pat, sing*. Observe children's letter formations.

Name _____

pencil   sun   six

sink   towel   soap

seal   sandwich   hat

seven   carrot   seesaw

Write the letters *Ss*. • Say the word that names each picture. • Listen for the sound at the beginning of each word. • Draw a circle around each picture whose name begins with the same sound as *soap*.

78   Unit 2 Introduce Initial /s/*s*

McGraw-Hill School Division

Pupil Edition, page 78

ADDITIONAL PHONICS RESOURCES

Practice Book, *page 78*
Phonics Workbook

McGraw-Hill School
TECHNOLOGY

Phonics **CD-ROM**
Activities for practice with Initial Letters

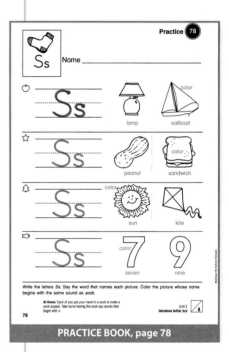

PRACTICE BOOK, page 78

Meeting Individual Needs for Phonics

EASY	ON-LEVEL	CHALLENGE	LANGUAGE SUPPORT
Have children sit in a circle and say words that begin with *s* as they "Pass the S." Give one child a tagboard cutout of the letter *s*, and have the child say a word that begins with /s/. This child then passes the *s* to the next child in the circle, and so on.	**Have** children write *S, s* on several index cards. Display a selection of word cards: *set, do, dad, sad, sip, my.* Ask children to turn over an *s* card for every word that begins with /s/. Read the cards aloud, and have the children repeat the initial /s/ sound.	**Have** children write *S* on a sheet of drawing paper as large or as small as they would like. Then they draw a picture or design that incorporates the letter. Display pictures and invite children to find the letters.	**Have** children use a hand mirror as they say the /s/ sound. Ask them to repeat short words, noting that their tongue is behind their teeth: *sit, sap, sun, so, sent.*

OBJECTIVES

Children will:

- recognize words with initial /s/
- classify food items at the fair

LANGUAGE SUPPORT

ESL Review some of the food items that are mentioned the story, including tacos, waffles, and desserts. Determine if children are familiar with these foods, using pictures as necessary. Have them describe colors, textures, and tastes of the foods.

Read the Big Book

Before Reading

Develop Oral Language

Sing "The Alphabet song" together. The song is on page 2 of the Big Book of Phonics Rhymes and Poems. Then ask a volunteer to point to the letters as you sing it again.

Remind children that they read a story about a street fair. Ask them to recall some of the things that the family did at the fair.

Set Purposes

Model: We read a story about a street fair. When we read the story today, let's think about what foods are described in the story. Let's also read the words that match the letters on the page.

Ss Super sandwiches   Tasty tacos Tt

The ABC Street Fair, pages 24–25

During Reading

Read Together

- Point to the uppercase and lowercase letters at the top of each page as you say the name of the letter. Run your finger under each word in the story as you read it and relate it to the initial letter. Have children repeat the word after you. *Concepts of Print*

- After you read page 2, have children determine that apples are a food at the fair. Have them describe the different colors. As you read the story, make a picture or word list of other foods at the fair. *Use Illustrations*

- After you read page 23, ask children: *How do you think Dad feels about the roses? How can you tell? Make Inferences*

- Make the /s/ sound and have children repeat it. Reread page 24, emphasizing the beginning sound of the words. Invite children to name other foods that begin with the /s/ sound. *Phonics*

The ABC Street Fair, page 24

After Reading

Retell the Story Invite children to retell the story, using illustrations from the book.

Literary Response **JOURNAL WRITING** Ask children to draw a picture of a food that they would like to eat at the fair and write about it.

ORAL RESPONSE Ask questions such as:

- *What is the name of this food? Have you ever eaten it?*

- *What does it taste like?*

ABC Activity Give each child an alphabet card. Begin with *a*, and have the child holding that card stand up. He or she tries to remember what words in the story started with *a*. Use the Big Book as needed, and continue through the alphabet.

CULTURAL PERSPECTIVES

STREET FAIRS Explain that there are street fairs all over the world. In Egypt, certain street fairs sell camels, goats, and donkeys. A street fair in France has an array of fresh vegetables and baked goods. A street fair in Turkey might offer rugs, spices, pottery, and toys.

Activity Stage a make-believe street fair or bazaar. Ask what each child would like to sell. Allow each child to prepare their wares using clay, paper, and markers. Have the children stand in two lines facing each other and stop at each of their stalls to see what they are selling.

Bring a basket and buy a little of what everyone is selling.

▶ **Linguistic**

Introduce Numbers

OBJECTIVES

Children will:

- identify numbers 6–10

MATERIALS

- *Warthogs in the Kitchen*
- number cards

TEACHING TIP

INSTRUCTIONAL

Encourage children to use their number lines 1–10 as they participate in number activities. Make sure children are confident counting 1–6 before asking them to understand greater numbers.

PREPARE

Review Numbers 1–6 Say a number between 1 and 6. Have children hold up that number of fingers. Then reverse the activity by holding up fingers and having children tell how many. Ask questions such as: *How many eyes do you have? How many noses?*

TEACH

Count and Recognize Numbers Display the Big Book *Warthogs in the Kitchen,* and invite children to share what they remember about the story. Reread the story, stopping and having children identify the number on each page. Ask children to count the corresponding items on the page. Let children search the classroom for groups that have the same number.

PRACTICE

Match Numbers and Groups Read the directions on page 79 to the children, and make sure they clearly understand what they are asked to do. Identify each picture, and complete the first item together. Then work through the page with children, or have them complete the page independently.

ASSESS/CLOSE

Review the Page Check children's work on the Pupil Edition page. Note areas where children need extra help.

Name_____

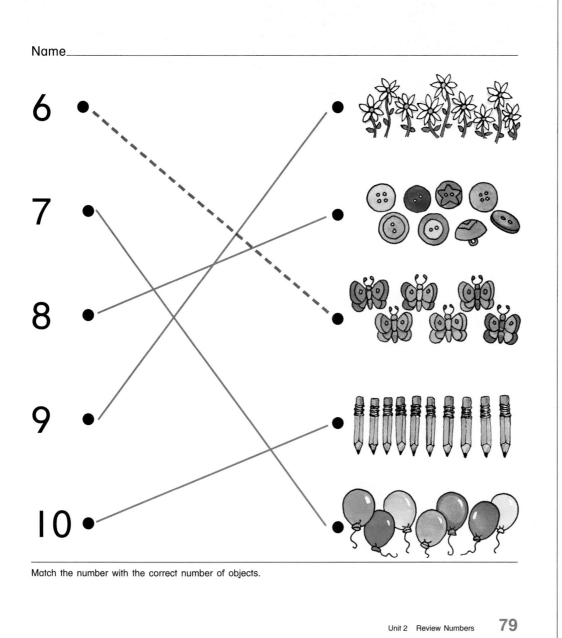

Match the number with the correct number of objects.

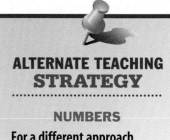

ALTERNATE TEACHING STRATEGY

....

NUMBERS

For a different approach to teaching this skill, see page T25.

▶ **Visual/Auditory/Kinesthetic**

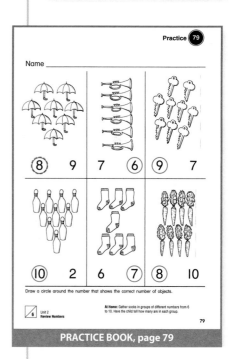

Practice 79

Name_____

Draw a circle around the number that shows the correct number of objects.

Unit 2 Review Numbers

At Home: Gather socks in groups of different numbers from 6 to 10. Have the child tell how many are in each group.

79

PRACTICE BOOK, page 79

Meeting Individual Needs for Beginning Reading Concepts

EASY	ON-LEVEL	CHALLENGE	LANGUAGE SUPPORT
Use number cards 7–10 and 10 crayons. Say the number 1, and ask a child to find the number card. Then he or she chooses 7 crayons. Ask the child to return the crayons, and repeat with numbers 8–10.	**Display** number cards for 7–10. Ask questions such as: *I'm thinking of a number that comes just after 8. What is it?* Volunteers then come and point to the number.	**Give** a child a number card from 7–10. He or she then draws something from the warthogs' kitchen to show the number. Other children count the items and verify.	**Continue** to use numbers frequently during the day to help children whose first language is not English. Give directions such as: *Please bring me one sheet of paper. Choose two books.*

79

Develop Phonological Awareness

Listen

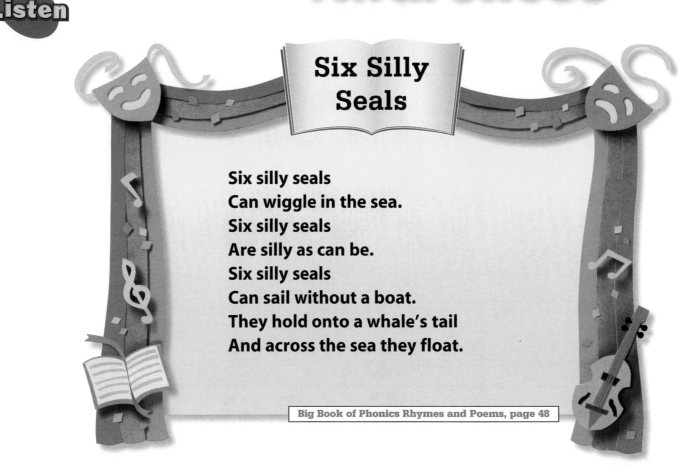

Six Silly Seals

Six silly seals
Can wiggle in the sea.
Six silly seals
Are silly as can be.
Six silly seals
Can sail without a boat.
They hold onto a whale's tail
And across the sea they float.

Big Book of Phonics Rhymes and Poems, page 48

Objective: Strengthen Awareness of Words

LISTEN TO THE POEM

- Read the poem "Six Silly Seals" to a small group of children. Then give each child six connecting cubes or small squares of paper.

- Explain that you are going to read the poem again, line by line. For each word in the line, children take a cube. When you stop after a line, children hook the cubes together and say how many words are in the line of the poem.

MODEL THE ACTIVITY

- Slowly say *six silly seals*. As you say each word, take a cube. Then connect the cubes and count them. Determine that the line of the poem has three words.

- Continue with the first four lines of the poem. When children are proficient with the activity, continue with the rest of the poem.

Objective: Listen for Initial /s/

LISTEN FOR THE SOUND

- Say the word *seal* and emphasize the initial /s/ sound. Have children say the sound with you.

- Read the title of the poem. Point out that all of the words in the title begin with the /s/ sound. Have children say the words.

REPEAT THE SOUND

- Talk about how seals clap their flippers. Place your wrists together and pretend to clap like a seal. Have children do the same.

- Read words from the poem. If a word begins with /s/, children clap like seals.

six	boat	sea	hold	sail	tail

From Phonemic Awareness to Phonics

Objective: Identify Initial /s/ *S, s*

IDENTIFY THE LETTER FOR THE SOUND

- Explain to children that the letter *s* stands for /s/. Say the sound and have children repeat it after you.

- Display page 48 in the Big Book of Phonics Rhymes and Poems. Point to the letters in the corner, identify them, and repeat the sound. Have children make the sound.

REREAD THE POEM

- Reread the poem, pointing to each word as you read. Children repeat each word that begins with /s/.

STAND FOR WORDS WITH S

- Write the letter *s* on a large index card. Have children sit in a circle and give the card to a volunteer.

- Read the poem slowly. When you say a word that begins with /s/, the child holding the card stands up. He or she then passes the card to the next child.

- Read the poem several times, until all children are standing.

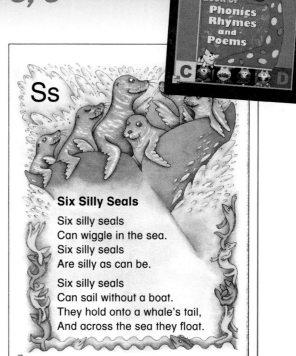

Ss

Six Silly Seals

Six silly seals
Can wiggle in the sea.
Six silly seals
Are silly as can be.

Six silly seals
Can sail without a boat.
They hold onto a whale's tail,
And across the sea they float.

48

Big Book of Phonics Rhymes and Poems, page 48

OBJECTIVES

Children will:

* identify the letters *S, s*
* identify and use /s/ *S, s*
* write the letters *S, s*

MATERIALS

* letter cards from the Word Play Book

TEACHING TIP

INSTRUCTIONAL As a warm-up to the lesson, have children repeat this chant: *Say the sound of Ssss,* emphasizing the initial /s/ sound. Ask children to see how long they can stretch the hissing sound, and invite them to trace the letter *s* in the air while they make the sound.

ALTERNATE TEACHING STRATEGY

INITIAL /s/s

For a different approach to teaching this skill, see page T28.

▶ **Visual/Auditory/ Kinesthetic**

Review Initial /s/s

TEACH

Identify and Use /s/ S, s
Ask children to make the sound of the letter *s* as you hold up the letter and identify it. Invite volunteers to suggest words that begin with *s*. Have children hold up their *s* letter cards when they hear a word that begins with *s* in the following: *Sally and her sister went for a sail. The sun came out. They had such fun.*

Write S, s
With your back to the children, trace the letter *S* in the air. Ask children to do the same. Then invite them to write the letters *S, s* on a sheet of paper. Ask them to hold up their papers when they hear a word that begins with *s*. Say: *mad, sad, sun, fun, sit, pit.*

PRACTICE

Complete the Pupil Edition Page
Read the directions on page 80 of the Pupil Edition, and make sure children clearly understand what they are being asked to do. Identify each picture, and complete the first item together. Then work through the page with children or have them complete the page independently.

ASSESS/CLOSE

Identify and Use S, s
Show pictures that represent objects whose names begin with *s* and objects that don't. Invite children to hold up their *s* papers when they see an object whose name begins with the letter *s*, for example: *sit, sad, sun, sink, sick, sock.*

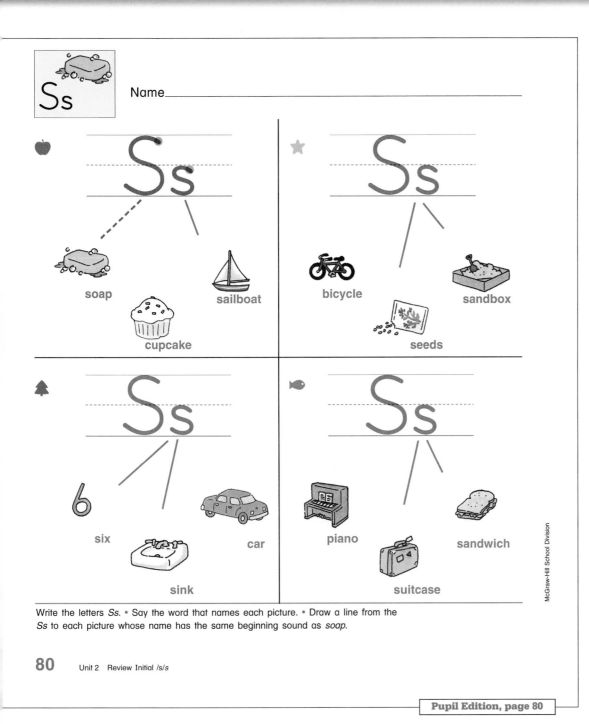

Ss Name

soap sailboat cupcake

bicycle sandbox seeds

six car sink

piano suitcase sandwich

Write the letters *Ss*. • Say the word that names each picture. • Draw a line from the *Ss* to each picture whose name has the same beginning sound as *soap*.

80 Unit 2 Review Initial /s/*s*

McGraw-Hill School Division

Pupil Edition, page 80

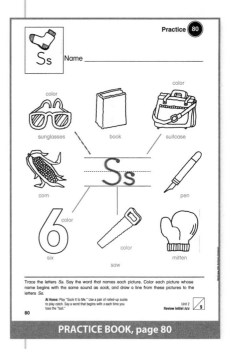

Practice **80**

Ss Name

sunglasses book suitcase
corn pen
six sow mitten

Trace the letters *Ss*. Say the word that names each picture. Color each picture whose name begins with the same sound as *sock*, and draw a line from these pictures to the letters *Ss*.

At Home: Play "Sock It to Me." Use a pair of rolled-up socks to play catch. Say a word that begins with *s* each time you toss the "ball."

80 Unit 2 Review Initial /s/*s* 9

PRACTICE BOOK, page 80

Meeting Individual Needs for Phonics

EASY	ON-LEVEL	CHALLENGE	LANGUAGE SUPPORT
Have children trace their *s* letter cards using a light-colored crayon, then show them how to go over the letter several times to make a thick layer of crayon on the paper. They can paint the paper with watercolor, watch their letter *s* appear, and say words that begin with *s*.	**Invite** children to pretend they are at a restaurant, and ask them to order things that begin with *s*, for example: *soup, salad, salmon, sandwich, salsa*. Have them write an *s* for each item ordered.	**Give** children sheets of paper with a large numeral 6 or 7 printed on the page. Point to the numbers one at a time and say their names, emphasizing the initial /s/ sound. Invite children to write a border using *s* around their numeral and to label the numeral with *s*.	**Say** action words that begin with *s*, and have children repeat the words and pantomime the actions with you, for example: *sit, sigh, sew, sip, see, say*. Each time you say a word, the children trace an *s* in the air with their fingers.

✓OBJECTIVES

- recognize words with initial /s/
- classify and categorize

TEACHING TIP

Use the story to reinforce counting skills. Show a number on the page and ask questions such as: *What number will come next? What number comes just before 6? Let's check to find out.*

Read the Big Book

Before Reading

Develop Oral Language

Sing this familiar song with the children:

I'm a Little Teapot
I'm a little teapot,
Short and stout.
Here is my handle,
Here is my spout.
When I get all steamed up,
Hear me shout,
Just tip me over
and pour me out!

Show children the actions, and sing the song together. Ask children where they might see a teapot. Ask children to recall some of the things they saw in the warthog's kitchen.

Set Purposes

Model: We know that this story is about warthogs who make cupcakes. The warthogs use some real ingredients and some silly ingredients. Let's find out what they are.

There's something in the bowl that shouldn't be there!

10

"Get out this instant, you greedy little bear."

Warthogs in the Kitchen, pages 10–11

11

During Reading

Read Together

- Before you begin to read, point to the first word in the first sentence. Explain that this is where you will begin to read. Continue to track print as you read the story. *Tracking Print*

- After you read page 9, ask children if the sugar is a real ingredient for cupcakes or a silly ingredient. As you continue to read the story, make a picture chart of Real and Silly ingredients. *Classify and Categorize*

- Reread page 12. Make the /s/ sound with children. Ask which words begin with that sound. (*scoops, some*) *Phonics and Decoding*

- Direct children to look at page 14. Frame the exclamation mark and the question mark, and discuss each one. Reread the question, asking children to listen to your voice inflection when you read the question. *Concepts of Print.*

"Get out this instant, you greedy little bear."

Warthogs in the Kitchen, page 11

After Reading

Retell the Story

Take a picture walk through the book, asking volunteers to retell the story.

Literary Response

JOURNAL WRITING Ask children to think of another silly ingredient that the warthogs could add to their cupcakes. Invite children to draw a picture to show it. Encourage them to incorporate a number, if appropriate. Help them to label their pictures.

ORAL RESPONSE Engage children in a discussion by asking questions such as:

- *How would ___ make the cupcake taste?*

- *What would the cupcakes look like?*

CULTURAL PERSPECTIVES

CUPCAKES Share that people all over the world love to bake sweet things. In Poland, people like to eat sweet breads with poppy seeds in them. In Greece, people eat baklava—a flaky dessert with sweet, sticky sauce. In the United States, many people love to eat cakes or cupcakes. Explain that it can be interesting to try different kinds of foods.

Activity Explain that the class will bake cupcakes. Give each child a special task in the preparation. Make cupcakes following the recipe on the back of *Warthogs in the Kitchen*.

▶ Logical

81B

TESTED

OBJECTIVES

Children will:

- classify and categorize to understand a story

MATERIALS

- *Warthogs in the Kitchen*

TEACHING TIP

INSTRUCTIONAL Have children each bring in one of the ingredients for the "Cupcake Recipe for Humans" at the back of the book. Make the muffins and eat them with the class. Compare the recipe to the warthogs' recipe.

Introduce Classify and Categorize

PREPARE

List Details Ask children to recall the story *Warthogs in the Kitchen*.

Have them name some of the items that the warthogs used in their recipe.

TEACH

Classify and Categorize Food Items Turn to page 6 and read the text. Ask if sugar would really be used in a recipe for cupcakes. Go through the story, classifying each food item as a real ingredient or a silly ingredient. You may wish to make a picture or a word list to record the information. Explain that children are sorting the items into two groups, or categories.

PRACTICE

Complete the Pupil Edition Page Read the directions on page 81 to the children, and make sure they clearly understand what they are asked to do. Identify each picture, and complete the first item together. Then work through the page with children, or have them complete the page independently.

ASSESS/CLOSE

Review the Page Review children's work, and note children who are experiencing difficulty.

Real Ingredients	Silly Ingredients
sugar butter eggs flour	Pickles

Name _____

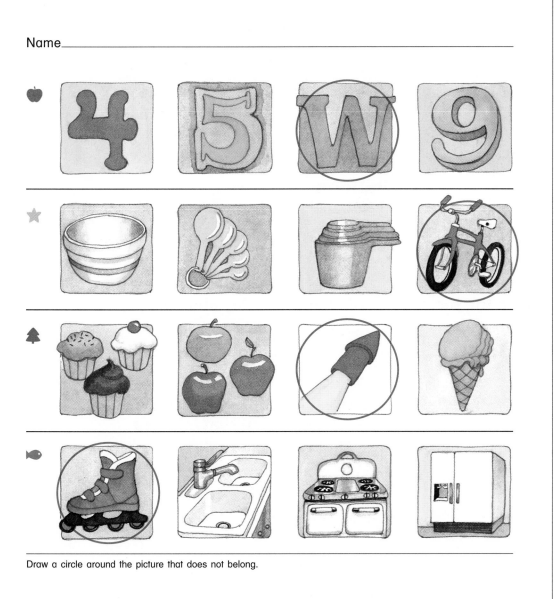

Draw a circle around the picture that does not belong.

Unit 2   Introduce Classify and Categorize   **81**

Pupil Edition, page 81

ALTERNATE TEACHING STRATEGY

CLASSIFY AND CATEGORIZE

For a different approach to teaching this skill, see page T29.

► **Visual/Auditory/Kinesthetic**

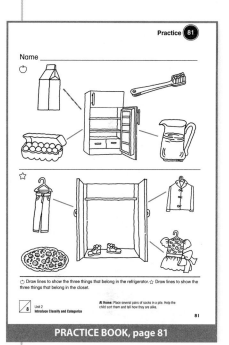

PRACTICE BOOK, page 81

Meeting Individual Needs for Comprehension

EASY	ON-LEVEL	CHALLENGE	LANGUAGE SUPPORT
Provide cooking utensils or pictures of utensils, such as bowls, spoons, measuring cups, and so on. Have children sort the items into groups.	**Use** animal cards, and have children think of ways to sort the cards into different groups, or categories. Give examples of characteristics, such as animals with horns; two feet; four feet; animals that swim; animals that fly.	**Choose** 10–15 classroom picture books with people or animals on the cover. Have children think of ways to sort the books. Encourage different ways of sorting. After they sort, have them describe their groups.	**Ask** children to draw a picture of their favorite type of muffin. After the pictures are completed, have children think of ways to sort the types of muffins. Begin with simple categories, such as *Fruit* and *No Fruit*. Then invite children to think of categories.

81

Develop Phonological Awareness

Listen

Six Silly Seals
a poem

Red Balloon
a poem

Six silly seals
Can wiggle in the sea.
Six silly seals
Are silly as can be.
Six silly seals
Can sail without a boat.
They hold onto a whale's
  tail,
And across the sea they
  float.

A lost balloon so big and red
Floated one day above my
  head.
That lost balloon so red and
  proud
Hid behind a large white cloud.
But I was glad that I did see
That red balloon fly over me.

Big Book of Phonics Rhymes and Poems, pages 16, 48

Objective: Develop Listening Skills

READ THE POEM Read the poem "Six Silly Seals." Invite children to join in on the repeating line.

PLAY "SEAL, WHERE ARE YOU?" Gather children in a circle. Demonstrate a seal's bark. Invite children to play "Seal, Where Are You?" Have a child sit in the circle with his or her eyes closed. Choose another child to be the seal. This child moves to any part of the room and makes a barking sound. The child in the circle points to the seal. The child who is the seal then sits in the circle.

IDENTIFY LOCATION Continue the game, having children tell the seal's location. For variety, invite children to make other animal sounds. The child in the circle must name the animal, as well as tell where the animal is.

Objective: Listen for /s/ and /d/

LISTEN FOR INITIAL /S/ Read the poem "Six Silly Seals" one sentence at a time. Emphasize the initial /s/ sound. Encourage children to echo each line.

MAKE A SEA OF STRING Have children sit in a circle. Invite them to make a sea of string. Hand a ball of string to one child. Then say a word and have the child with the string repeat the word. If the word begins with the /s/ sound, the child holds one end of the string and rolls the ball to a classmate. Continue until everyone has had a chance to roll the string. Have the last child roll the string to you.

> sun sing pig soft hot

LISTEN FOR /D/ Read "Red Balloon," stressing words with initial and final /d/. Have children say /d/. Say aloud words with initial or final /d/. Have children stand up if the word ends with /d/, and sit down if the word begins with /d/.

> door fed pad date Ned lid

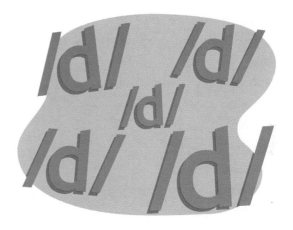

From Phonemic Awareness to Phonics

Read Together

Objective: Identify /s/ S, s and /d/ D, d

IDENTIFY THE LETTERS Display the Big Book of Phonics Rhymes and Poems, pages 48 and 16. Point to the letters and identify them. Say each sound the letters stand for.

READ THE POEMS Reread the poems. Point to each word, stressing those with the initial /s/ sound and initial and final /d/ sound.

FIND WORDS WITH S, s, d Have children find words with S, s or d in the poems. Provide self-stick dots to place under the letters.

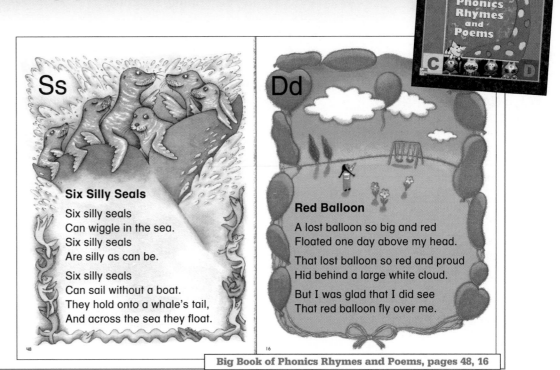

Ss

Six Silly Seals

Six silly seals
Can wiggle in the sea.
Six silly seals
Are silly as can be.

Six silly seals
Can sail without a boat.
They hold onto a whale's tail,
And across the sea they float.

48

Dd

Red Balloon

A lost balloon so big and red
Floated one day above my head.

That lost balloon so red and proud
Hid behind a large white cloud.

But I was glad that I did see
That red balloon fly over me.

16

Big Book of Phonics Rhymes and Poems, pages 48, 16

82B

OBJECTIVES

Children will:

- identify and use /s/ *S, s* and /d/ *D, d*
- write the letters *S, s* and *D, d*

MATERIALS

- letter cards from the Word Play Book

TEACHING TIP

INSTRUCTIONAL

Children can dramatize the rhyme in the Teach activity. Show them how to *dig for potatoes.* Model common gestures and body language that indicate *I don't* and *Do you?* Have all the children chant the rhyme with you as volunteers act it out.

ALTERNATE TEACHING STRATEGY

LETTERS /s/s, /d/d

For a different approach to teaching this skill, see page T28.

▶ **Visual/Auditory/ Kinesthetic**

Review /s/ s, /d/ d

Discriminate Between /s/ *S, s* and /d/ *D, d*

Tell children they will identify the sounds /s/ and /d/ and write the letters *S, s* and *D, d*. Write the letters on the chalkboard. Have them repeat the sounds after you; then ask them to identify the first and last letters of the word *said*. Place the following word cards on the chalkboard ledge, and invite children to sort them into words that begin with *d*, words that end with *d*, and words that begin with *s: dip, pad, sat, red, sun, dot.*

Write *S, s* and *D, d*

Write *S, s* on one side of the chalkboard and *D, d* on the other side. Say the following rhyme, and have children point to the letter *s* or *d* when they hear a word that begins with one of these letters: *Sam said, "I don't dig tomatoes." Sue said, "Sam, do you dig potatoes?"* Draw a line under each letter when children point to it; then have children write an *s* or *d* for each underlined letter. Point out that *said* begins with one sound and ends with the other.

PRACTICE

Complete the Pupil Edition Page

Read the directions on page 82 of the Pupil Edition, and make sure children clearly understand what they are being asked to do. Identify each picture, and complete the first item together. Then work through the page with children or have children complete the page independently.

ASSESS/CLOSE

Identify and Use *S, s* and *D, d*

Show pictures of the following objects: *soup, door, sock, dot, deer, sink.* Ask children to write the letter each one begins with on a self-stick note and use the notes as labels for the pictures.

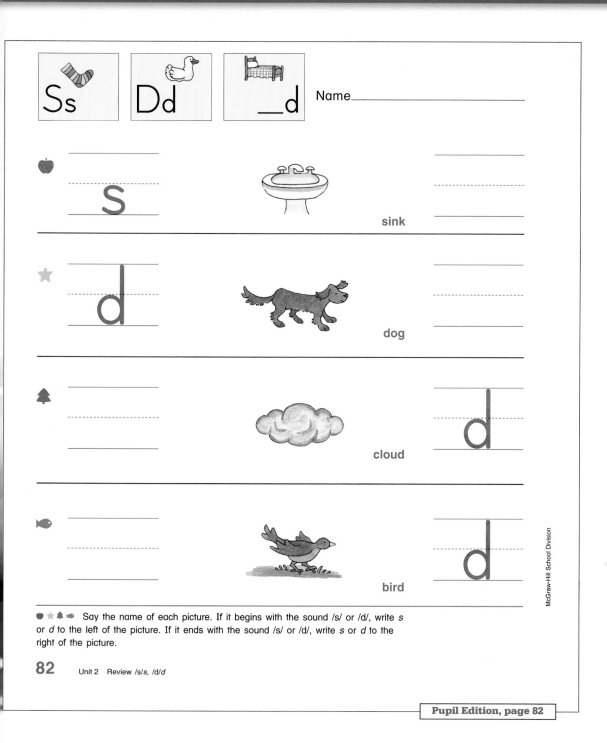

Name_____

Ss **Dd** **__d**

s

d

sink

dog

cloud

d

bird

d

● ★ ▲ ➤ Say the name of each picture. If it begins with the sound /s/ or /d/, write *s* or *d* to the left of the picture. If it ends with the sound /s/ or /d/, write *s* or *d* to the right of the picture.

82 Unit 2 Review /s/s, /d/d

McGraw-Hill School Division

Pupil Edition, page 82

ADDITIONAL PHONICS RESOURCES

Practice Book, *page 82*
Phonics Workbook

McGraw-Hill School
TECHNOLOGY

Phonics CD-ROM
Activities for practice with Initial and Final Letters

PRACTICE BOOK, page 82

Meeting Individual Needs for Phonics

EASY	ON-LEVEL	CHALLENGE	LANGUAGE SUPPORT
Give children letters *S, s, D,* and *d* cut out of sandpaper. With their eyes closed, have children sort for *s* and *d* and arrange the letters in two groups on their table. Then have children repeat the activity, sorting for capital *S* and *D*.	**Give** groups of children a selection of word cards such as: *sad, sit, Sam, did, dog,* Dan. Have one group sort for initial *s* or *d* and another group sort for capital or lowercase letters.	**Have** small groups of children look through storybooks for words that begin with *S* and begin or end with *d*. Have children make a list of five words and read them aloud.	**Help** children learn to distinguish /s/ from other consonants by having them recite this rhyme with you: *I saw a zebra, I saw a lion, I saw a tiger, too. I saw them all at the zoo.* Children hold up a letter card when words begin with *s*.

Teacher Read Aloud

Listen

The Legend of Bluebonnet

An Old Tale of Texas
Retold by Tomie dePaola

"Great Spirits,
the land is dying. Your People
are dying, too,"
the long line of dancers sang.
"Tell us what we have done to
anger you.
End this drought. Save your People.
Tell us what we must do so you will
send the rain that will bring back
life."

For three days,
the dancers danced to the sound of
the drums,
and for three days, the People
called Comanche
watched and waited.

And even though the hard winter
was over,
no healing rains came.

Drought and famine are hardest
on the very young and very old.

Among the few children left
was a small girl named She-Who-
Is-Alone.
She sat by herself watching the
dancers.
In her lap was a doll made from
buckskin—a warrior doll.
The eyes, nose and mouth were
painted on with the juice of
berries. It wore beaded leggings
and a belt of polished bone.

Continued on page T4

Oral Comprehension

LISTENING AND SPEAKING Ask children to describe wildflowers that they have seen. Explain that wild flowers grow in fields and forests because their seeds are spread by the wind and by forest animals. Tell children that the story is a folk tale from Texas—a story that has been told over and over by many different people. You may also wish to explain the meaning of the words *drought* and *famine* before you begin the story.

Ask children if they remember what the little girl's doll is made of. Remind them that the doll is made of bone,

beads, feathers, and the juice of berries. Ask them to classify which of these materials come from animals and which come from plants or stones.

Explain that the Comanche people are just one of many Native American tribes who live in the United States. Share that they hunted buffalo and rode horses.

Real-Life Reading

How does a bluebonnet grow?

1. Plant a seed.

seed

2. Sunshine and rain help it grow.

stem

roots

10

3. The first leaves and buds appear.

buds

leaves

4. The plant in full bl...

f...

11

Big Book of Real-Life Reading, pages 10–11

Objective: Diagram

READ THE PAGE Ask children to name some of their favorite flowers. Then remind them of the story "The Legend of Bluebonnet." Explain that children will see a diagram of how a bluebonnet seed grows. A diagram can use pictures and words to explain something. Then read the text and discuss the pictures.

ANSWER THE QUESTION Note the numbers that show the sequence of the pictures. Point to the number 1, and ask a volunteer to explain the picture. Continue and ask: *How are the seed and the plant changing?* Provide watercolors and paper. Ask children to paint a flower they like. Help them to label the petals, stem, and leaves.

CULTURAL PERSPECTIVES

TEPEES Explain that the girl in the story belongs to a Native American tribe called the Comanches. When the Comanches hunted buffalo, they lived in tepees. A tepee was a great home for people on the move because it could be packed up and set up again quickly. Other "moving homes" include house-boats in Thailand for fishermen and tents in India for gypsies. These houses let their inhabitants move wherever they wanted, whenever they wanted.

Activity Children will make a miniature tepee using paper, craft sticks, and glue. Encourage children to decorate their tepees any way they want.

▶ Spatial

OBJECTIVES

Children will:

• identify and read the high-frequency word *I*

....

MATERIALS

• word cards from the Word Play Book

TEACHING TIP

INSTRUCTIONAL When you write sentences with the word *I*, leave ample space before and after the letter. Use examples from classroom picture books, pointing out when the letter stands alone and when it is part of a word.

Introduce High-Frequency Words: *I*

PREPARE

Listen to Words   Explain to children that they will be learning a new word: *I*. Say the following sentence: "I think I can." Say the sentence again, and ask children to raise their hands when they hear the word *I*.

TEACH

Model Reading the Word in Context   Give a word card to each child, and read the word. Reread the sentence, and have children raise their hands when they hear the word.

Identify the Word   Write the sentence above on the chalkboard. Track print and read each sentence. Children hold up their word cards when they hear the word *I*. Then ask volunteers to point to and underline the word *I* in the sentences.

PRACTICE

Complete the Pupil Edition Page   Read the directions on page 83 to the children, and make sure they clearly understand what they are asked to do. Complete the first item together. Then work through the page with children, or have them complete the page independently.

ASSESS/CLOSE

Review the Page   Review children's work, and note children who are experiencing difficulty or need additional practice.

Name

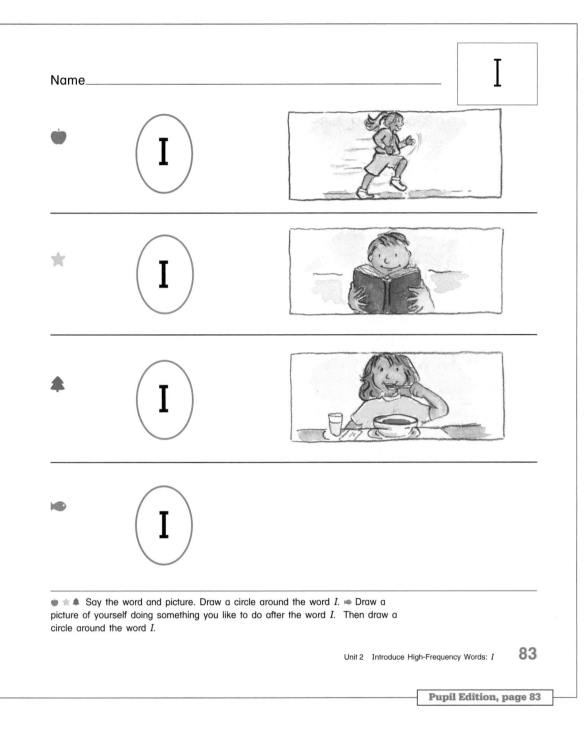

I

🍎 ⭐ 🌲 Say the word and picture. Draw a circle around the word *I*. 🐟 Draw a picture of yourself doing something you like to do after the word *I*. Then draw a circle around the word *I*.

Pupil Edition, page 83

PRACTICE BOOK, page 83

Meeting Individual Needs for Vocabulary

EASY	ON-LEVEL	CHALLENGE	LANGUAGE SUPPORT
Using objects such as pencils, rulers, and paper clips, have the children build the word *I*. Then they use the word in sentences.	**Write** the phrase *I like ___.* on chart paper. Read the phrase. Then volunteers point to the word *I* and complete the sentence with a word or a phrase.	**Have** children write or dictate a sentence about their physical appearance, such as: *I have blue eyes.* Children illustrate their sentences, and trace the letter *I*.	**Put** classroom objects in a bag, and write the letter *I* on chart paper. Each child takes something from the bag and says: "I have a (block)." Point to the word on the chart paper.

Develop Phonological Awareness

Listen

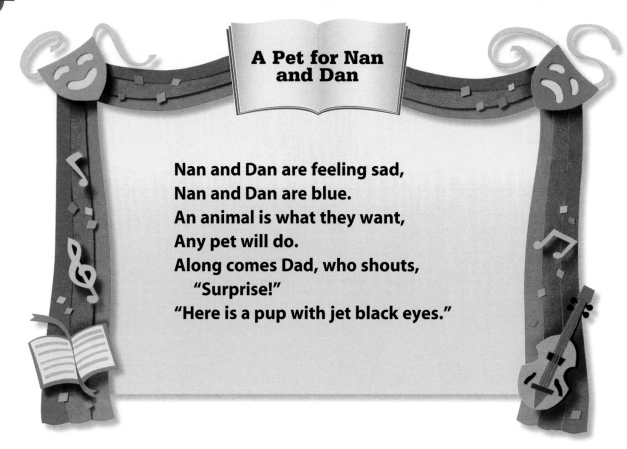

A Pet for Nan and Dan

Nan and Dan are feeling sad,
Nan and Dan are blue.
An animal is what they want,
Any pet will do.
Along comes Dad, who shouts,
    "Surprise!"
"Here is a pup with jet black eyes."

Objective: Focus on Syllables

READ THE POEM Have children sit in a circle. Read the poem "A Pet for Nan and Dan." Ask: *What present did Nan and Dan get?* Explain that *pup* is a short form of the word *puppy*. Say the last line of the poem and substitute the word *puppy*.

CLAP THE SYLLABLES Say the word *puppy* as you clap once for each syllable. Repeat the word again and have children clap out the syllables.

NAME OTHER PETS Invite children to suggest other pets that Nan and Dan could have received.

> gerbil iguana turtle kitten

LISTEN AND CLAP Using the children's pet suggestions, reread the poem several times substituting a different pet each time. After each reading, have children name the pet you mentioned. Then repeat the name of the pet, pausing slightly between syllables. Have children clap out the syllables.

Objective: Blending Short *a* with /s/

LISTEN TO THE POEM Read the poem "A Pet for Nan and Dan." Ask children to listen carefully to find out how Nan and Dan feel because they do not have a pet. Help children determine that Nan and Dan are sad.

LISTEN TO THE SOUNDS Provide each child with three connecting cubes. Then read the first line of the poem, segmenting the word *sad* into sounds. Have children set out one cube for each sound. Say the word again, pausing after each sound. Have children determine there are three sounds.

/s/-/a/-/d/

BLEND SOUNDS Have children say each sound in the word *sad* as they point to the cubes in left to right order. Increase the speed until the word is blended smoothly. Continue this activity by having children blend the following words.

/n/-/a/-/n/ /d/-/a/-/n/ /d/-/a/-/d/

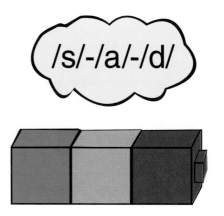

/s/-/a/-/d/

Read Together

From Phonemic Awareness to Phonics

Objective: Identify Short *a* Words

IDENTIFY THE LETTERS Write the word *sad* on the chalkboard, using a different color chalk for each letter. Point to the letters, one at a time, and have children identify them and say the sounds they stand for.

COUNT THE LETTERS In advance, write the word *sad* in large print and duplicate copies for children. Provide each child with three different colored cubes and the paper with the word *sad*. Say

the names of the letters in the word *sad* in order as children place one cube on each letter. Have children count the cubes and determine that the word *sad* has three letters.

LOCATE THE LETTERS Have children use the paper with the word *sad* to help them answer the following questions.

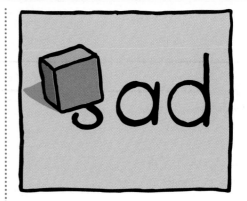

What letter is at the end of the word *sad*?
What letter is at the beginning of the word *sad*?
What letter is in the middle of the word *sad*?

OBJECTIVES

Children will:

- identify /a/*a*
- blend and read short *a* words
- write short *a* words
- review /s/ and /d/

MATERIALS

- letter cards from the *Word Play Book*

TEACHING TIP

INSTRUCTIONAL Write the following question on the chalkboard, and read it aloud: *Why are Nan and Dan sad?* Ask volunteers to underline the words that have /a/*a* in the middle. Have children brainstorm possible answers to the question.

ALTERNATE TEACHING STRATEGY

BLENDING SHORT *a*
For a different approach to teaching this skill, see Unit 1, page T32.

▶ **Visual/Auditory/ Kinesthetic**

Review Blending with short *a*

> **TEACH**

Identify *a* as the Symbol for /a/
Tell children that today they will be reading and writing a new word with the letter *a* that stands for the sound /a/.

- Display the *a* letter card and say /a/. Have children repeat the sound /a/ after you as you point to the *a*.

BLENDING Model and Guide Practice
- Review the word *ad* by placing a *d* letter card to the right of the *a*. Blend the sounds together and have children repeat: *ad*.

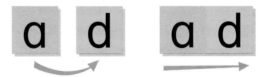

- Ask children what would happen to the word *ad* if you put an *s* in front of it. Place an *s* letter card to the left of the *a* and say *sad*.

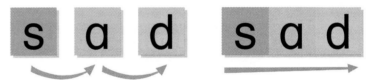

- Blend the sounds in the word to read *sad*. Have children repeat.

Use the Word in Context
- Ask children if they have ever been *sad*. Invite children to complete the following sentence: *Once I felt sad when…*

Repeat the Procedure
- Then ask children if they know someone who was *sad* about wanting a pet. Have children complete the following sentence: (Person's name) was sad because…

> **PRACTICE**

Complete the Pupil Edition Page
Read the directions on page 84 of the Pupil Edition, and make sure children clearly understand what they are being asked to do. Identify each picture, and complete the first item together. Work through the page with children, or have them complete it independently.

> **ASSESS/CLOSE**

Write Short *a* Words
Observe children as they complete page 84. Then have them write the word *sad*.

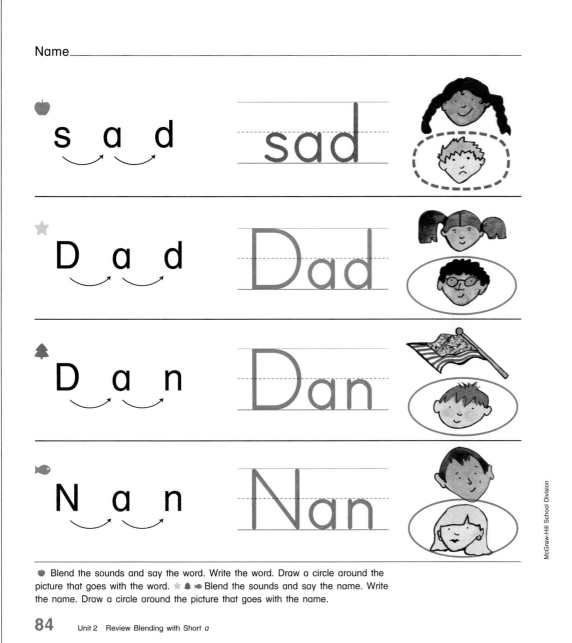

Name _____

🍎 s a d   sad

⭐ D a d   Dad

🌲 D a n   Dan

🐟 N a n   Nan

McGraw-Hill School Division

🍎 Blend the sounds and say the word. Write the word. Draw a circle around the picture that goes with the word. ⭐🌲🐟 Blend the sounds and say the name. Write the name. Draw a circle around the picture that goes with the name.

84   Unit 2   Review Blending with Short *a*

Pupil Edition, page 84

Meeting Individual Needs for Phonics

EASY	ON-LEVEL	CHALLENGE	LANGUAGE SUPPORT
Review the sounds of the letters *a, d,* and *s* by having children blend and read the following word: *sad*. Using tactile letters, have children trace the first letter while saying its sound. Repeat this with the middle and last letters. Then ask children to put the sounds together.	**Give** each child three paper squares, each with one of the following letters: *a, d, s*. First ask children to make the word *ad* by gluing the letters with sounds /a/ and /d/ to a piece of paper. Then have children make the word *ad* into *sad* by gluing on the letter with the sound /s/.	**Write** the words *sad* and *dad* on the chalkboard. Blend the words to read them aloud. Review the meaning of the words. Invite children to think of a reason why a Dad might be sad. Then have them draw and label a picture of a "Sad Dad."	**Make** a "sad face" and tell children that the way you look is described as *sad*. Blend the word as you say it. Then give each child a mirror. Have children make "sad faces" into the mirrors and blend and say the word *sad*.

Guided Instruction

BEFORE READING

PREVIEW AND PREDICT Take a brief **picture walk** through the book, focusing on the illustrations.

- Who is this story about? Where does it take place?

- Do you think the story is realistic or make-believe? Why?

SET PURPOSES Brainstorm a list of ideas the children have about what they may want to find out about as they read the story. Spark children's interest by asking questions such as: *Why are these children picking pumpkins?*

TEACHING TIP

To put the book together:

1. Tear out the story page.

2. Cut along dotted line.

3. Fold each section on fold line.

4. Assemble the book.

INSTRUCTIONAL Talk about the time of year when pumpkins are ready to pick. Then name some uses for pumpkins.

Dad, Dan, and I

Dan and I

3

Dad, Dan, and I

2

Dad and Dan

4

Guided Instruction

DURING READING

☑ **Letter *s***

☑ **Classify and Categorize**

☑ **Concepts of Print**

☑ **High-Frequency Word: *I***

① **CONCEPTS OF PRINT** Model how to run your finger from left to right under each word as you read. Read the title, and then have children repeat the words as they track print.

② **HIGH-FREQUENCY WORD: *I*** Ask children to point to the last word on page 2 and to read it together: *I*. Point out that when capital *I* stands alone, it is a word. Have children read the word with you.

③ **CONCEPTS OF PRINT** Ask children how many words are on page 13. (3) Ask which word has one letter. (I)

④ **USE ILLUSTRATIONS** Have children look at the picture on page 4. Ask them what they think Dad and Dan are doing. (Dad is helping Dan carry the pumpkin.)

LANGUAGE SUPPORT

ESL Beginning on page 6 and through page 8, provide facial expressions as you read the words. Then ask children to make facial expressions as you say the words *sad*, *happy*, and *surprised*.

Guided Instruction

DURING READING

5 **CLASSIFY AND CATEGORIZE** Have children discuss the picture on page 5. Ask how the pumpkins are the same and how they are different. (same shape and color; different sizes)

6 **PHONICS: LETTER _s_** Have children point to the first letter of the word on page 6. Ask them to say the letter. (S) Then have them make the _s_ sound. Blend the sounds and read the word together: _s a d_ sad

7 **USE ILLUSTRATIONS** Look at the small picture on page 7. What word does the picture stand for? (happy) What kind of face does the pumpkin have? (happy)

8 **CLASSIFY AND CATEGORIZE** Ask children to look at the people's faces on page 8. How are they the same? (They have the same expression—surprise) Then ask children to identify the differences among the pumpkin's expressions. (one is sad, one is happy, and one is surprised) Ask them which pumpkin has the same expression as the people. (the one on the right)

INFORMAL ASSESSMENT

CLASSIFY AND CATEGORIZE

HOW TO ASSESS
Set out a variety of classroom objects and ask children to classify them by color, size, and shape.

FOLLOW-UP
For children having difficulty, model the different ways in which items were classified.

Dad and I

5

sad and

7

sad

6

Sad and and !

8

Guided Instruction

RETURN TO PREDICTIONS AND PURPOSES
Ask children to check if their predictions about the story were correct.

RETELL THE STORY Work as a class to retell the story. Children can take turns by retelling their favorite parts. Ask children to think about what happened at the beginning, in the middle, and at the end of the story. Then reread the story together.

LITERARY RESPONSE To help children respond to the story, ask:

- Which pumpkin face was your favorite? Why?

- Did you ever decorate a pumpkin? What did it look like?

Invite children to draw a pumpkin face and to write about it. Encourage them to name the expression on the pumpkin face.

CENTER Activity

Cross Curricular: Math

PUMPKIN PATCH Cut out orange pumpkin shapes of different sizes. Children put them in size order.

▶ Logical/Mathematical

OBJECTIVES

Children will:

- classify and categorize to understand a story

....

MATERIALS

- *Dad, Dan, and I*

TEACHING TIP

INSTRUCTIONAL Display pictures of different fruits and vegetables. Have children describe how they are alike and how they are different.

Introduce Classify and Categorize

PREPARE

Discuss Characters and Events

Ask children to recall the story *Dad, Dan, and I.* Ask how the story begins and who the characters are. Then have children talk about what happens in the story.

TEACH

Understand Differences and Similarities

Reread the story, stopping after each spread and talking about how the pumpkins are alike and how they are different. Explain that when children classify and sort, they look for ways that items are the same and ways that they are different.

PRACTICE

Complete the Pupil Edition Page

Read the directions on page 87 to the children, and make sure they clearly understand what they are asked to do. Identify each picture, and complete the first item together. Then work through the page with children or have them complete the page independently.

ASSESS/CLOSE

Review the Page

Review children's work, and note children who are experiencing difficulty.

Name_____

Look at the pictures in each row. • Draw a circle around the picture that does not belong.

Pupil Edition, page 87

ALTERNATE TEACHING STRATEGY

CLASSIFY AND CATEGORIZE

For a different approach to teaching this skill, see page T29.

▶ **Visual/Auditory/ Kinesthetic**

Practice 87

Name_____

○ Draw lines to show the three things that belong in the classroom. ☆ Draw lines to show the three things that belong in the garden.

Unit 2
Review Classify and Categorize

At Home: Play "Categories." Name three things that belong together. Ask your child to name one more.

87

PRACTICE BOOK, page 87

Meeting Individual Needs for Comprehension

EASY	ON-LEVEL	CHALLENGE	LANGUAGE SUPPORT
Bring in some real pumpkins, or show pictures of pumpkins. Talk about how they are alike and how they are different. Ask questions about shape, size, color, stems, and so on.	**Divide** a sheet of mural paper into thirds, and draw a happy face, a sad face, and a surprised face at the top of each section. Then children draw or cut out pictures of people with these expressions. Point out that children are adding to categories.	**Give** each child an orange circle. Provide markers and pieces of construction paper and invite children to create a jack-o-lantern. Then have them describe their jack-o-lanterns, and think of categories for sorting them.	**Have** children experiment making happy, sad, and surprised faces. Then play a game of "Simon Says," giving directions about showing these expressions.

87

Develop Phonological Awareness

Listen

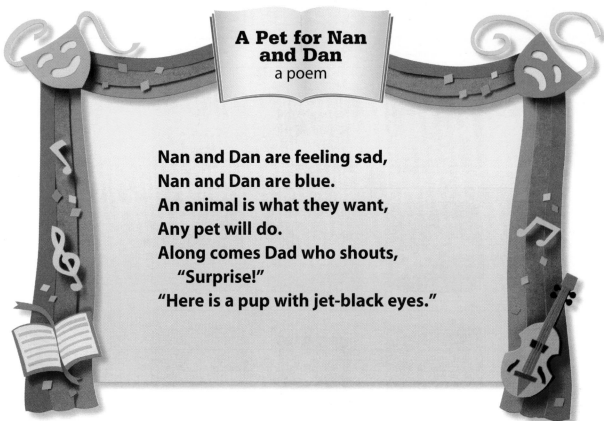

A Pet for Nan and Dan
a poem

Nan and Dan are feeling sad,
Nan and Dan are blue.
An animal is what they want,
Any pet will do.
Along comes Dad who shouts,
  "Surprise!"
"Here is a pup with jet-black eyes."

Objective: Focus on Sounds and Speech

READ THE POEM Read the poem "A Pet for Nan and Dan." Reread the last two lines of the poem. Then repeat the lines again and invite children to join in. Encourage them to shout Dad's words.

> **Surprise! Here is a pup with jet-black eyes.**

WHISPER WORDS Reread the poem and substitute the word *whispers* for *shouts*. Have children finish the poem in a whisper. Repeat the poem several times, interchanging the words *whispers* and *shouts*. Children listen for the word and finish the poem in the voice indicated.

PLAY A GAME Set a chair at the front of the room. Have children sit behind it. Then ask a volunteer to sit in the chair. Have children take turns repeating Dad's words in a whisper. The volunteer guesses the name of the child who is speaking.

Objective: Blending Short *a* with /s/, /d/, and /n/

LISTEN FOR WORDS Read the poem "A Pet for Nan and Dan." Then tell children you are going to say a sentence about the poem, but one word will sound funny. Explain that children need to blend the sounds on their own to identify the word. Say: */n/-/a/-/n/ wants a pet.* Have children identify the word *Nan*. Continue the activity, saying other sentences about the poem.

> **/d/-/a/-/n/ wants a pet.**
> **The children are feeling /s/-/a/-/d/.**
> **/d/-/a/-/d/ has a pup.**

BLEND SOUNDS Say the word *sad*. Say the word again, this time segmenting the sounds. Have children repeat the segmented word after you. Then choose three volunteers and assign each a sound. Have children stand in a left-to-right line and say their sounds in order. Repeat several times, increasing the tempo until *sad* is clearly audible.

BLEND OTHER WORDS Choose new volunteers and repeat the activity using the words below.

> **Dan   Dad   Nan**

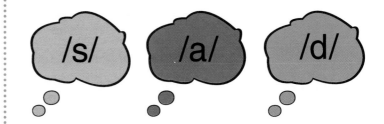

Read Together

From Phonemic Awareness to Phonics

Objective: Identify Word Endings

LISTEN FOR RHYMING WORDS Gather children in a circle. Then say a series of three words, two of which end with the letter *ad* or *an*. Ask children to identify the rhyming words. Write the words on separate cards and then set them aside to use later.

> | tan | dog | pan |
> | leg | mad | lad |
> | sad | pad | sail |
> | ran | car | van |

IDENTIFY THE LETTERS Write *can* on the board. Point to and identify the letters *an*. Have children say the sounds the letters stand for. Repeat with the word *pad*, identifying the letters *ad*.

MATCH RHYMING WORDS Display a word card and say the word. Have children repeat it. Then ask a volunteer to match the card to one of the rhyming words on the board. Have children repeat the rhyming pair after you.

> **tan   sad   van   mad**

FIND WORDS Work with a small group. Display three word cards, two of which rhyme. Do not say the words. Ask children to look at the ending letters to find the two words that rhyme. Say the words children choose and ask them to repeat the words if they rhyme.

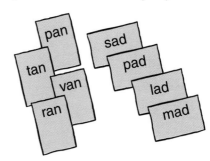

Review Blending with short a

^{TESTED} OBJECTIVES

Children will:

- blend and read short *a* words
- write short *a* words
- review /n/*n*, /s/*s*, and /d/*d*

MATERIALS

- letter cards from the *Word Play Book*
- overhead projector
- two rubber bands

TEACHING TIP

INSTRUCTIONAL Place a stuffed dog with black eyes in a paper bag. Write the following questions on the chalkboard and read them aloud: *Why are Nan and Dan sad? Why did Dad shout, "Surprise!"?* Read aloud the questions, and have volunteers underline words with the letter *a* in the middle. After children answer the questions, display the bag and ask them to guess its contents. Invite a volunteer to take the dog out of the bag to reveal the answer.

ALTERNATE TEACHING STRATEGY

BLENDING SHORT *a*
For a different approach to teaching this skill, see Unit 1, page T32.

▶ **Visual/Auditory/ Kinesthetic**

TEACH

Blend /a/*a* with /s/*s*, /d/*d* and /n/*n*
- Tell children they will review the /a/, /s/, /d/, and /n/ sounds and the letters *a*, *s*, *d*, and *n*. Turn to page T88A and read aloud the poem. Point to the letters *a*, *s*, *d,* and *n* in the first line and identify them. Read aloud the poem. Then ask children to identify words in the first line with blended /a/ and /s/, /d/, or /n/ sounds.

Identify Blended *an, ad, da, sa,* and *na*
- Write the words *sad* and *Dad* on an overhead projector. Have volunteers place rubber bands around the letters that blend to say /ad/, one rubber band around each set of letters. Have children blend and say the sounds. Remove the rubber bands and place one around the *sa* in *sad* and the *Da* in *Dad*. Have children blend and say those sounds. Take off the rubber bands, and have children say the words. Repeat the activity with the words *Nan* and *Dan*.

PRACTICE

Complete the Pupil Edition Page
Read the directions on page 88 of the Pupil Edition, and make sure children clearly understand what they are being asked to do. Identify each picture, and complete the first item together. Then work through the page with children, or have them complete the page independently.

ASSESS/CLOSE

Identify and Use Short *a* and *s, d,* and *n*
Write the following sentences on the chalkboard: *Nan is sad. Dan is sad. Dad is not sad. Dad is glad.* Say the sentences, point to each word, and have children hold up their fingers to count the number of times you say *sad*. After children identify that you've said the word four times, repeat the game and play it with the words *Dan* and *Dad*.

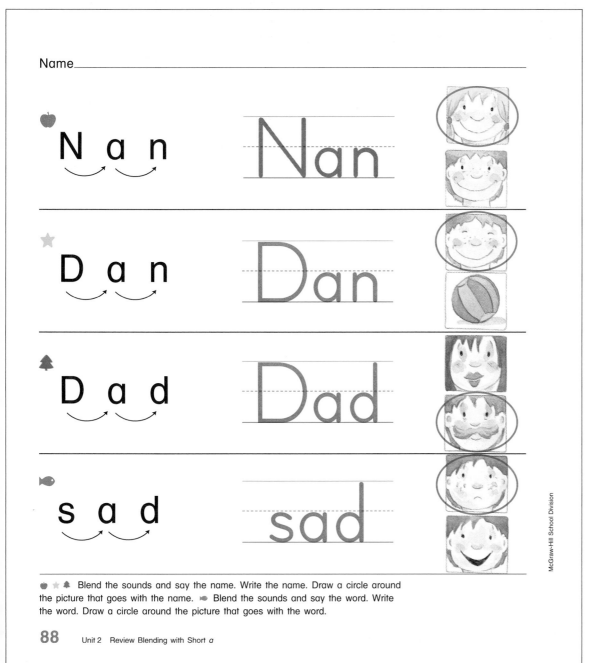

Name _____

N a n   Nan

D a n   Dan

D a d   Dad

s a d   sad

🍎 ⭐ 🌲 Blend the sounds and say the name. Write the name. Draw a circle around the picture that goes with the name. 🐟 Blend the sounds and say the word. Write the word. Draw a circle around the picture that goes with the word.

McGraw-Hill School Division

88   Unit 2   Review Blending with Short *a*

Pupil Edition, page 88

ADDITIONAL PHONICS
RESOURCES

Practice Book, *page 88*
Phonics Workbook

McGraw-Hill School
TECHNOLOGY

Phonics CD-ROM
Activities for practice with
Blending and Segmenting

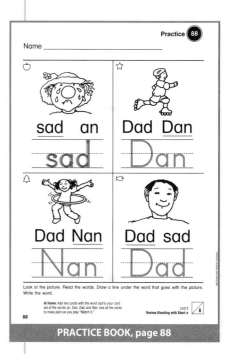

PRACTICE BOOK, page 88

Meeting Individual Needs for Phonics

EASY	ON-LEVEL	CHALLENGE	LANGUAGE SUPPORT
Hold up letter cards *a, s, d,* and *n*. Ask children to smile when they see *s*. Play the game with *a* and *d*. Put the letter cards together. Tell children that when you say the word that the cards make, they are to change their smiles into frowns. Blend and say *sad* as children frown.	**Write** an incomplete version of the first line of "A Pet for Nan and Dan" on the chalkboard: ____ and ____ are feeling ____. Read the incomplete sentences as well as complete sentences from the poem. Have children tape a word card on a blank to complete the sentence.	**Make** a set of index-card word cards with the following words: *Nan, Dan, sad, an, Dad*. Give children blank index cards as well. Invite children to arrange the cards to make one or more sentences, adding words to blank index cards to fill in missing words.	**Tell** children that rhyming words have the same sounds at the end. Display the word cards *Nan, Dan, sad,* and *Dad* in random order. Help children blend and say the words. Invite volunteers to use clothespins to clip together the words that rhyme.

88

Reread the Decodable Story

Dad, Dan, and I

☑ **Letter s**
☑ **Classify and Categorize**
☑ **High-Frequency Word: I**
☑ **Use Illustrations**

Dad, Dan, and I

INFORMAL ASSESSMENT

LETTER s
HOW TO ASSESS
Write the letter s, and have children underline the letter in the word *sad*. Read the word together.

FOLLOW UP
Have children use clay to form the letter s. Then have them make the /s/ sound.

Guided Reading

SET PURPOSES Tell children that when they read the story again they can find out more about what happened. Explain that you also want them to look for words with the initial S. Remind them that they know the word *I* and will see it again in this story.

REREAD THE BOOK As you reread the story, keep in mind any problems children experienced during the first reading. Use the following prompts to guide reading.

- **USE ILLUSTRATIONS** Read the text together, and have children point to Dad and Dan. Ask who the word *I* refers to. (Nan)

- **CLASSIFY AND CATEGORIZE** Talk about the clothing that the characters are wearing. Ask what season it is and what other clothes would be appropriate for that season of the year.

RETURN TO PURPOSES Ask children if they found out more about what they wanted to know about the story. Ask them how many times they saw a word with the initial S and how many times they saw the word *I*.

LITERARY RESPONSE Ask children to write a different ending to the story by thinking of a different kind of pumpkin that Dan could make. Have them use clay to show their pumpkin faces.

<u>Read the</u> Patterned Book

TEACHING TIP

MANAGEMENT Provide a quiet space in the classroom for children to read with partners. You may wish to block off a shelved area to eliminate distractions for readers.

Sid and I

- ☑ **Initial /s/s**
- ☑ **Classify and Categorize**
- ☑ **High-Frequency Word:** *and*
- ☑ **Concepts of Print**

LANGUAGE SUPPORT

 Read the story aloud. Then have partners read the story together. Have children act out words from the story, such as *saw* and *sand*.

Guided Reading

PREVIEW AND PREDICT Read the title and the author's and the illustrator's names. Take a **picture walk** through pages 2–4, noting that the animals are seals and describing what they are doing. Have children make predictions about what will happen in the story.

SET PURPOSES Have children decide what they want to find out from the story and predict what the seals might be building. Tell them that the story contains words with *initial s*.

READ THE BOOK Use the following prompts while the children are reading or after they have read independently. Remind them to run their fingers under each word as they read.

Pages 2–3: Point to the second word. *Let's read it together: and. High-Frequency Words*

Pages 4–5: Point to the word Sid. *I notice the word Sid begins with the /s/ sound. Let's read it together: Sid. Phonics*

Pages 6–7: *Think of all the things that the seals did. How are they the same? Classify and Categorize*

Page 8: *Look at the words on this page. Let's count how many words are on this page. (4) Point to each word as you count. Concepts of Print*

RETURN TO PREDICTIONS AND PURPOSES Ask children if they found out what they needed to know from the story. Check to see if their predictions were correct.

LITERARY RESPONSE The following questions will help focus children's responses:

- Did you ever build something? Draw a picture or write about it in your journal.

- How did the seals work together? Do you like to work alone or with a friend when you do a project? Why?

CENTER Activity

Cross Curricular: Social Studies

FLOAT OR SINK
Provide a small bowl of water and various classroom objects. Have children predict which items will float and which will not. Then have them test to find out. Help them make generalizations based on their findings.

OBJECTIVES

Children will:

- identify and read the high-frequency word *I*

MATERIALS

- word cards from the Word Play Book
- *Dad, Dan, and I*

TEACHING TIP

INSTRUCTIONAL If children have difficulty recognizing letters, provide additional activities. Children can trace tactile letters, and discriminate between pairs of letters. Concentrate on children's understanding of the word *I*.

Review I, and, my

PREPARE

Listen to Words Explain to the children that they will be reviewing the word: *I*. Say the word together. Then ask children to say rhyming words, such as *pie, sky, fly*, and so on.

TEACH

Model Reading the Word in Context Have children reread the decodable book. Ask children to listen for the word: *I*.

Identify the Word Ask children to look at their word cards, and then ask them to say the word: *I*. Have children reread the sentences and track print. Have them put a self-stick note below the word. Have children move the self-stick note from page to page.

Review High-Frequency Words Hold up word cards for the following words: *the, a, my, that, and*. Children say the words.

PRACTICE

Complete the Pupil Edition Page Read the directions on page 89 to children and make sure they clearly understand what they are being asked to do. Complete the first item together. Then work through the page with children or have them complete the page independently.

ASSESS/CLOSE

Review the Page Review children's work, and note children who are experiencing difficulty or need additional practice.

Name _____

Nan and (I)

My dad (and) Nan

(My) dad and I

(I)

Say each group of words and the picture names. ● Draw a circle around the word *I*. ★ Draw a circle around the word *and* . ♠ Draw a circle around the word *my*. ☞ Next to the word *I* draw a picture yourself doing something. Then draw a circle around the word *I*.

Unit 2   Review *I, and, my*   **89**

Pupil Edition, page 89

ALTERNATE TEACHING STRATEGY
....

HIGH-FREQUENCY WORDS

For a different approach to teaching this skill, see page T27.

▶ **Visual/Auditory/ Kinesthetic**

PRACTICE BOOK, page 89

Meeting Individual Needs for Vocabulary

EASY	ON-LEVEL	CHALLENGE	LANGUAGE SUPPORT
Give a word card to partners. Have them tell a short story about themselves, using the word *I*. Give an example, such as: *I like to play with my friend, Jan.* Children hold up the word card when they say *I*.	**Invite** children to think of rhymes using the word *I*. Give partners a sheet of paper and have them draw pictures of words that rhyme with *I*. (*sky, pie, fly*) Have them write *I* at the top of the page.	**Give** each child a word card. Then have each child take turn saying something special about themselves such as: *I play piano. I can run far.* Have children hold up their *I* cards when they hear the word *I*.	**Have** children draw pictures of themselves doing their favorite hobbies. Then have children share their pictures beginning with the word: *I*.

GRAMMAR/SPELLING CONNECTIONS

Model subject-verb agreement, complete sentences, and correct tense so that students may gain increasing control of grammar when speaking and writing.

Interactive Writing

Make a List

Prewrite

LOOK AT THE STORY PATTERN Reread the story *Warthogs in the Kitchen*. Talk about how the numbers follow a pattern in the story. Then ask children what they like to eat for breakfast. Have them follow a similar number pattern in their responses: *1 glass of juice, 2 slices of toast, 3 slices of apple*, and so on.

Draft

MAKE A LIST Tell children that they are going to make a menu that shows foods for a Breakfast Party. If possible, display a menu and talk about what is included on it.

- Have children help you think of breakfast food categories, such as *bread, eggs, cereal, drinks, fruit*. Write the categories on chart paper with words and pictures. Then have children help you think of foods for each category. Have children help you write the words as appropriate, and note when the word *and* is used.

- After the list is complete, ask children what foods they would like to include for the Breakfast Party. Each child creates a personal menu using the lists and drawing and writing selections. Remind children to write their menus in list form, starting at the top of the page. Have children illustrate their menus.

Publish

CREATE THE BOOK Ask each child to read and describe his or her menu. Then combine all of the menus to make a class book for children to share.

Presentation Ideas

HAVE A PARTY Plan a class party, GROUP choosing a menu that was written earlier, or working together to make a class menu. Invite parents to help you prepare the food.

▶ **Representing/Speaking**

ROLE PLAY Have pairs of children role play PARTNERS cooking the foods on their personal menus. You may wish to provide simple kitchen props, pictures of food, or play food.

▶ **Speaking/Representing**

COMMUNICATION TIPS

- **Listening** When children role play, remind them to take turns and listen to each other.
- **Representing** Talk about table manners before your Breakfast Party. Demonstrate how to use napkins, chew and swallow before talking, and try unfamiliar foods.

TECHNOLOGY TIP

Children may wish to use their food lists to create a computer-generated menu. If possible, print out their work, and allow them to illustrate their pages.

LANGUAGE SUPPORT

ESL Use a breakfast menu and discuss the different kinds of foods. Talk about taste, appearance, and texture.

Meeting Individual Needs for Writing

EASY

Food Pairs Have children think of foods that go together: ham and eggs, eggs and toast, peanut butter and jelly, and so on. Make a word/picture list, and highlight the word *and*.

ON-LEVEL

Rewrite the Story Children rewrite the story, substituting different foods that the warthogs eat. Have them follow the number pattern.

CHALLENGE

Write a Menu Invite pairs of children to write a menu for a different meal, such as dinner. Encourage them to use words and pictures, and create a balanced meal.

I Am Sam!

Children will read and listen to stories about friends who pool their talents and have fun together.

I Am Sam!

Listening
Library
Audiocassette

**Decodable Story,
pages 97–98 of the
Pupil Edition**

Our Mobile

by Matt Stuart

illustrated by Angela Adams

**Patterned Book,
page 101B**

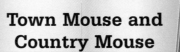

**Town Mouse and
Country Mouse**
Retold and illustrated
by Lorinda Bryan Cauley

**Teacher Read Aloud,
page 95A**

The
ABC
Street
Fair

Written By Constance Keremes
Illustrated By Lindy Burnett

Listening
Library
Audiocassette

**ABC Big Book,
pages 91A–91B**

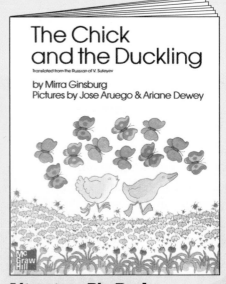

The Chick
and the Duckling
Translated from the Russian of V. Suteyev

by Mirra Ginsburg
Pictures by Jose Aruego & Ariane Dewey

Listening
Library
Audiocasse

**Literature Big Book,
pages 93A–93B**

Pupil Edition,
pages 90–101

Big Book of Real-Life Reading,
page 12

Big Book of Phonics Rhymes and
Poems, pages 33, 34–35

 **Listening**
Library
Audiocassette

ADDITIONAL RESOURCES

Practice Book,
pages 90–101

- **Phonics Kit**
- **Language Support Book**
- **Alternate Teaching Strategies,**
  pages T26, T27, T30

McGraw-Hill School
TECHNOLOGY

Phonics CD-ROM Provides
extra phonics support.

inter NET
CONNECTION Research & Inquiry Ideas.

Visit www.mhschool.com

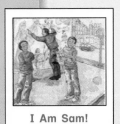

I Am Sam!

READING AND LANGUAGE ARTS

- Phonological Awareness
- **Phonics** initial and final /m/m
- Comprehension
- Vocabulary
- Beginning Reading Concepts
- Listening, Speaking, Viewing, Representing

Available on CD-Rom

Suggested Lesson Planner

DAY 1

Focus on Reading Skills

Develop Phonological Awareness, 90G–90H
"Molly" *Big Book of Phonics Rhymes and Poems,* 33

**Introduce Initial /m/m,** 90I–90
Practice Book, 90
Phonics/Phonemic Awareness
Practice Book

 **CD-ROM**

Read the Literature

Read *The ABC Street Fair* Big Book, 91A–91B
Shared Reading

Build Skills

☑ Shapes: Circle, Triangle, 91C–91
Practice Book, 91

DAY 2

The Chick and the Duckling
by Mitra Ginsburg
Pictures by Jose Aruego & Ariane Dewey

Focus on Reading Skills

Develop Phonological Awareness, 92A–92B
"Where Is Tim?" *Big Book of Phonics Rhymes and Poems,* 34–35

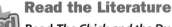**Introduce Final /m/m,** 92C–92
Practice Book, 92
Phonics/Phonemic Awareness
Practice Book

 CD-ROM

Read the Literature

Read *The Chick and the Duckling* Big Book, 93A–93B
Shared Reading

Build Skills

☑ Story Details, 93C–93
Practice Book, 93

- Cross Curriculum

 Language Arts, 91B

 Math, 93B

- Writing

 Writing Prompt: Draw and describe your favorite person from the story.

 Journal Writing, 91B
Letter Formation, 90I

 **Writing Prompt:** Write about how the chick and duckling are alike.

Journal Writing, 93B
Letter Formation, 92C

☑ = **Skill Assessed in Unit Test**

DAY 3

Town Mouse and Country Mouse

Focus on Reading Skills

Develop Phonological Awareness, 94A–94B
"Molly" and "Where Is Tim?" *Big Book of Phonics Rhymes and Poems*, 33–35
**Review /m/m,** 94C–94
Practice Book, 94
Phonics/Phonemic Awareness Practice Book

Phonics **CD-ROM**

Read the Literature

Read "Town Mouse and Country Mouse" Teacher Read Aloud, 95A–95B
Shared Reading
Read the Big Book of Real-Life Reading, 12–13
☑ Diagram

Build Skills

☑ High-Frequency Words: *is*, 95C–95
Practice Book, 95

Activity Cultural Perspectives, 95B

Writing Prompt: If you could take a trip to a big city or to the countryside, which would you choose? Write about your trip.

DAY 4

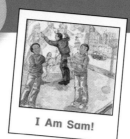
I Am Sam!

Focus on Reading Skills

Develop Phonological Awareness, 96A–96B
"Sam the Clown"
Review Blending with Short *a*, 96C–96
Practice Book, 96
Phonics/Phonemic Awareness Practice Book

Phonics **CD-ROM**

Read the Literature

Read "I Am Sam!" Decodable Story, 97/98A–97/98D

☑ Initial and Final /m/m; Blending
☑ Story Details
☑ High-Frequency Words: *is*
☑ Concepts of Print

Build Skills

☑ Story Details, 99A–99
Practice Book, 99

**Activity** Art, 97/98D

Writing Prompt: What mask would you wear? Draw and describe it.

Letter Formation
Practice Book, 97–98

DAY 5

I Am Sam! — Our Mobile
by Matt Stuart
Illustrated by Angela Adams

Focus on Reading Skills

Develop Phonological Awareness, 100A–100B
"Sam the Clown"
Review Blending with Short *a*, 100C–100
Practice Book, 100
Phonics/Phonemic Awareness Practice Book

Phonics **CD-ROM**

Read the Literature

Reread "I Am Sam!" Decodable Story, 101A

Read "Our Mobile" Patterned Book, 101B
Guided Reading
☑ Initial and Final /m/m; Blending
☑ Story Details
☑ High-Frequency Words: *is*
☑ Concepts of Print

Build Skills

☑ High-Frequency Words: *is, I, and, that,* 101C–101
Practice Book, 101

Activity Art, 101B

Writing Prompt: Write about a fun time you had playing with a friend. Draw a picture of both of you playing.

Interactive Writing, 102A–102B

90F

Develop Phonological Awareness

Listen

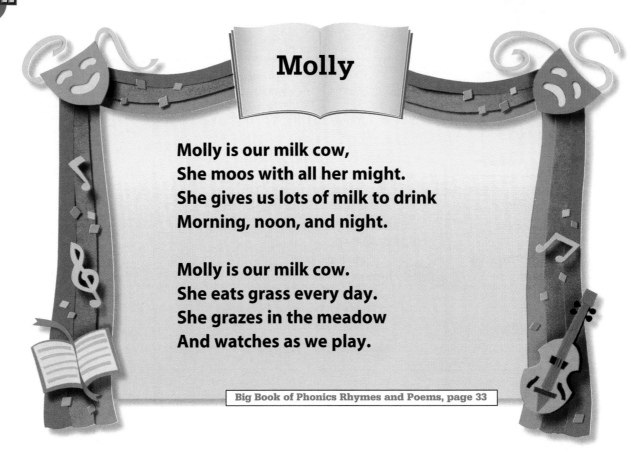

Molly

Molly is our milk cow,
She moos with all her might.
She gives us lots of milk to drink
Morning, noon, and night.

Molly is our milk cow.
She eats grass every day.
She grazes in the meadow
And watches as we play.

Big Book of Phonics Rhymes and Poems, page 33

Objective: Develop Listening Skills

LISTEN TO THE POEM

- Read the poem "Molly" to the children. Then ask them specific questions about the poem.

> **Who is Molly?**
> **What sound does she make?**
> **What does she eat?**

SUBSTITUTE WORDS IN THE POEM

- Invite children to substitute other words for the first two lines of the poem. Model by giving an example.

> **Molly is a pony.**
> **She neighs with all her might.**

- Have children think of words to substitute for the first two lines in the second verse.

> **Molly is our pony.**
> **She eats hay every day.**

- Continue with other animals.

Objective: Listen for Initial /m/

SEGMENTING

- Read the title of the poem, and emphasize the initial /m/ sound. Have children repeat the sound with you. Then segment the sound.

> **M -- olly**

- Repeat with the word *moos.*

LISTEN TO RIDDLES

Have children listen to the following riddles. Tell children the answer is a word that begins with the /m/ sound.

- I am thinking of an animal. It rhymes with house. (mouse)

- It is something the postman brings. It rhymes with pail. (mail) Repeat with other /m/ words.

> **meat   mom   moon**

DIFFERENTIATE BETWEEN INITIAL SOUNDS

- Say the following pairs of words. Children choose the word that begins with /m/.

> **man/fan   more/tore**
> **sat/mat   room/moon**

Read Together

From Phonemic Awareness to Phonics

Objective: Identify Initial /m/ *M, m*

IDENTIFY THE LETTER FOR THE SOUND

- Explain to children that the letters *M, m* stand for the sound /m/. Say the sound and have children repeat it.

- Display page 33 in the Big Book of Phonics Rhymes and Poems, and point to the letters in the corner. Identify the letters and have children repeat the sound.

REREAD THE POEM

- Read the poem again, stopping at each word that begins with

/m/. Children repeat the words, emphasizing the initial /m/.

RECOGNIZE WORDS WITH *M, m*

- Make the sound "m-m-m-m," and ask children to rub their bellies when they hear that sound. Reread the poem slowly.

- Then frame a word that begins with the letter m. Tell children to say "m-m-m" only when you point.

> **milk lots morning day Molly**

Molly

Molly is our milk cow.
She moos with all her might.
She gives us lots of milk to drink
Morning, noon, and night.

Molly is our milk cow.
She eats grass every day.
She grazes in the meadow
And watches as we play.

33

Big Book of Phonics Rhymes and Poems, page 33

90H

OBJECTIVES

Children will:

- identify the letters *M, m*
- identify /m/ *M, m*
- form the letters *M, m*

....

MATERIALS

- letter cards from the Word Play Book

TEACHING TIP

MANAGEMENT In this lesson, you will use the Big Book of Phonics Rhymes and Poems. Use the poem as a visual resource for the children.

Introduce Initial /m/m

TEACH

Identify /m/ M, m Display page 33 in the *Big Book of Phonics Rhymes and Poems,* and reread the poem. Emphasize words that begin with /m/, and write *M, m* on the chalkboard. Tell children they will learn to write the sound /m/ with the letters *M, m*. Say the sound and have children repeat it. Then ask children to clap when they hear a word in the poem that begins with *m*. Reread the poem slowly.

Form M, m Display letters *M, m*, and with your back to the children, trace *M, m* in the air. Ask children to do the same. Then play "Up and Down the Mountain." Draw a large *M* on the chalkboard and mark off stages of this "mountain" that must be climbed. Each time someone says a word that begins with *m*, write a small, lowercase *m* at the next stage of the climb. Give children strips of paper, and ask them to write one capital *M* for the mountain and one lowercase *m* for each stage of the climb.

PRACTICE

Complete the Pupil Edition Page Read the directions on page 90 of the Pupil Edition, and make sure children clearly understand what they are being asked to do. Identify each picture and complete the first item together. Then work through the page with children or have them complete the page independently.

ASSESS/CLOSE

Identify and Use M, m Say the following list of words, and have children hold up their *M, m* strips when they hear a word that begins with the letter *m*: *sad, mat, not, man, Max, Dad.*

ALTERNATE TEACHING STRATEGY

....

INITIAL /m/m

For a different approach to teaching this skill, see page T30.

▶ **Visual/Auditory/ Kinesthetic**

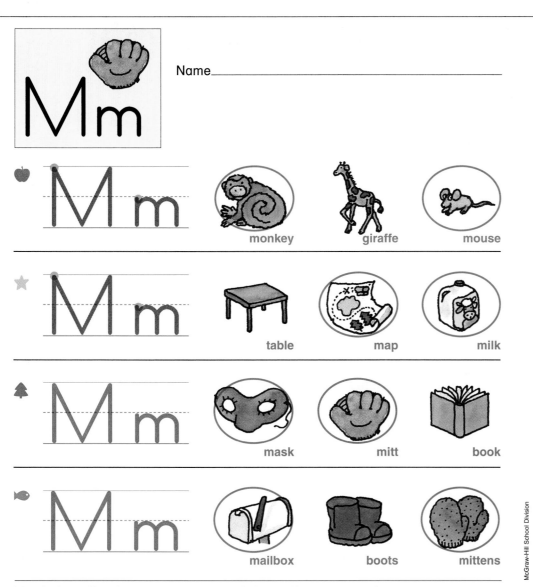

Name_____

monkey giraffe mouse

table map milk

mask mitt book

mailbox boots mittens

McGraw-Hill School Division

Write the letters *Mm*. • Say the word that names each picture. • Listen for the sound at the beginning of each word. • Draw a circle around each picture whose name begins with the same sound as *mitt*.

90 Unit 2 Introduce Initial /m/*m*

Pupil Edition, page 90

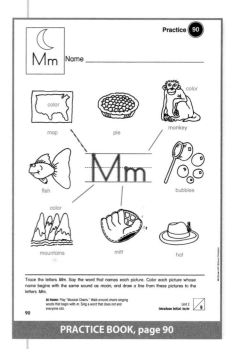

Practice 90

Mm Name_____

color color monkey

map pie

fish bubbles color

mountains mitt hat

Trace the letters *Mm*. Say the word that names each picture. Color each picture whose name begins with the same sound as *moon*, and draw a line from these pictures to the letters *Mm*.

At Home: Play "Musical Chairs." Walk around chairs singing words that begin with *m*. Sing a word that does not and everyone sits.

90 Unit 2 Introduce Initial /m/*m*

PRACTICE BOOK, page 90

Meeting Individual Needs for Phonics

EASY	ON-LEVEL	CHALLENGE	LANGUAGE SUPPORT
Give children magazine or catalog pictures of objects whose names begin with *m*, such as *mask, mop, mitten, money, mirror, moon*. Have them label each picture with the letter *m*. Staple the pages together to make a book. Ask children to write *M, m* on the cover.	**Ask** children to sort the following word cards to show words that do or do not begin with *m*: *Max, sat, nap, man, mix, win*. Have them write the letter *m* for each initial /m/ word.	**Have** children play "What's in Your Mind?" Think of a word that begins with *m*, and give children clues, for example: *The word in my mind rhymes with nap.* Each time someone guesses the word, have children repeat it and write an *m*.	**Invite** children to play the game "Mother, May I?" One child is *Mother*. The others line up across the room and try to reach him or her by asking, "Mother, May I?" and then give instructions such as "Take two steps." Have children emphasize the initial /m/ sounds.

90

Children will:

- recognize words with initial *m*
- answer questions using sentences

TEACHING TIP

You may wish to keep a chart for each child to record when he or she consistently recognizes each letter of the alphabet.

Read the Big Book

Before Reading

Develop Oral Language   Sing "The Monkey Alphabet" with the children. The song is on page 4 in the Big Book of Phonics Rhymes and Poems. Then sing the song again. When children hear the letter that begins their last name, have them raise a hand.

Remind children that they read a story about a street fair. Ask them what parts of the story they remember.

Set Purposes   Tell children that as they reread the story, they will supply words in the story. They will also use sentences to answer questions about the story.

Mm Marvelous marbles   Nice necklaces Nn

How many marbles?

The ABC Street Fair, pages 18–19

During Reading

Read Together

• Point to the uppercase and lowercase letters at the top of each page as you say the name of the letter. Then point to the word and have a volunteer use the picture and the letter to read the word. Confirm their response by saying, "That's right. The word *apples* begins with *a*." *Concepts of Print*

• After you read the words on page 2, ask: What color are Anna's apples? Have children answer in a complete sentence. Continue with other pages in the book. *Use Illustrations*

• Make the /m/ sound and have children say it with you. After you read page 18, have children repeat the words, emphasizing the initial /m/. *Phonics*

• After you read page 30, ask children to look closely at the zebra. Ask, "How many people do you think are inside the zebra costume?" Ask them to give reasons for their answers. *Story Details*

The ABC Street Fair, page 18

After Reading

Literary Response

JOURNAL WRITING Invite children to draw and write in their journals about an activity they would like to do at the fair.

ORAL RESPONSE Encourage them to answer questions in sentences. Ask:

• *Why did you choose this activity?*

ABC Activity

Write the letters of the alphabet on construction paper, and make a path in the classroom. Children take off their shoes and "walk" on the path, saying each letter as they walk.

INFORMAL ASSESSMENT

LETTER IDENTIFICATION

HOW TO ASSESS

Point to letters in the ABC Big Book. Ask children to identify the letters. Then point to the letter *m* and have children identify whether you are pointing to a capital or lowercase *m*.

FOLLOW-UP

Have children find examples of *Mm* in the ABC Big Book.

Cross Curricular: Art

QUILTING ABC Display a small quilt or a picture of a quilt. Have children make an ABC quilt. Have 26 large squares that are precut, with the letters written in the lower right-hand corner. Children can choose squares to illustrate with a picture or a design. When all the squares are completed, arrange them in order and make a "quilt" display on the wall.

▶ **Kinesthetic/Spatial**

OBJECTIVES

Children will:

- identify and describe circles and triangles

MATERIALS

- *The ABC Street Fair*
- large paper circles and triangles

TEACHING TIP

INSTRUCTIONAL Make sure children understand the terms *straight* and *curved*. Draw straight and curved lines, and have children identify them. Then draw two lines, and introduce the term *corner*.

Introduce Shapes: Triangle, Circle

PREPARE

Match Shapes Hold up a paper circle, and ask children to find objects in the classroom that have the same shape. Emphasize matching the shape, not the size. Repeat for triangles.

TEACH

Recognize Shapes Hold up a paper circle and identify it. Discuss the attributes of the shape such as round, no corners. Ask children to find objects with this shape. Then repeat with a paper triangle, noting that it has three straight sides and three corners. Display the Big Book *The ABC Street Fair,* and take a picture walk through the book. Have children look for objects that have the shape of a triangle or a circle.

PRACTICE

Find Circles and Triangles Read the directions on page 91 to the children, and make sure they clearly understand what they are asked to do. Identify each picture, and complete the first item together. Then work through the page with children, or have them complete the page independently.

ASSESS/CLOSE

Review the Page Check children's work on the Pupil Edition page. Note areas where children need extra help.

Name _____

Find the circles in the picture. • Color them yellow. • Find the triangles in the picture. • Color them blue.

Unit 2   Introduce Shapes: Triangle, Circle   **91**

ALTERNATE TEACHING STRATEGY

SHAPES: CIRCLE, TRIANGLE

For a different approach to teaching this skill, see page T31.

▶ **Visual/Auditory/ Kinesthetic**

PRACTICE BOOK, page 91

Meeting Individual Needs for Beginning Reading Concepts

EASY	ON-LEVEL	CHALLENGE	LANGUAGE SUPPORT
Provide different sizes of circles and triangles cut from heavy tagboard. Encourage children to trace the shapes with their fingers, and help them name the shape. Then have children sort the shapes.	**Provide** circle and triangle templates in several different sizes. Have children name the shapes, and use different colors of crayons to trace around them. Then ask questions such as: *Is the green circle larger than or smaller than the red circle?*	**Cut** out circles and triangles of different colors and sizes. Have children identify the shapes. Then begin a pattern, and have children identify and extend it. Invite children to create their own patterns.	**Draw** a square and a circle on oversized paper. Then give children paper triangles and circles of different sizes, and ask them to glue each shape in the matching larger shapes. Have children name each shape.

91

Develop Phonological Awareness

Listen

Where Is Tim?

Tim, Tim!
We are looking for him.
We want him to play
on the jungle gym.

Tim, Tim!
We are looking for him.
We want him to go outside
for a swim.

Tim, Tim!
It's him! It's him!
He's playing a game
with his sister, Kim.

Big Book of Phonics Rhymes and Poems, pages 34–35

Objective: Listen for the Number of Syllables

LISTEN FOR SYLLABLES IN THE POEM

- Read the poem "Where Is Tim?" aloud.
- Give each child a card with 1 or 2 on it.
- Then say the word *Tim*. Clap once as you say the word. Ask how many syllables the word has.
- Then ask children who have a card with one dot to hold it up.

1 OR 2 SYLLABLES?

- Continue the activity with the following words from the poem: *we, looking, play, outside, swim, playing, game, sister*.

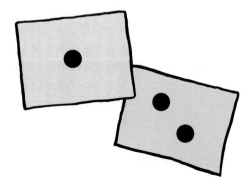

Objective: Listen for Final /m/

SEGMENTING

- Say the name *Tim*. Segment the final /m/ and have children repeat with you. Explain that the /m/ sound can be at the beginning, middle, or end of a word.

> **Ti - m**

LISTEN, LISTEN!

- Explain that children will play a listening game. Say the following rhyme:

  Listen, listen, loud and clear.
  What is the last sound that you hear?

  Say the word *him* and have children say the /m/ sound if it is in the final position.

- Continue the game with the following words: *for, gym, swim, gate, game, cab, bus, Kim*. Invite children to join in on the rhyme.

Read Together

From Phonemic Awareness to Phonics

Objective: Identify Final /m/

IDENTIFY THE LETTER FOR THE SOUND

- Explain to children that the letter *m* stands for the sound /m/. Ask children to say the sound with you.

- Display the Big Book of Phonics Poems and Rhymes, pages 34–35. Point to the letter in the corner. Identify the letter as *m* and say the sound. Have children say the sound with you.

REREAD THE POEM

- Read the poem again, pointing to each word. When you say a word that ends with /m/, stop and have children repeat it after you.

FIND FINAL *m*

- Write lowercase *m* on stick-on notes. Have volunteers place a note on words that end with *m*.

Mm

Where is Tim?

Tim, Tim!
We are looking for him.
We want him to play
On the jungle gym.

Tim, Tim!
We are looking for him.
We want him to go outside
For a swim.

34

Big Book of Phonics Rhymes and Poems, pages 34–35

Children will:

- identify /m/ *m*
- form the letter *m*

MATERIALS

- letter cards from the Word Play Book

TEACHING TIP

MANAGEMENT Children will benefit from tactile experiences with letters. Cut fairly large letters out of heavy sandpaper and thin foam panels such as those used for packing electronics. Soak yarn letters in starch and let them dry until they are stiff. Bend letters out of pipe cleaners, and glue drinking straws or craft sticks together to shape letters. Sort by letter and store in large labeled envelopes.

ALTERNATE TEACHING STRATEGY

FINAL /m/m

For a different approach to teaching this skill, see page T30.

▶ **Visual/Auditory/Kinesthetic**

Introduce Final /m/m

TEACH

Identify /m/ m Tell children they will listen for the sound /m/ and write the letter *m*. Say *jam, dim,* and ask children to say the sound that is the same in both words. Write the words on the chalkboard and invite volunteers to underline the letter that stands for the sound /m/. Ask if the letter is at the beginning or the end of the word.

Form m With your back to the children, trace a large lowercase letter *m* in the air. Ask children to do the same. On strips of paper, ask children to write a letter *m* for every picture you show them whose name ends in *m*. Examples: *ham, mop, jam, swim, net, drum.*

PRACTICE

Complete the Pupil Edition Page Read the directions on page 92 of the Pupil Edition, and make sure children clearly understand what they are being asked to do. Identify each picture and complete the first item together. Then work through the rest of the page with children or have them complete the page independently.

ASSESS/CLOSE

Identify and Use m Ask children to hold up their *m* strips when they hear a word that ends in /m/ in the following story: *Tim and Pam live on a farm with their mom and dad. Tim likes to hum. Pam plays the drum. Together, they hum and drum.*

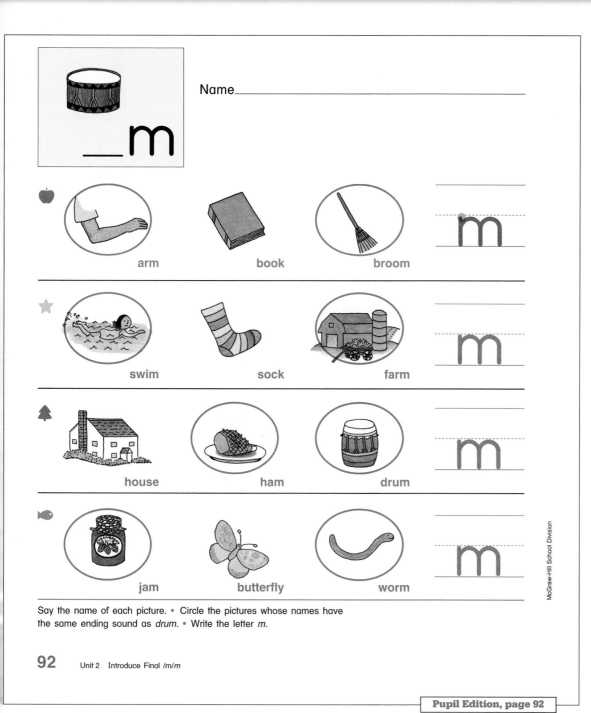

Name _____

__m

🍎 arm	book	broom	m
⭐ swim	sock	farm	m
🌲 house	ham	drum	m
🐟 jam	butterfly	worm	m

Say the name of each picture. • Circle the pictures whose names have
the same ending sound as *drum*. • Write the letter *m*.

92   Unit 2   Introduce Final /m/m

McGraw-Hill School Division

Pupil Edition, page 92

PRACTICE BOOK, page 92

Meeting Individual Needs for Phonics and Decoding

EASY	ON-LEVEL	CHALLENGE	LANGUAGE SUPPORT
Give children laminated *m* letter cards, and have them use an erasable pen to trace the letter several times. Then ask them to sort a selection of *a, d, s,* and *m* letter cards into groups. Also ask them to think of a word that ends with the sound /m/.	**Ask** children to suggest all of the names they can think of that end in *m*, such as *Jim, Kim, Tim, Adam, Tom, Pam, Sam*. Ask children to write the letter *m* for each name they suggest.	**Read** the Dr. Seuss story *Green Eggs and Ham*. Have children hold up their *m* strips when they hear a word that ends in *m*, or give them self-stick notes to label words in the story that end with the letter *m*. Other story books can be used for this activity as well.	**Children** who have trouble distinguishing between *n* and *m* can practice writing the letters on the chalkboard with paintbrushes dipped in water. Write the letters above their workspace so that they can use them for reference, and have children repeat each sound.

OBJECTIVES

- recognize words with final *m*
- use story details

MIRRA GINSBURG grew up in a Russian village, where she heard many folktales. She writes and edits books for children and adults and lives in New York City.

JOSE ARUEGA AND ARIANE DEWEY have worked together on illustrations for numerous children's picture books. Mr. Aruega designs the page and draws the outlines, and Ms. Dewey fills in the color.

LANGUAGE SUPPORT

ESL Invite children to pantomime the action words in the story: *digging, pulled, caught, swimming*. Children can act out the words, and others can guess what the action is. Encourage children to think of animals that do these actions.

Read the Big Book

Before Reading

Build Background

EVALUATE PRIOR KNOWLEDGE Talk about farms that children have seen in real life or on television. Ask what types of animals live on a farm. Make a picture first.

MAKE A MURAL Draw a simple barnyard scene on mural paper. Invite children to draw and cut out an animal that could live on the farm.

Preview and Predict

DISCUSS AUTHOR AND ILLUSTRATOR Read the title of the book and display the cover. Talk about what children see, pointing out the duckling and the chick. Name the author and illustrators, and share information about them. Explain that the story was first written by a Russian writer, V. Suteyev.

TAKE A PICTURE WALK Then take a picture walk through about one third of the book.

MAKE PREDICTIONS Ask children to make predictions about what will happen in the story.

Set Purposes

Tell children you will read to find out what things the chick and the duck do together.

The Chick and the Duckling, pages 8–9

During Reading

Read Together

- Before you begin to read, point to the first word in the first sentence. Explain that this is where you will begin to read. Continue to track print as you read the story. *Tracking Print*

- Have children look carefully at the illustrations on the title page, copyright page, and the dedication page. Ask children what the hen and the chick did. (Laid eggs and then left the eggs.) *Story Details*

- Make the /m/ sound and have children repeat it after you. Then reread page 5. Ask children to say two words that end with that sound. (came, am) *Phonemic Awareness*

- After you read page 20, ask children what they think the chick will say and do. *Make Predictions*

"Not me," said the Chick.

The Chick and the Duckling, page 32

After Reading

Return to Predictions and Purposes

Ask children if their predictions about the story were correct.

Literary Response

JOURNAL WRITING

- Point out that the chick always followed what the duckling did until the end of the story. Invite children to draw a picture of something the duckling did and the chick followed. Have them write about the picture.

ORAL RESPONSE Engage children in a discussion by asking questions such as:

- *Did you ever learn to do something from a friend? What did you do?*

- *Did you ever try to do something that was hard for you? What was it?*

INFORMAL ASSESSMENT

STORY DETAILS
HOW TO ASSESS
Have children recall details from the story by naming all of the activities the chick and the duckling did together.

FOLLOW-UP
Remind children to refer back to their books to help them recall story details.

CENTER Activity

Cross Curricular: Math

COUNTING TIME Explain to children that eggs need sun and warmth to hatch. It takes about 21 days for a chick to hatch and about 29 days for a duckling to hatch.

Place 21 counters in a paper cup that is labeled with a picture of a chick. Place 29 counters in a paper cup that is labeled with a duckling. Have children match one to one to find out which takes longer to hatch.

▶ Logical/Mathematical

OBJECTIVES

Children will:

- use story details to understand a story

. . . .

MATERIALS

- *The Chick and the Duckling*

TEACHING TIP

INSTRUCTIONAL Explain that one reason ducks are better swimmers than chicks is that ducks have oil on their feathers. Illustrate by putting a cotton ball in water and watch it sink. Then dip a cotton ball in vegetable oil and watch it float.

Introduce Story Details

PREPARE

Discuss the Sequence of Events
Ask children to recall the story *The Chick and the Duckling*. Ask how the story begins, and who the characters are. Then ask what kinds of things the duck and the chick did together. Make a picture or word list.

TEACH

Review Details in the Story
Revisit the title and copyright pages. Point out that looking carefully at the illustrations adds to the enjoyment of the story. Then reread the story, stopping frequently and checking the list that the children made. Change the list if necessary. Explain that noting details of the story makes it more interesting to read.

PRACTICE

Complete the Pupil Edition Page
Read the directions on page 93 to the children, and make sure they clearly understand what they are asked to do. Identify each picture, and complete the first item together. Then work through the page with children or have them complete the page independently.

ASSESS/CLOSE

Review the Page
Review children's work, and note children who are experiencing difficulty.

Name _____

Think about the story "The Chick and the Duckling." • In each row, circle the
pictures that show something from the story.

Pupil Edition, page 93

ALTERNATE TEACHING
STRATEGY
....
STORY DETAILS
For a different approach
to teaching this skill, see
page T26.

► **Visual/Auditory/
Kinesthetic**

PRACTICE BOOK, page 93

Meeting Individual Needs for Comprehension

EASY	ON-LEVEL	CHALLENGE	LANGUAGE SUPPORT
Ask children to draw their favorite part of the story. Encourage them to use as many details as possible. Then have others guess what part of the story children illustrated.	**Revisit** pages 30–31 and ask how the chick is feeling. Have children look for clues and details in the picture to support their answers. Invite children to choose other parts of the book and describe how Chick and Duck are feeling.	**Show** children photographs of chickens and ducks. Have them describe the animals, using as many details as possible. Ask questions about variations in color, size, shape, and so on.	**Take** children on a picture walk through the story. Have children name different things in each picture, using as many details as possible.

Develop Phonological Awareness

Listen

Molly
a poem

Where Is Tim?
a poem

Molly is our milk cow.
She moos with all her
    might.
She gives us lots of milk to
    drink
Morning, noon, and night.

Molly is our milk cow.
She eats grass every day.
She grazes in the meadow
And watches as we play.

Tim, Tim!
We are looking for him.
We want to play on the jungle
    gym.

Tim, Tim!
We are looking for him.
We want him to go outside
    for a swim.

Tim, Tim!
It's him! It's him!
He's playing a game with his
    sister, Kim.

Big Book of Phonics Rhymes and Poems, pages 33, 34–35

Objective: Focus on Sounds

READ THE POEM Read the poem "Molly." Ask children to imitate the sound Molly makes.

PLAY AN ANIMAL SOUND GAME Name animals and invite children to make each animal's sound. Then ask children to close their eyes as you make an animal sound. Have children name the animal. Increase the game's difficulty by making a sequence of two or three animal sounds.

quack oink heehaw meow

OMIT A SOUND Make a series of animal sounds. Repeat the series in order, leaving out one sound. Encourage children to identify the missing sound.

bow-wow

Objective: Listen for /m/

LISTEN FOR INITIAL /M/ Read the poem "Molly." Say /m-m-m/ to emphasize words with the initial /m/ sound. Have children say the /m/ sound. Then say names of foods. Have children say /m-m-m/ if the word begins with the /m/ sound.

> **muffin peas milk meat nut**

LISTEN FOR FINAL /M/ Read the poem "Where Is Tim?" emphasizing the final /m/ sound. Have children repeat the sound with you. Say the word *him*. Segment the final /m/ and have children repeat with you. Next, say a word. Have children add a final /m/ sound to make a new word.

> **far (farm)   tea (team)   tie (time)**

IDENTIFY WORDS WITH /M/ Ask: *Could Tim be...?*, completing the sentence with names of people or places. Children clap when they hear the /m/ sound.

> **Could Tim be in his room?**
> **Could Tim be with his mother?**

Read Together

From Phonemic Awareness to Phonics

Objective: Identify /m/ M, m

IDENTIFY THE LETTERS
Display the Big Book of Phonics Rhymes and Poems, pages 33 and 34–35. Point to the letters and identify them. Say the sound the letters stand for.

REREAD THE POEMS Reread the poems. Point to each word and emphasize those with the /m/ sound.

COUNT THE WORDS WITH M, m Reread the poems line by line. Have children count the words that begin or end with M or m.

Mm

Where is Tim?

Tim, Tim!
We are looking for him.
We want him to play
On the jungle gym.

Tim, Tim!
We are looking for him.
We want him to go outside
For a swim.

Tim, Tim!
It's him! It's him!
He's playing a game
with his sister, Kim.

34

35

Big Book of Phonics Rhymes and Poems, pages 34–35

94B

OBJECTIVES

Children will:

- identify and use letters *M, m*
- write the letter *M, m*

MATERIALS

- letter cards from the Word Play Book

TEACHING TIP

INSTRUCTIONAL Have children sort tactile letters *a, d, s, n,* and *m* to further familiarize themselves with the letter forms they have studied. Invite them to compare and contrast two different letters, for example, lowercase *a* and *d* or capital and lowercase *n* and *m*. Encourage them to talk about how the letter shapes feel as well as guiding them to notice visual clues, such as the fact that capital *M, N,* and *A* all show triangles.

ALTERNATE TEACHING
STRATEGY

FINAL /m/*m*

For a different approach to teaching this skill, see page T30.

▶ **Visual/Auditory/ Kinesthetic**

Review /m/ m

TEACH

Identify and Use /m/ *M, m*

Tell children they will review the sound /m/ and the letters *M, m*. Give them letter cards *d, m, n, s, a,* and ask them to show the letter *m* card and to make the sound of this letter. Say the following sentence, and have children hold up their *m* letter cards when they hear a word that begins with *m: Max's mom gave him a map of the moon.* Repeat, and ask which words end with the letter *m*.

Write and Use *M, m*

Give each child an incomplete word card that has a blank space at the beginning or at the end of a word, such as *_an, hi_, ja_, _y, su_, _at.* Have children write the missing *m*'s. Collect the cards and read them aloud, asking children to repeat after you.

PRACTICE

Read the directions on page 94 of the Pupil Edition, and make sure children clearly understand what they are being asked to do. Identify each picture, and complete the first item together. Then work through the rest of the page with children or have them complete the page independently.

ASSESS/CLOSE

Identify and Use *M, m*

Say the following list of words, and have children tap their feet when they hear a word that ends in *m: man, map, Pam, mix, ham, my, him.* Repeat for words that begin with *m*. Then ask children to write the letter *m* several times.

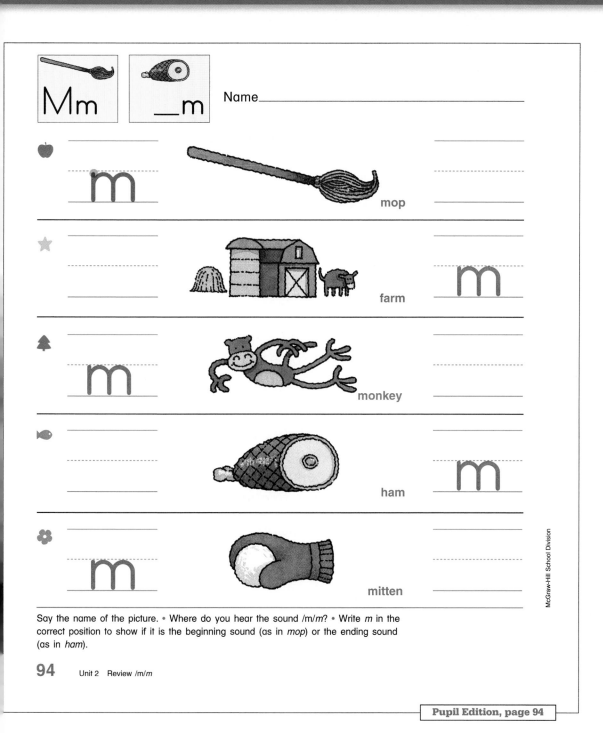

Mm | __m | Name_____

🍎 _____ m _____ mop _____

⭐ _____ farm m _____

🌲 m monkey _____

🐟 _____ ham m _____

✿ m mitten _____

Say the name of the picture. • Where do you hear the sound /m/m? • Write *m* in the correct position to show if it is the beginning sound (as in *mop*) or the ending sound (as in *ham*).

94   Unit 2   Review /m/m

McGraw-Hill School Division

Pupil Edition, page 94

ADDITIONAL PHONICS RESOURCES

Practice Book, *page 94*
Phonics Workbook

McGraw-Hill School
TECHNOLOGY

Phonics CD-ROM
Activities for practice with Initial and Final Letters

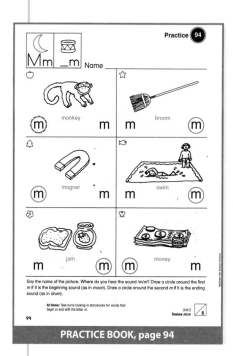

PRACTICE BOOK, page 94

Meeting Individual Needs for Phonics and Decoding

EASY	ON-LEVEL	CHALLENGE	LANGUAGE SUPPORT
Give children a selection of tactile letter *M*'s and *m*'s to choose from, such as foam or sandpaper cutouts. Have children lay the letters out in an *M, m* pattern.	**Have** children sit in a circle and spin a spinner. The child who the spinner points to says a word that begins or ends in *m*. Invite the other children to hold up their *m* letter cards and repeat the words.	**Tell** this story and ask children to fill in the missing words by saying a word that begins or ends with *m*: *My dad and ____ took ____ to the theater to see a ____ about a ____ and his dog.* Have children write an *m* for each /m/ they hear.	**Write** the following words, one at a time, on the chalkboard: *man, am, Sam, sat, mat,* and. Ask children to turn thumbs down if the word does not begin or end in *m* and to turn thumbs up and say *Mmm!* if it does. Ask them to write an *m* for each *m* they see.

94

Teacher Read Aloud

Listen

The Town Mouse and the Country Mouse

retold by Lorinda Bryan Cauley

The Country Mouse lived by himself in a snug little hole in an old log in a field of wild flowers.

One day he decided to invite his cousin the Town Mouse for a visit, and he sent him a letter.

When his cousin arrived, the Country Mouse could hardly wait to show him around. They went for a walk, and on the way they gathered a basket of acorns.

They picked some wild wheat stalks.

They stopped by the river and sat on the bank, cooling their feet.

And on the way home for supper, they picked some wild flowers for the house.

The Country Mouse settled his cousin in an easy chair with a cup of fresh mint tea and then went about preparing the best country supper he had to offer.

He made a delicious soup of barley and corn.

He simmered a root stew seasoned with thyme.

Then he made a rich nutcake for dessert, which he would serve hot from the oven.

Continued on page T6

Oral Comprehension

LISTENING AND SPEAKING Ask children to talk about the differences between living in the city and living in the country. Make a picture or word list. Then explain that children will hear a fictional (make-believe) story about two mice who live in different places. As they listen, ask children to think about how life was different for the country mouse and the city mouse.

After you finish the story, ask children if they would prefer to visit the country mouse or the city mouse.

Encourage children to give reasons to support their choice. Then take a class vote.

 **Activity** Ask children to draw a picture of the country mouse or the city mouse, showing where the mouse lives. Ask children to give the mouse a name.

▶ **Spatial/Linguistic**

Real-Life Reading

Who is the Town Mouse?
Who is the Country Mouse?

ear

hat

nose

jacket

briefcase

tail

shoe

12

nose

shirt

overalls

tail

boot

13

Big Book of Real-Life Reading, pages 12–13

Objective: Use a Diagram

READ THE PAGE Remind children of "The Town Mouse and the Country Mouse." Have children explain how the mice were alike and how they were different. Tell children that they will see a diagram that shows each mouse. A diagram uses pictures and words to explain something. Read the text and discuss the pictures.

ANSWER THE QUESTION Ask children how they can tell which mouse is the city mouse and which is the country mouse. Ask what each mouse is wearing. *Why do you think the country mouse is wearing overalls and boots?* Provide pencils and paper. Ask children to draw a mouse and draw arrows to its ears, mouth, tail, and feet.

CULTURAL PERSPECTIVES

PUPPET THEATER Story telling is a special art in many countries. In Bali, people often use shadow puppets to tell a story.

Activity Have children select a favorite story that includes several characters. Ask children to draw the story's characters on thin cardboard. Cut out the characters. Ask for volunteers to retell the story using shadow puppets. Hold up a large piece of paper as a screen in front of a lamp. Have puppeteers perform behind the lamp and the screen. The audience will see the shadows of the puppets appear on the screen.

▶ **Interpersonal/Kinesthetic**

OBJECTIVES

Children will:

- identify and read the high-frequency word *is*

MATERIALS

- word cards from the Word Play Book

Introduce High-Frequency Words: *is*

PREPARE

Listen to Words Explain to children that they will be learning a new word: *is*. Say the following sentence: "The pup is hot." Say the sentence again, and ask children to raise a finger when they hear the word *is*. Repeat with the question: *Is Mom mad?*

TEACH

Model Reading the Word in Context Give a word card to each child, and read the word. Reread the sentences, and have children raise their hands when they hear the word.

Identify the Word Write the sentences above on the chalkboard. Track print and read each sentence. Children hold up their word cards when they hear the word *is*. Then ask volunteers to point to and underline the word *is* in the sentences.

PRACTICE

Complete the Pupil Edition Page Read the directions on page 95 to children, and make sure they clearly understand what they are asked to do. Complete the first item together. Then work through the page with children, or have them complete the page independently.

ASSESS/CLOSE

Review the Page Review children's work, and note children who are experiencing difficulty or need additional practice.

Name_____

Sam <u>is</u> sad.

_____

Nan <u>is</u> mad.

_____

Dan <u>is</u> a man.

_____

That <u>is</u> my dad.

Read the sentences. • Then draw a line under the word *is* in each sentence.

Unit 2   Introduce High-Frequency Words: *is*   95

Pupil Edition, page 95

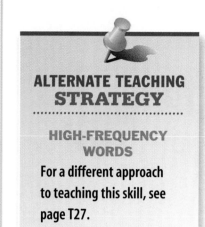

ALTERNATE TEACHING STRATEGY

HIGH-FREQUENCY WORDS

For a different approach to teaching this skill, see page T27.

▶ **Visual/Auditory/Kinesthetic**

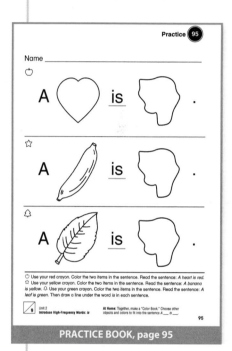

PRACTICE BOOK, page 95

Meeting Individual Needs for Vocabulary

EASY	ON-LEVEL	CHALLENGE	LANGUAGE SUPPORT
Give children a letter card with *i* or *s*. Children find a partner to form the word *is*. Then each child uses the word in a sentence.	**Have** children dictate sentences that use the word *is*. After you write and reread the sentences, volunteers circle the word in each sentence.	**Invite** children to use the word *is* to begin a question. Have them ask questions to other children, such as: *Is it time for lunch? Is it cold today?* Partners answer, using the word *is*.	**Have** children sit in a circle. One child describes the child sitting next to him or her, using the word *is*: *Tom is friendly. Sara is wearing a blue dress.* Encourage children to make positive statements about their classmates.

Develop Phonological Awareness

Listen

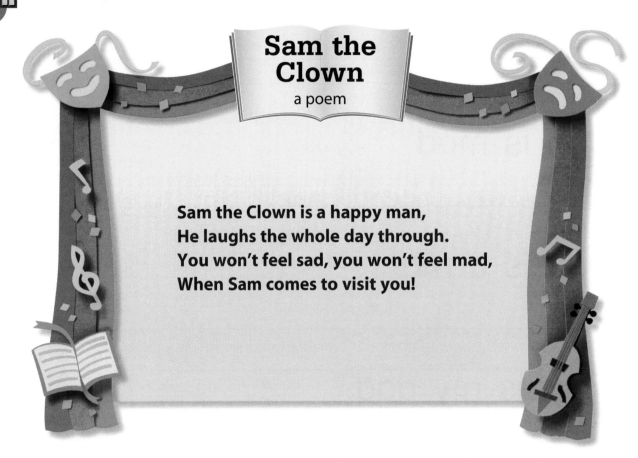

Sam the Clown
a poem

Sam the Clown is a happy man,
He laughs the whole day through.
You won't feel sad, you won't feel mad,
When Sam comes to visit you!

Objective: Focus on Sentence Length

READ THE POEM Read aloud the poem "Sam the Clown" several times. Invite children to join in on familiar words. Then encourage children to share their experiences with clowns.

COUNT WORDS Provide each child with six blocks. Then say: *Sam is a clown.* Repeat the sentence slowly and set one block on the table for each word. Starting at the left, point to each block as you repeat the sentence. Encourage children to join in. Help children determine that there are four words in the sentence. Have children use their blocks to repeat the activity.

> **Sam is a clown.**

MAKE LONGER SENTENCES Say other sentences having six words or less. Have children work in pairs, using their blocks to determine the number of words in each sentence. Then invite a volunteer to model each sentence.

> **Sam came to see me.**
> **He made me laugh.**
> **I don't feel sad or mad.**

Objective: Blending Short *a* with /m/

LISTEN FOR THE SEGMENTED WORD Invite children to listen as you read the poem "Sam the Clown." Explain that you will reread the poem, but one word will be said differently. Then read the poem again, segmenting each sound in *Sam*. Have children determine that *Sam* was read differently.

> **/s/ /a/ /m/**

BLEND THE SOUNDS On the chalkboard, draw an outline of a simple clown face. Tell children that the clown is Sam and that Sam is happy. Add three small circles to form a smiling mouth. Then starting at the left, point to the circles in the smiling mouth as you say the sounds in the name *Sam*. Repeat several times and invite children to join in. Increase the speed to blend the sounds.

PRACTICE BLENDING Have each child draw a clown face. Then give each three self-stick dots to use as the mouth. Encourage children to move their fingers from dot to dot as they blend the sounds /s/-/a/-/m/.

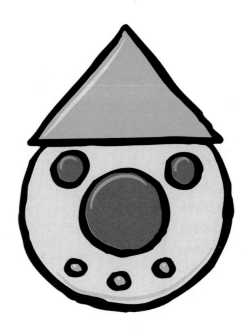

Read Together ## From Phonemic Awareness to Phonics

Objective: Identify Word Endings

LISTEN FOR RHYMING WORDS Read the following rhyming lines: *There is Sam. He likes ham.* Ask children to identify the words that rhyme. Write the rhyming words on the board.

> **Sam   ham**

IDENTIFY THE LETTERS Invite a volunteer to circle the letters in the rhyming words that are the same. Then identify the letters. Ask children to say the sound each letter stands for.

NAME OTHER RHYMING WORDS Ask children to name other words that rhyme with *Sam* and *ham*. Write the words on the board and circle the ending letters.

> **yam   jam   dam**
> **Pam   ram**

SUBSTITUTE WORDS Point to one of the rhyming words on the board and say it aloud. Have children repeat the word. Then substitute the chosen word for the word *ham* in the couplet: *There is Sam. He likes ham.* Read the new rhyme, inviting children to join in. Have children determine if the rhyme makes sense.

> **There is Sam.**
> **He likes Pam.**

OBJECTIVES

Children will:

- identify and blend /a/*a* words
- read and write short *a* words
- review /m/*m*

....

MATERIALS

- letter cards from the Word Building Book

TEACHING TIP

INSTRUCTIONAL Say the following sentence: *Sam is a man.* Ask children to hold up their *a* letter cards when they hear a word with the /a/ sound. Write the sentence on the chalkboard, and ask children to circle the two words with the /a/ sound.

ALTERNATE TEACHING STRATEGY

....

BLENDING SHORT *a*

For a different approach to teaching this skill, see Unit 1, page T32.

▶ **Visual/Auditory/ Kinesthetic**

96C   *I Am Sam!*

Review Blending with short a

TEACH

Identify *a* as a Symbol for /a/

Tell children they will continue to read and write short *a* words.

- Display the *a* letter card and say /a/. Have children repeat the sound /a/ after you as you point to the card.

BLENDING Model and Guide Practice

- Place an *n* card after the *a* card. Blend the sounds together and have children repeat after you: _an.

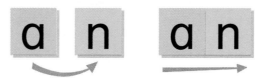

- Place an *m* letter card before the *a, n* cards. Blend the sounds in the word to read *man*. Have children repeat after you.

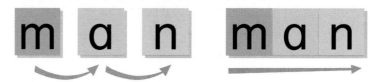

Use the Word in Context

- Have children use *man* in a sentence, perhaps by discussing a story or nursery rhyme they know well.

Repeat the Procedure

- Use the following words to continue modeling and for guided practice with short *a*: am, dam, sam, sad, mad, an, Nan.

PRACTICE

Complete the Pupil Edition Page

Read the directions on page 96 to the children, and make sure they clearly understand what they are being asked to do. Identify each picture, and complete the first item together. Then work through the page with children, or have them complete the page independently.

ASSESS/CLOSE

Write Short *a* Words

Observe children as they complete page 96. Display letter cards *m, s, d, n* and ask them to write four short *a* words that begin or end in *m*. Have children read their words aloud and write them on the chart.

Name_____

🍎 S a m   Sam

⭐ d a m   dam

🌲 m a n   man

🐟 m a d   mad

🍎 Blend the sounds and say the name. Write the name. Draw a circle around the picture that goes with the name. ⭐🌲🐟 Blend the sounds and say the word. Write the word. Draw a circle around the picture that goes with the word.

96   Unit 2 Review Blending with Short *a*

McGraw-Hill School Division

Pupil Edition, page 96

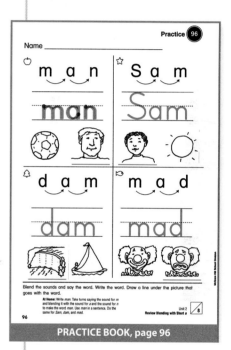

PRACTICE BOOK, page 96

Meeting Individual Needs for Phonics

EASY	ON-LEVEL	CHALLENGE	LANGUAGE SUPPORT
Display word cards *man, mad, dam, am, Sam*. Have children repeat as you blend sounds to read the words. Let children read the words and take the word card. When all the cards have been taken, ask each child to read the word again.	**Ask** children to form a circle and pass a hat with short *a* words such as: *am, Sam, dam, mad, man*. Have the first child choose a card and blend sounds to read the word aloud. The next child uses the word in a sentence. Continue until all words have been used.	**Have** children draw a picture that shows a man standing near a dam. Ask children to label the man and the dam. You may also want children to dictate a sentence about their pictures.	**Help** children distinguish between /m/ and /n/ by blending sounds to read these words aloud: *am, an, dam, Dan, Nan, man*. Point out that *man* includes both sounds.

96

Guided Instruction

BEFORE READING

PREVIEW AND PREDICT Take a brief **picture walk** through the book, focusing on the illustrations.

- Who is this story about? Where does it take place?

- Do you think the story is realistic or make-believe? Why?

SET PURPOSES Discuss some reasons children may have for wanting to read the story. Ask children questions such as, Who do you think is under the costumes?

I Am Sam!

I am Sam!

3

Is that Sam?

2

Is that Dan?

4

Guided Instruction

DURING READING

☑ **Final** *m*
☑ **Story Details**
☑ **Concepts of Print**
☑ **High-Frequency Word:** *is*

① CONCEPTS OF PRINT Have children run fingers from left to right as they track print on the title page. Ask children to point to the last character. Explain that this is an exclamation mark and that it is used to show excitement.

② HIGH-FREQUENCY WORD: *is* Have children point to the first word on page 2. Track print and read it together: *is*. Then have children read it again.

③ PHONICS: FINAL *m* Have children look at page 3. Then show them the letter card for *m*. Identify the letter and make the sound together. Ask which word ends with *m*. (Sam)

④ CONCEPTS OF PRINT Ask children to point to the question mark on page 4, and explain what it means. (ask a question)

LANGUAGE SUPPORT

ESL Talk about the words *costume* and *mask*. Point out the costumes and masks throughout the story, repeating the words. Then have children locate the pictures of costumes and masks in the story, saying the words as they find the pictures.

Guided Instruction

DURING READING

⑤ CONCEPTS OF PRINT Point to the exclamation mark on page 5 and identify it. Reread the sentence with an excited voice. Ask why Dad and Dan are laughing.

⑥ STORY DETAILS Have children look closely at the picture on page 6. Then ask them to describe the costume, using descriptive language.

⑦ MAKE INFERENCES After reading page 7, ask why Sam is puzzled. (He doesn't know where Dad is.)

⑧ BLENDING WITH SHORT *a* Have children locate the short *a* words on page 8. (That, dad) Ask children to make the short *a* sound. Then have them blend the sounds to read the word.

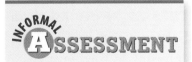

INFORMAL ASSESSMENT

STORY DETAILS

HOW TO ASSESS
Have children compare how they think Sam is feeling on page 7 to how he is feeling on page 8.

FOLLOW-UP
Point out that on page 7 Sam looks frightened because he doesn't know who is behind the mask and on page 8 he looks happy because he discovered it was his dad.

I am Dan!

5

Dad?

7

Is that Dad?

6

That is my dad!

8

Guided Instruction

AFTER READING

RETURN TO PREDICTIONS AND PURPOSES
Discuss children's previous predictions about the story. Ask children if they found out where the story took place and who was under the costumes.

RETELL THE STORY Have small groups retell the story by acting it out. Have volunteers act out the story while other children provide the details.

LITERARY RESPONSE To help children respond to the story, ask:

• What costume was your favorite? Why?

Invite children to draw and write about a costume they would like to wear.

Activity

Cross Curricular: Art

MASK MAKING Provide paper bags and craft materials. Invite children to make their own masks. You may wish to provide books with photos of different types of masks. Then have groups of children act out the story.

▶ **Kinesthetic/Intrapersonal**

OBJECTIVES

Children will:

- use story details to understand a story

....

MATERIALS

- *I Am Sam!*

TEACHING TIP

INSTRUCTIONAL Display a familiar classroom object. Ask children to use as many words as possible to describe it without naming the object. Point out that children are using details to describe the object.

Introduce Story Details

PREPARE

Discuss Story Details   Ask children to recall the story *I Am Sam!* Ask how the story begins, and who the characters are. Then ask what clues helped them guess the identity of the person behind the mask.

TEACH

Review Details in the Story   Reread the story, stopping after each spread and talking about what clues help children to guess who is behind each mask. Focus on as many details as possible, such as height, body type, and so on.

PRACTICE

Complete the Pupil Edition Page   Read the directions on page 99 to the children, and make sure they clearly understand what they are asked to do. Identify each picture, and complete the first item together. Then work through the page with children or have them complete the page independently.

ASSESS/CLOSE

Review the Page   Review children's work, and note children who are experiencing difficulty.

Name _____

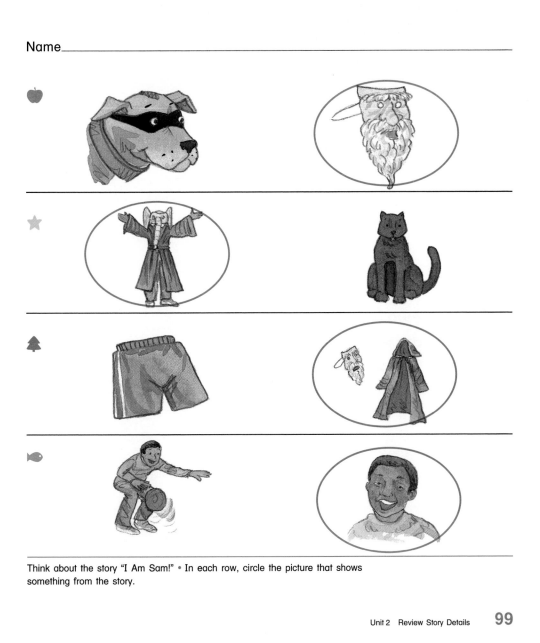

Think about the story "I Am Sam!" • In each row, circle the picture that shows something from the story.

Pupil Edition, page 99

ALTERNATE TEACHING STRATEGY

STORY DETAILS

For a different approach to teaching this skill, see page T26.

▶ Visual/Auditory/ Kinesthetic

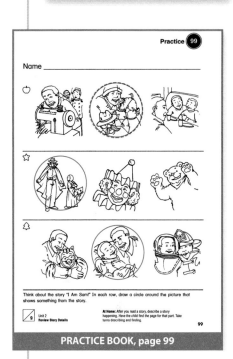

PRACTICE BOOK, page 99

Meeting Individual Needs for Comprehension

EASY	ON-LEVEL	CHALLENGE	LANGUAGE SUPPORT
Ask children to look at the costume Dad is wearing on page 6 of the book. Have children describe it in terms of color, shape, size, and so on. Then have children describe their own clothing, using as many details as possible.	**Give** each child a sheet of large drawing paper. Have them draw a picture of themselves in a costume, adding as many details as possible. Invite children to then describe their costumes.	**Have** small groups sit in a circle. One child chooses something in the classroom and gives clues to describe it, using as many details as possible. Others try to guess the object. Children take turns.	**Explain** that children need to look carefully to notice details. Place several classroom objects on a tray, naming each item as it is placed. Children close their eyes as you take one away. Then have children tell you what is missing.

99

Develop Phonological Awareness

Listen

Sam the Clown

a poem

Sam the Clown is a happy man,
He laughs the whole day through.
You won't feel sad, you won't feel mad,
When Sam comes to visit you!

Objective: Identify Action Words

ACT LIKE A CLOWN Gather children in a circle and read the poem "Sam the Clown." Then invite volunteers to demonstrate actions clowns might do.

> **jump   skip   hop**

SUBSTITUTE ACTION WORDS Reread the second line in the poem and identify the action word *laugh*. Then invite children to name other action words. Substitute their responses for the word *laugh* as you reread the line. Encourage children to perform the action as you repeat the entire poem.

> **He skips the whole day through.**

PERFORM THE ACTIONS IN ORDER Have children stand. Explain that you will say two actions, and children are to do them in the order named. Then say: *Hop three times; touch your nose.* Continue the activity by naming two or three actions in a row.

> **spin around; jump two times; skip to the door; pat your knee**

Objective: Blending Short *a* with /m/, /s/, /d/, and /n/

SOUND OUT A WORD Read the poem "Sam the Clown." Ask children to name the clown in the poem. Then encourage children to say *Sam* sound by sound. Ask children how many sounds they hear. Have children determine that they hear three different sounds.

> /s/ /a/ /m/

LISTEN AND BLEND Tell children you will say a sentence, but one word will be said differently. Tell children to listen to the sentence, and then repeat it with the word blended together.

> **The /m/-/a/-/n/ is happy.**

MORE BLENDING Continue the activity with the following sentences.

> /s/-/a/-/m/ **is a clown.**
> **Nan is** /s/-/a/-/d/.
> **Dan is not** /m/-/a/-/d/

Read Together

From Phonemic Awareness to Phonics

Objective: Identify Word Endings

LISTENING FOR RHYMING WORDS Read the third line of the poem "Sam the Clown," whispering the rhyming words. Ask children to name the rhyming words and then write them on the board.

> **sad   mad**

IDENTIFY THE LETTERS Circle the letters in the words that are the same. Identify the letters and say the sounds. Then write the rhyming pairs *jam- ham* and *pan-man* in separate columns on the board. Circle the ending letters and repeat the letter and sound identifications.

MATCH WORD ENDINGS Write words ending with the letters *an, am,* and *ad* on index cards. Give each child a card. Then invite children to play a game. Have children walk among their classmates gathering everyone who has the same word ending as shown on their card. When the group is complete, children sit down. Have group members hold up their cards. Read the words aloud. Encourage children to give the thumbs up sign if all the words rhyme.

Nan	Dan	fan	man	pan
Dad	glad	pad	mad	sad
Sam	jam	ham	yam	Pam

OBJECTIVES

Children will:

- identify and blend /a/*a* words

- read and write short *a* words

- review /m/*m*, /s/*s*, /d/*d*, /n/*n*

MATERIALS

- letter cards from the Word Building Book

TEACHING TIP

INSTRUCTIONAL Make word cards for the following words: *Nan, and, Dan, an, man, am, sad*. Ask children to read the words and then to sort them into two groups: words that begin with the /a/ sound and words with the /a/ sound in the middle.

ALTERNATE TEACHING STRATEGY

BLENDING SHORT *a*

For a different approach to teaching this skill, see Unit 1, page T32.

▶ **Visual/Auditory/ Kinesthetic**

Review Blending with short *a*

TEACH

Identify *a* as a Symbol for /a/

Tell children they will continue to read and write short *a* words.

- Display the *a* letter card and say /a/. Have children repeat after you.

BLENDING Model and Guide Practice

- Place a *d* card after the *a* card. Blend the sounds together and have children repeat after you: _ad.

- Place a *d* letter card before the *a, d* cards. Blend the sounds in the word to read *dad*. Have children repeat.

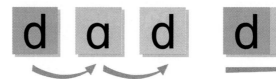

Use the Word in Context

- Have children use *dad* in a sentence. They could say something they admire about their dad or someone else's dad.

Repeat the Procedure

- Use the following words to continue modeling and for guided practice with short *a*: *an, Dan, man, mad, sad, Sam, am*.

PRACTICE

Complete the Pupil Edition Page

Read the directions on page 100 to the children and make sure they clearly understand what they are being asked to do. Identify each picture, and complete the first item together. Then work through the page with children, or have them complete the page independently.

ASSESS/CLOSE

Build a Short *a* Word

Observe children as they complete page 100. Then give each child three *a* letter cards and several *m, s, d, n* cards to build three words with short *a* in the middle.

Name_____

N a n   Nan

m a n   man

m a d   mad

s a d   sad

McGraw-Hill School Division

🍎 Blend the sounds and say the name. Write the name. Draw a circle around the picture that goes with the name. ⭐ 🌲 🐟 Blend the sounds and say the word. Write the word. Draw a circle around the picture that goes with the word.

100   Unit 2 Review Blending with Short *a*

Pupil Edition, page 100

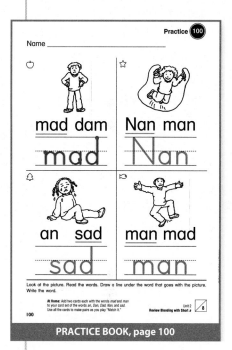

ADDITIONAL PHONICS RESOURCES

Practice Book, *page 100*
Phonics Workbook

McGraw-Hill School
TECHNOLOGY

📀 **Phonics** **CD-ROM**
Activities for practice with
Blending and Segmenting

Practice 100

Name _____

mad dam	Nan man
mad	Nan
an sad	man mad
sad	man

Look at the picture. Read the words. Draw a line under the word that goes with the picture. Write the word.

At Home: Add two cards each with the words *mad* and *man* to your card set of the words *an, Dan, Dad, Nan,* and *sad.* Use all the cards to make pairs as you play "Match it."

100   Unit 2 Review Blending with Short *a*   8

PRACTICE BOOK, page 100

Meeting Individual Needs for Phonics

EASY	ON-LEVEL	CHALLENGE	LANGUAGE SUPPORT
Write *Sam* and *sad* on the chalkboard and have children repeat as you blend sounds to read the words aloud. Ask how the words are alike and different. Continue using *mad, man, Dan, dad.*	**Have** children complete sentences using the following words: *sad, dad, mad, dam, Nan.* For example: *The water fell over the ___. The children in the story are Dan and ___. Mom and ___ are cleaning the house.* Children can write their answers and then read them aloud.	**Give** children these letter cards: *n, a, d, s, m.* Ask them to form as many words as they can that have the /a/ sound at the beginning or in the middle of the word. Children can write the words they build. (Possible words: *an, Nan, Dan, Dad, sad, man, mad, am, Sam, dam*)	**Reinforce** blending with short *a* by having children repeat the following sentences: *The man is Sam. Dan is the dad.* Write the sentences on the chalkboard. Ask children to circle the words with the /a/ sound.

Reread the Decodable Story

I Am Sam!

☑ **Phonics: Letter** *m*
☑ **Story Details**
☑ **High-Frequency Word:** *is*
☑ **Concepts of Print**

I Am Sam!

Guided Reading

SET PURPOSES Tell children that when they read the story again, they can find out more about what happened. Explain that you also want them to look for words with the initial and final letter *m*. Remind children that they know the word *is* and they will see it again in this story.

REREAD THE BOOK As you reread the story, keep in mind any problems children experienced during the first reading. Use the following questions to guide reading.

- **CONCEPTS OF PRINT** Remind children that words on a page are read from left to right. Invite children to read a page, while tracking print.

- **STORY DETAILS** Have children describe the costume shop. Explain what types of items are sold at costume shops and why.

RETURN TO PURPOSES Ask children if they found out more about what they wanted to know. Ask them if they were able to locate words with the letter *m*.

LITERARY RESPONSE Ask children to act out a different ending to the story. Brainstorm ideas together.

WRITING

Read the Patterned Book

Our Mobile

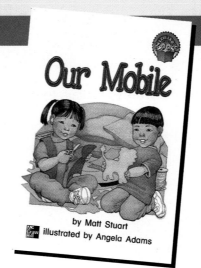

by Matt Stuart
illustrated by Angela Adams

☑ **Initial and final /m/m**

☑ **Classify and Categorize**

☑ **High-Frequency Word:** *is*

☑ **Concepts of Print**

Guided Reading

PREVIEW AND PREDICT Read the title and the author's and the illustrator's names. Take a **picture walk** through pages 2–4, paying attention to the details in the illustrations. Have children make predictions about what they think will happen in the story.

SET PURPOSES Have children decide what they want to find out from the story and predict what the children might be making. Tell them that the story contains words with initial and final *m*.

READ THE BOOK Use the following prompts while the children are reading or after they have read independently. Remind them to run their fingers under each word as they read.

Pages 2–3: Point to the word *is*. *Let's read this word together: is. High-Frequency Words*

Pages 4–5: Point to the word *monkey*. *The word monkey begins with the /m/ sound. Let's read it together: monkey. Phonics*

Pages 6–7: *What did the boy make?* (moose) *What does it look like? Story Details*

Page 8: Point to the space between the words *this is. This is a space. Words have spaces between them. Who can find another space on this page? Concepts of Print*

RETURN TO PREDICTIONS AND PURPOSES Ask children if they found out what they needed to know from the story. Check to see if their predictions were correct.

LITERARY RESPONSE The following questions will help focus children's responses:

- What kind of mobile would you like to make? Draw a picture or write about it in your journal.

- What animals did the children in the story make?

LANGUAGE SUPPORT

ESL Discuss the word *mobile*, making sure that children have a clear idea of what a mobile is. Read the story aloud. On each page point to the word that names an animal. Then point to the picture and have the children say the name of the animal with you. Then have partners read the story together.

CENTER Activity

Cross Curricular: Social Studies

ANIMAL MOBILES Have children make their own animal mobiles. Children can draw or cut out pictures from magazines. Hang the pictures from coat hangers. Children may wish to work together and choose animals in a particular category, such as dogs or mammals.

OBJECTIVES

Children will:

- identify and read the high-frequency word *is*

MATERIALS

- word cards from the *Word Play Book*
- *I Am Sam!*

TEACHING TIP

INSTRUCTIONAL Play a game to reinforce high-frequency words. Have children sit in a circle and close their eyes. Tap a child on the shoulder, who then leaves the circle and hides. As children open their eyes, say, "Who is missing?" Children guess who is missing and guess where the child is hiding.

Introduce High-Frequency Words: *is*

PREPARE

Listen to Words   Explain to the children that they will review the word *is*.

Read the following sentences, and have children raise a hand when they hear the word *is: That is my dad. Is that my dad?*

TEACH

Model Reading the Word in Context   Reread the decodable book. Ask children to listen for the word *is*.

Identify the Word   Ask children to look at their word cards, and then ask them to look for the word in sentences. Read the sentences, tracking print, and ask children to come up and point to the word *is*. Have volunteers put a self-stick dot below the word.

Review High-Frequency Words   Give each child word cards for *the, a, my, that,* and *I*. Say the words, and have children hold up the appropriate cards.

PRACTICE

Complete the Pupil Edition Page   Read the directions on page 101 to the children, and make sure they clearly understand what they are asked to do. Complete the first item together. Then work through the page with children or have them complete the page independently.

ASSESS/CLOSE

Review the Page   Review children's work, and note children who are experiencing difficulty or need additional practice.

Name_____

🍎 (I) am Sam and that is Nan.

_____

⭐ Is that Dad (and) Dan?

_____

🌲 Dad (is) that man.

_____

🐟 (That) is Dad.

_____

🍎 Draw a circle around the word *I*.   ⭐ Draw a circle around the word *and*.
🌲 Draw a circle around the word *is*.   🐟 Draw a circle around the word *that*.

Unit 2   Review *is, I, and, that*   **101**

Pupil Edition, page 101

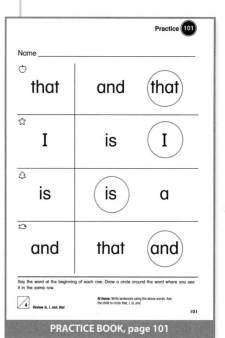

PRACTICE BOOK, page 101

ALTERNATE TEACHING STRATEGY
··
HIGH-FREQUENCY WORDS: *is*

For a different approach to teaching this skill, see page T27.

▶ **Visual/Auditory/ Kinesthetic**

Meeting Individual Needs for Vocabulary

EASY	ON-LEVEL	CHALLENGE	LANGUAGE SUPPORT
Give children letter cards for *i* and *s*, and have them form the word *is*. Then show a picture from a magazine, and ask questions such as: *Where is the (boy)? What is the (dog) doing?*	**Invite** children to bring in photos from home. Use the word card *is*, and read the word together. Then ask questions such as: *Who is this person? Where is this cabin?* Point to the word *is* when appropriate.	**Some** children may express interest and be ready to write the word *is*. Provide dashed letters, and show children how to form the letters. Children can trace the letters and say the word.	**Display** an alphabet chart, and ask children to find the letters *i* and *s*. Write *is* and read it together. Use the word in questions that children can answer.

Interactive Writing

Make a Calendar

GRAMMAR/SPELLING CONNECTIONS

Model subject-verb agreement, complete sentences, and correct tense so that students may gain increasing control of grammar when speaking and writing.

Prewrite

LOOK AT THE STORY PATTERN Reread the story *The Chick and the Duckling*. Ask what the animals liked to do together, and then talk about the pattern in the story. Ask: *What did the Chick do whenever the Duckling did something?* Then talk about what the children like to do with their friends.

Draft

WRITE A CLASS CALENDAR Display a calendar and explain its purpose. Talk about why and how a calendar is used.

- Begin by making a calendar grid for one week. Have children help you label the days of the week, and point out that there are seven days in a week.

- Invite children to think of something that two friends can do in the classroom each day of the week. Write their suggestions, beginning each phrase: *You can . . .*

Publish

CREATE THE CALENDAR Reread the calendar together. Then ask children to choose one of the days of the week, and illustrate the information on the calendar. Have children label their drawings as appropriate. Display the illustrations near the calendar.

Presentation Ideas

ACT OUT THE CALENDAR Invite partners
to act out the events on the calendar.
PARTNERS Others describe what they see, using
the sentence: *You can (play games) with a
friend.*

▶ **Speaking/Listening**

MAKE A POSTER Invite each child to
make a poster showing one of the
PARTNERS days of the week. Children show
what they would like to do with a friend at
school. Have children line up, showing
Monday to Friday, and describe their posters.

▶ **Representing/Viewing**

COMMUNICATION TIPS

- **Speaking** When children
speak to the class, remind
them to make eye contact.
Explain that it is important
to let others know that you
are speaking to them.

- **Representing** Remind children to use words and actions
when they role play. Before
children begin role-playing
activities, brainstorm possible ideas for them to try.

TECHNOLOGY TIP

Use a calendar graphic from a
computer program to input
children's data.

LANGUAGE SUPPORT

ESL Familiarize chil-
dren with differ-
ent types of calendars, making
sure that children understand
that days and months are
always included. Invite them to
find their birthdays and other
special events on a calendar.

Meeting Individual Needs for Writing

EASY	ON-LEVEL	CHALLENGE
Draw Pictures Ask children to draw something that they did during the day. Then help them to label the picture with the day of the week.	**Make a Calendar** Help children to make a calendar for two weeks. Have them help you label the calendar. Then draw pictures on the calendar to mark special classes, such as music or art, special days or activities, and so on.	**Journal Entry** Ask children to draw and write about something they like to do on Saturday or Sunday. Remind children to sound out words as they write.

Sid Said

The variety of literature in this lesson will offer children many opportunities to read and listen to stories about friends who work and play together.

Sid Said

Listening Library Audiocassette

**Decodable Story,
pages 109–110 of the
Pupil Edition**

Come In!

by Jane Tower
illustrated by John Wallner

**Patterned Book,
page 113B**

**Mary Had a
Little Lamb**
by Sarah Josepha Hale

**Teacher Read Aloud,
page 107A**

The
ABC
Street
Fair

Written By Constance Keremes
Illustrated By Lindy Burnett

Listening Library Audiocassette

**ABC Big Book,
pages 103A–103B**

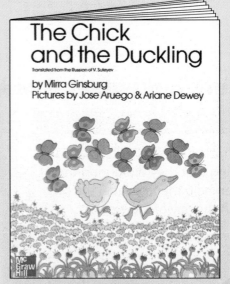

The Chick
and the Duckling

Translated from the Russian of V. Suteyev

by Mirra Ginsburg
Pictures by Jose Aruego & Ariane Dewey

Listening Library Audiocassette

**Literature Big Book,
pages 105A–105B**

**Pupil Edition,
pages 102–113**

**Big Book of Real-Life Reading,
page 14**

**Big Book of Phonics Rhymes and
Poems, pages 25, 26–27**

 **Listening
Library
Audiocassette**

ADDITIONAL RESOURCES

**Practice Book,
pages 102–113**

- **Phonics Kit**
- **Language Support Book**
- **Alternate Teaching Strategies,**
  pages T24–T32

McGraw-Hill School
TECHNOLOGY

Phonics CD-ROM Provides
extra phonics support.

interNET CONNECTION Research & Inquiry Ideas.

Visit www.mhschool.com

Sid Said

Suggested Lesson Planner

READING AND LANGUAGE ARTS

- **Phonological Awareness**

- **Phonics** initial and medial /i/i; blending with short *i*

- **Comprehension**

- **Vocabulary**

- **Beginning Reading Concepts**

- **Listening, Speaking, Viewing, Representing**

DAY 1

Focus on Reading Skills

Develop Phonological Awareness, 102G–102H
"Iggy the Iguana" *Big Book of Phonics Rhymes and Poems,* 25

 **Introduce Initial /i/i,** 102I–102
Practice Book, 102
Phonics/Phonemic Awareness
Practice Book

💿 **Phonics** **CD-ROM**

Read the Literature

Read *The ABC Street Fair* Big Book, 103A–103B
Shared Reading

Build Skills

☑ Shapes: Square, Rectangle, 103C–103
Practice Book, 103

DAY 2

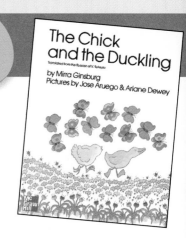

The Chick and the Duckling
by Mirra Ginsburg
Pictures by Jose Aruego & Ariane Dewey

Focus on Reading Skills

Develop Phonological Awareness, 104A–104B
"I Miss My Mouse" *Big Book of Phonics Rhymes and Poems,* 26–27

 **Introduce Medial /i/i,** 104C–104
Practice Book, 104
Phonics/Phonemic Awareness
Practice Book

💿 **Phonics** **CD-ROM**

Read the Literature, 105A–105B

Read *The Chick and the Duckling* Big Book, 105A–105B
Shared Reading

Build Skills

☑ Classify and Categorize, 105C–105
Practice Book, 105

- **Cross Curriculum**

 Language Arts, 103B

 Science, 105B

- **Writing**

 Writing Prompt: How would you have your face painted? Draw and describe.

 Journal Writing, 103B
Letter Formation, 102I

 Writing Prompt: Describe something else the chick and duckling can do.

 Journal Writing, 105B
Letter Formation, 104C

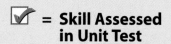

DAY 3

Mary Had a Little Lamb

Focus on Reading Skills

Develop Phonological Awareness,
106A–106B
"Iggy the Iguana" and "I Miss My Mouse" *Big Book of Phonics Rhymes and Poems*, 25–27

 **Review** /i/*i* 106C–106
Practice Book, 106
Phonics/Phonemic Awareness Practice Book

 **CD-ROM**

Read the Literature

Read "Mary Had a Little Lamb" Teacher Read Aloud, 107A–107B
Shared Reading
Read the Big Book of Real-Life Reading, 14–15
  ☑ Diagram

Build Skills

  ☑ High-Frequency Words: *said*, 107C–107
  Practice Book, 107

 Science, 107A

 Writing Prompt: Write about your favorite thing to do at school. Draw a picture of it.

DAY 4

Sid Said

Focus on Reading Skills

Develop Phonological Awareness,
108A–108B
"Bedtime"
 **Introduce Blending with Short *i*,** 108C–108
Practice Book, 108
Phonics/Phonemic Awareness Practice Book

 **CD-ROM**

Read the Literature

Read "Sid Said" Decodable Story, 109/110A–109/110D

  ☑ Initial and Medial /i/*I*; Blending
  ☑ Classify and Categorize
  ☑ High-Frequency Words: *said*
  ☑ Concepts of Print

Build Skills

  ☑ Classify and Categorize, 111A–111
  Practice Book, 111

 Arts, 109/110D

 Writing Prompt: Write about a special friend you made this year.

Letter Formation
  Practice Book, 109–110

DAY 5

Come In!
by Jane Tower
illustrated by John Wallner

Sid Said

Focus on Reading Skills

Develop Phonological Awareness,
112A–112B
"Bedtime"
 **Review Blending with Short *i*, *a*,** 112C–112
Practice Book, 112
Phonics/Phonemic Awareness Practice Book

 **CD-ROM**

Read the Literature

Reread "Sid Said" Decodable Story, 113A

Read "Come In!" Patterned Book, 113B
  Guided Reading
  ☑ Initial and Medial /i/*I*; Blending
  ☑ Classify and Categorize
  ☑ High-Frequency Words: *said*
  ☑ Concepts of Print

Build Skills

  ☑ High-Frequency Words: *said*, *I*, *is*, 113C–113
  Practice Book, 113

 Math, 113B

 **Writing Prompt:** Sometimes friends disagree. Write about how you solve the problem.

Interactive Writing, 114A–114B

102F

Develop Phonological Awareness

Listen

Iggy the Iguana

Is Iggy Iguana in his cage,
Or is he out today?
If Iggy Iguana is running
around,
I won't come in to play.

Big Book of Phonics Rhymes and Poems, page 25

Objective: Create Rhyming Words

LISTEN FOR RHYMES

- Have children sit in a circle. Read the poem aloud. Ask children which two words in the poem rhyme.

> today   play

- Explain that children will play a game called "Is Iggy In?" Begin by turning to the child next to you, and say, "Is Iggy in a bin?"
- The child answers by using a word that rhymes with *bin* to say, "No, Iggy is in a [pin]."
- If children can't think of a rhyme, they say, "I don't know what Iggy is in."

START WITH A NEW RHYME

- Then begin the game with a new word to rhyme, such as: *"Is Iggy in a hat?"*

Objective: Listen for Initial /i/

LISTEN FOR THE SOUND

- Reread the title of the poem. Emphasize the initial /i/ sound in the name. Have children repeat the sound after you.
- Say the following words. Children raise a hand if the word begins with /i/.
- Have children think of other words that begin with /i/.

> it big in kit
> is mitt if

 **Read Together**

From Phonemic Awareness to Phonics

Objective: Identify Initial /i/ *i*, I

IDENTIFY THE LETTER FOR THE SOUND

- Explain to children the letters *I, i* stand for the sound /i/. Say the sound and have children repeat it.
- Then display page 25 in the Big Book of Phonics Rhymes and Poems. Point to the letters in the corner of the page and identify them. Have children repeat the sound after you.

REREAD THE POEM

- Read the poem again, emphasizing words that begin with /i/.

FIND WORDS WITH *I, i*

- Play "I Spy an *I*." Say "Do you spy an *I*?"
- Volunteers find the letters in the poem.
- Point out that the letters *I, i* can be found in the beginning, middle, or end of a word.

Iggy the Iguana

Is Iggy Iguana
in his cage?
Or is he out today?
If Iggy Iguana is
running around,
I won't come in to play.

Big Book of Phonics Rhymes and Poems, page 25

102H

OBJECTIVES

Children will:

- identify the letters *I, i*
- identify /i/ *I, i*
- form the letter *I, i*

MATERIALS

- letter cards from the Word Play Book

TEACHING TIP

INSTRUCTIONAL Introduce the short *i* sound by playing a simple version of "20 Questions." Tell children that you are thinking of an object in plain sight and that they must guess what it is by asking questions that begin with *Is it . . . ?* Your reply will be either *It is* or *It is not.* You may wish to give children clues, always beginning by saying *It is . . . .*

ALTERNATE TEACHING STRATEGY

....

INITIAL /i/i

For a different approach to teaching this skill, see page T31.

▶ **Visual/Auditory/ Kinesthetic**

Introduce Initial /i/ i

TEACH

Identify /i/ I, i
Tell children they will learn to write the sound /i/ with the letters *I, i*. Hold up an *i* letter card and say /i/; then ask children to repeat the sound as they hold up their letter cards. Have them hold up the cards when they hear a word that begins with the sound /i/ and say "Isabel sat in her igloo and wrote a letter in ink."

Form I, i
Display letter *I, i* and trace them with your finger. With your back to the children, trace large letters *I, i* in the air. Ask children to do the same. They can trace their *i* letter cards and then write *I, i* on strips of paper. Show them how to fold the strip accordion-style and how to use the fold lines as guides for writing the letters.

PRACTICE

Complete the Pupil Edition Page
Read the directions on page 102 of the Pupil Edition, and make sure children clearly understand what they are being asked to do. Identify each picture and complete the first item together. Then work through the rest of the page with children or have them complete the page independently.

ASSESS/CLOSE

Identify and Use I, i
Make word cards for the following words, and place them on the chalkboard ledge. Ask children to hold up their letter strips when they hear a word that begins with the sound /i/: *igloo, ill, lap, itch, is, sat*. Then have them write *I, i* and observe their letter formations.

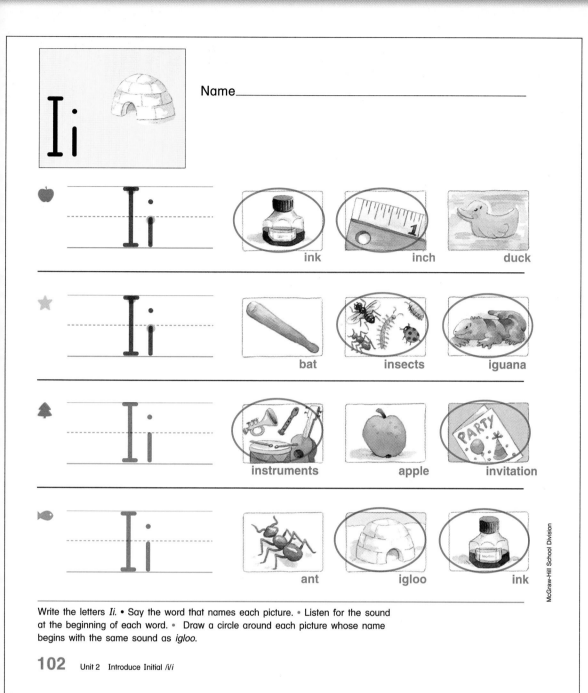

Name _____

ink · inch · duck

bat · insects · iguana

instruments · apple · invitation

ant · igloo · ink

Write the letters Ii. • Say the word that names each picture. • Listen for the sound at the beginning of each word. • Draw a circle around each picture whose name begins with the same sound as *igloo*.

McGraw-Hill School Division

102 Unit 2 Introduce Initial /i/i

Pupil Edition, page 102

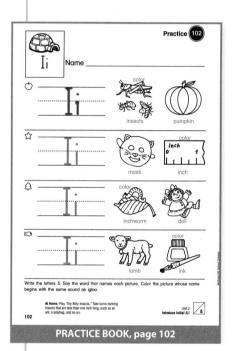

Practice **102**

Ii Name _____

color
insects · pumpkin

color
mask · inch

color
inchworm · doll

color
lamb · ink

Write the letters Ii. Say the word that names each picture. Color the picture whose name begins with the same sound as *igloo*.

At Home: Play "Itty Bitty Insects." Take turns naming insects that are less than one inch long, such as an ant, a ladybug, and so on.

102 · Unit 2 Introduce Initial /i/ · 8

PRACTICE BOOK, page 102

Meeting Individual Needs for Phonics and Decoding

EASY	ON-LEVEL	CHALLENGE	LANGUAGE SUPPORT
Give children index cards that have a long vertical line and a short vertical line. Write *I, i* on the board. Ask children to write *I* twice by the longer line; then write *i* twice by the shorter line. When they write a letter, ask them to make the sound /i/.	**Play** "In or Out." Place an open box on the table and label it *I, i.* Hold up word cards and read them aloud; then follow children's instructions. They say *In* (the box) if the word begins with the sound /i/; otherwise they say *Out*. Then they write *i* for each *i* word.	**Write** the sentence, *It is in.* on the chalkboard. Read the sentence to children and ask several volunteers to identify the words. Then ask children to write the sentence at the bottom of a sheet of drawing paper, and draw a picture to illustrate the sentence.	**To** help children understand these three key *i* words, have them chant the following: *Is it in? Or is it out?* Emphasize the /i/ sounds, and have them act out the chant, using a box and classroom objects as props.

OBJECTIVES

Children will:

- recognize words with short *i*
- identify capital and lowercase letters

LANGUAGE SUPPORT

ESL Help ESL children understand the meaning of the word *perform*. Explain that a performer usually sings, acts, or dances for other people. Have children name performers that they like, and have children role-play what the performers do.

Read the Big Book

Before Reading

Develop Oral Language
Read "The Alphabet Name Game" with children on page 5 in the Big Book of Phonics Rhymes and Poems. Have children use their last names and do the actions to the song.

Remind children that they have read "The ABC Street Fair." Ask what parts of the book they enjoyed the most.

Set Purposes
Explain to children that as they reread the story, they will make a list of the performers at the fair. Have children describe what these performers do. Explain that they will also think of the order of the letters in the alphabet.

The ABC Street Fair, pages 14–15

During Reading

Read Together • Point to the uppercase and lowercase letters at the top of each page as you say the name of the letter. Run your finger under each word in the story as you read it. Have children repeat the word after you. *Concepts of Print*

• After you read pages 2–3, have children identify the words with the capital *B* and the lowercase *b*. *Concepts of Print*

• After you read pages 4–5, determine that the clowns are performers at the fair. Make a picture or word list of the performers as you continue the story. *Use Story Details*

• Make the short /i/ sound, and have children make the sound with you. After you read pages 12–13, determine that the words begin with this sound. Repeat the words together. *Phonics*

Red roses **Rr**

The ABC Street Fair, page 23

After Reading

Literary Response **JOURNAL WRITING** Ask children to draw a picture and write about a performer at the street fair.

ORAL RESPONSE Ask questions such as:

• *What is this performer doing?*

• *If you could be a performer at the fair, what would you do?*

ABC Activity Write the letters of the alphabet on the chalkboard. Invite a child to point to a letter, identify it, and erase it. Continue until all the letters are erased.

INFORMAL ASSESSMENT

IDENTIFY CAPITAL AND LOWERCASE LETTERS
HOW TO ASSESS
Point to a page and ask children to identify the words with capital and lowercase letters.

FOLLOW-UP
Write children's names on index cards. Highlight the initial letter in red. Have children identify each other's capital letter.

CENTER Activity

Cross Curricular: Language Arts

NAME THAT LETTER Use a large piece of tagboard and make a 6 by 4 grid. Write letters of the alphabet in random order on the grid. Children drop a counter or coin on a square and say the letter. Partners take turns.

▶ **Kinesthetic**

103B

Children will:

- identify and describe squares and rectangles

MATERIALS

- *Warthogs in the Kitchen*
- Large paper squares and rectangles

TEACHING TIP

INSTRUCTIONAL Some children may have difficulty distinguishing between squares and rectangles. Review the terms *long* and *short*, and emphasize that the rectangle has two longer sides and two shorter sides.

Review Shapes: Square, Rectangle

PREPARE

Match Shapes Hold up a paper square, and ask children to find objects in the classroom that have the same shape. Emphasize matching the shape, not the size. Repeat for rectangles.

TEACH

Recognize Shapes Hold up a paper square and identify it. Discuss its attributes, noting that it has four sides that are the same length and four corners. Ask children to find objects with this shape. Then repeat with a paper rectangle. Ask children how the rectangle is different from the square. Then display the Big Book *Warthogs in the Kitchen*. Take a picture walk through the book, having children note objects that have the shape of a square or rectangle.

PRACTICE

Find Squares and Rectangles Read the directions on page 103 to the children, and make sure they clearly understand what they are asked to do. Identify each picture, and complete the first item together. Then work through the page with children, or have them complete the page independently.

ASSESS/CLOSE

Review the Page Check children's work on the Pupil Edition page. Note areas where children need extra help.

Name_____

Find the squares in the picture. • Color them blue. • Find the rectangles in the
picture. • Color them red.

Unit 2   Review Shapes: Square, Rectangle   **103**

ALTERNATE TEACHING
STRATEGY
·····················

SHAPES: SQUARE,
RECTANGLE

**For a different approach
to teaching this skill, see
page T31.**

▶ **Visual/Auditory/
Kinesthetic**

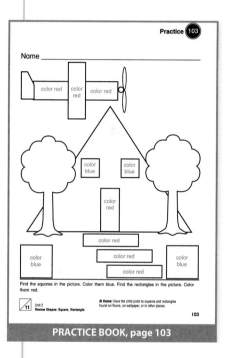

PRACTICE BOOK, page 103

Meeting Individual Needs for Beginning Reading Concepts

EASY	ON-LEVEL	CHALLENGE	LANGUAGE SUPPORT
Draw a triangle and a rectangle, using a heavy marker. Invite children to trace the shapes with their fingers, counting each side as they trace. Have children identify the shapes. Then provide templates, and have them trace around the shapes.	**Cut** out squares and rectangles of different sizes and colors. Then cut each shape in half. Children match to make shapes, and identify each.	**Provide** paper shapes of different types and sizes of circles, triangles, squares and rectangles. Have children sort the shapes, then use them to create patterns for partners to extend.	**Some** children may confuse names of shapes. Continue to incorporate shape vocabulary into daily activities by referring to the shapes of objects as children use them.

Develop Phonological Awareness

Listen

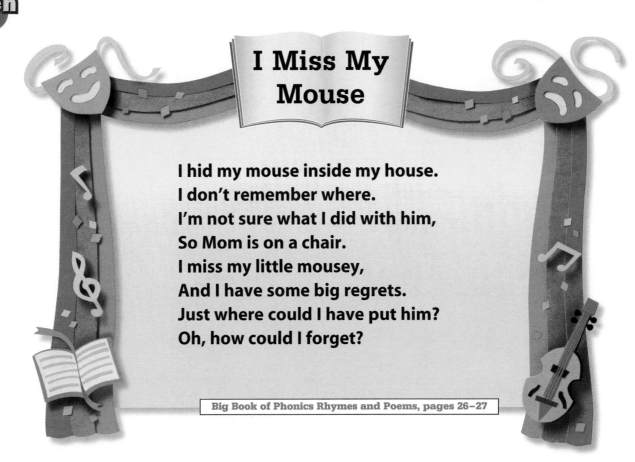

I Miss My Mouse

I hid my mouse inside my house.
I don't remember where.
I'm not sure what I did with him,
So Mom is on a chair.
I miss my little mousey,
And I have some big regrets.
Just where could I have put him?
Oh, how could I forget?

Big Book of Phonics Rhymes and Poems, pages 26–27

Objective: Develop Listening Skills

LISTEN TO THE POEM

- Read the poem "I Miss My Mouse" to the children. Have them retell the story of the poem.
- Then reread the poem, changing the word order.

> **I hid my house inside my mouse.**

- Have children say the words that were changed.

CHANGE OTHER WORDS

- Change the word order in other lines of the poem.

> **So chair is on a Mom.**
> **I'm not sure what I it with did.**

COUNT WORDS IN SENTENCE Say the title of the poem. Have children clap and count the number of words in the sentence with you. Repeat with other sentences.

Objective: Listen for Medial *i*

LISTEN FOR THE SOUND

- Say the word *miss*. Emphasize the short *i* sound and have children say the sound with you. Then say the word *hid* and have children repeat it. Point out that both words have the /i/ sound.

TOUCH YOUR CHIN

- Say the word *chin* and have children repeat it. Point out that it has the /i/ sound. Have children touch their *chins* when you say a word with that sound.

hit	car	pull	sit
road	pig	cake	pin
lid	row	thick	leave

LISTEN FOR RHYMES

- Say the words *chin* and *pin*. Have children touch their chins if the words rhyme. Continue with other pairs of words that rhyme with chin. Point out the /i/ sound.

Read Together

From Phonemic Awareness to Phonics

Objective: Identify /i/ *I, i*

IDENTIFY THE LETTER FOR THE SOUND

- Explain to children that the letter *i* stands for the sound /i/. Invite children to say the sound with you.

- Display the Big Book of Phonics Rhymes and Poems, page 26–27. Point to the letters in the upper left corner and identify them. Have children say the sound with you.

REREAD THE POEM

- Reread the poem. Frame each word that has a medial *i*, and emphasize the /i/ sound. Have children say the words with you.

FIND WORDS WITH /i/

- Make word cards to match words in the poem with medial *i*. Ask volunteers to find the words in the poem. Point out the medial *i*. Read them together.

Ii

I Miss My Mou___

I hid my mouse
Inside my house.
I don't remember where.
I'm not sure
What I did with him,
So mom is on a chair.

26

Big Book of Phonics Rhymes and Poems, pages 26–27

OBJECTIVES

Children will:

- identify the letter *i*
- identify /i/*i*
- form the letter *i*

....

MATERIALS

- letter cards from the Word Play Book

TEACHING TIP

INSTRUCTIONAL Ask children questions they can answer with words that have medial short *i*, such as: *The opposite of little is what? (big) What do you do in a chair? (sit)* Write the words on the chalkboard, and read them aloud. Ask children to make the sound /i/.

ALTERNATE TEACHING STRATEGY

....

MEDIAL /i/*i*

For a different approach to teaching this skill, see page T32.

▶ **Visual/Auditory/ Kinesthetic**

Introduce Medial /i/ i

TEACH

Identify /i/*i* Tell children they will write the sound /i/ with the letter *i*. Write the letter on the chalkboard, and have them repeat the /i/ sound after you, then say, "Did she sit next to Sid?" Ask children to listen as you repeat the question and to clap when they hear a word that has the short *i* sound in the middle.

Form *i* With your back to the children, trace a large letter *i* in the air and ask them to do the same. Remind them to dot the *i*. Show them how to fold a sheet of paper in fourths and to write four *I*'s on one side and four *i*'s on the other side.

PRACTICE

Complete the Pupil Edition Page Read the directions on page 104 of the Pupil Edition, and make sure children clearly understand what they are being asked to do. Identify each picture, and complete the first item together. Then work through the page with children or have them complete the page independently.

ASSESS/CLOSE

Identify and Use *i* Give children incomplete word cards *d_d, d_m, s_t,* and *T_m,* and have them write the medial *i*. Collect the cards, and use each word in a sentence, asking children to trace *i* in the air when they hear a word that has the /i/ sound in the middle.

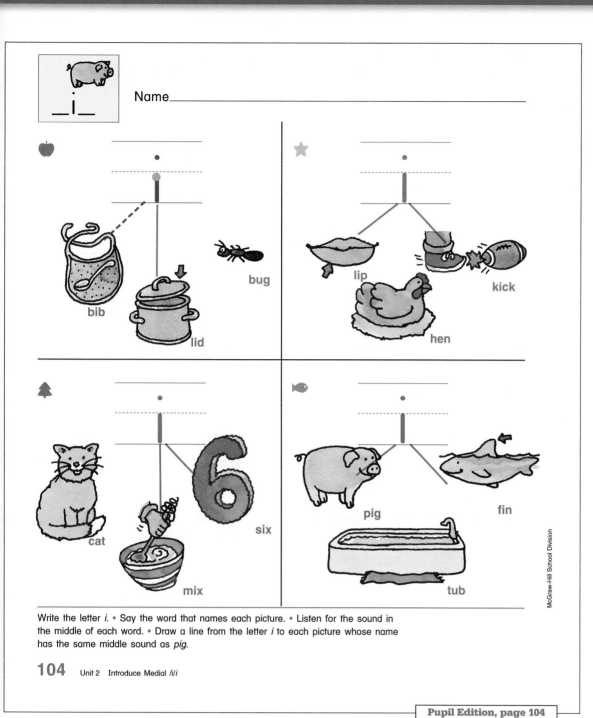

_i_ Name _____

bib
lid
bug

lip
kick
hen

cat
mix
six

pig
fin
tub

Write the letter _i_. • Say the word that names each picture. • Listen for the sound in the middle of each word. • Draw a line from the letter _i_ to each picture whose name has the same middle sound as _pig_.

104 Unit 2 Introduce Medial /i/i

McGraw-Hill School Division

Pupil Edition, page 104

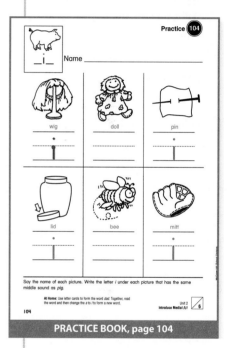

PRACTICE BOOK, page 104

Meeting Individual Needs for Phonics

EASY	ON-LEVEL	CHALLENGE	LANGUAGE SUPPORT
Say this rhyme slowly, then ask children to repeat it after you, holding up their _i_ cards when they hear a word that has short _i_ in the middle: _Did Sid sit here? Did Sid sit there? Did Sid sit on the tip of the chair?_	**Read** the following pairs of words to children. Have them repeat the words in each pair and tell which word has the sound /i/ in the middle: _hit, hat; Sam, fish; pig, hog; sick, sack; bib, bat._ Have children write an _i_ on the chalkboard for each word they identify.	**Write** _big, little_ on the chalkboard, pointing out the short _i_'s. Display pictures of objects such as _house, elephant, bridge,_ and have children decide if the object is big or little. Have children draw a picture of something _big_ or _little_ and label it.	**Ask** children to trace lowercase _i_ in the air when they hear the /i/ sound in the middle of a word, and say, "Did Tim win the tin toy? Yes, Tim did win. Did Kim win the big pig? No, Kim did not win."

OBJECTIVES

Children will:

- recognize words with short /i/
- classify and categorize

TEACHING TIP

When you reread the story, use two distinct voices for the duckling and the chick. Since the chick is the follower, you may wish to give the chick a more timid voice.

Read the Big Book

Before Reading

Develop Oral Language

Sing the following familiar song with the children:

THE MORE WE GET TOGETHER

The more we get together,
Together, together,
The more we get together,
The happier we'll be.

For your friends are my friends,
And my friends are your friends.
The more we get together,
The happier we'll be.

Talk about friendship, and what it means to be a good friend. Talk about how children know that the duckling and the chick were good friends.

Set Purposes

Model: We read a story about two friends, the duckling and the chick. The duckling and the chick were alike in many ways. Let's find out how the two friends are alike and how they are different.

"I am digging a hole," said the Duckling.

The Chick and the Duckling, pages 10–11

During Reading

Read Together
- Before you begin to read, point to the first word in the first sentence. Explain that this is where you will begin to read. Continue to track print as you read the story. *Tracking Print*

- Say the short /i/ sound. Say the word *chick* and emphasize the vowel sound. Reread page 7 and ask children to say a word with the short /i/ sound. (swim) *Phonemic Awareness*

- Have children look at the pictures of the duckling and the chick on pages 10–11. Tell children they are both birds. Ask children to describe what birds look like. *Classify and Categorize*

- Have children look at the illustration on page 16, and ask how the duckling caught a butterfly. (with its beak) Then have children look at page 19, and ask how the chick caught the butterfly. (with its claws) *Story Details*

"Not me," said the Chick.

The Chick and the Duckling, page 32

After Reading

Return to Purposes
Help children to recall how the duckling and the chick were alike and how they were different. Include animal and personality characteristics.

Retell the Story
Help children to make simple finger puppets or craft-stick puppets for the duckling and the chick. Have partners act out the story.

Literary Response
JOURNAL WRITING Ask children to draw a picture about a way they could be a leader. Ask how they could help someone who is younger. Have them write a note or caption about their pictures.

ORAL RESPONSE Engage children in a discussion of the story by asking questions such as:

- *How did the duckling help the chick?*
- *What did the chick learn about itself?*

CLASSIFY AND CATEGORIZE
HOW TO ASSESS
Tell children you will say three words. Ask children to tell how they are the same: whale, dolphin, shark.

FOLLOW UP
Have children classify picture cards of fish, birds, farm animals.

Cross Curricular: Science

WHERE DOES IT BELONG?
Provide animal cards that show different farm animals. Begin by having children sort the pictures into two groups: *Large Animals* and *Small Animals*. Then provide picture or word cards that give different classifying characteristics, such as *Two Legs, Four Legs, Flies, Runs, Swims, Has Feathers, Insect* and so on. Invite children to sort the pictures into different groups. Encourage children to think of other sorting categories.

▶ **Linguistic**

OBJECTIVES

Children will:

- classify and categorize to understand a story

....

MATERIALS

- *The Chick and the Duckling*

TEACHING TIP

MANAGEMENT Provide large, brightly colored sheets of construction paper for children to use during sorting activities.

Introduce Classify and Categorize

PREPARE

Discuss Characters and Events
Ask children to recall the story *The Chick and the Duckling*. Ask how the story begins and who the characters are. Ask them to describe what chicks and ducklings look like.

TEACH

Understand Differences and Similarities
Reread the story, stopping after pages 6 and 7 to talk about how the chick and the duckling are alike and how they are different. Point out that they can both be classified as animals and birds. Then continue through the story, noting how the chick and the duckling are alike and how they are different. Ask if they can both do the same things.

PRACTICE

Complete the Pupil Edition Page
Read the directions on page 105 to the children and make sure they clearly understand what they are asked to do. Identify each picture and complete the first item together. Then work through the page with children or have them complete the page independently.

ASSESS/CLOSE

Review the Page
Review children's work and note children who are experiencing difficulty.

Name _____

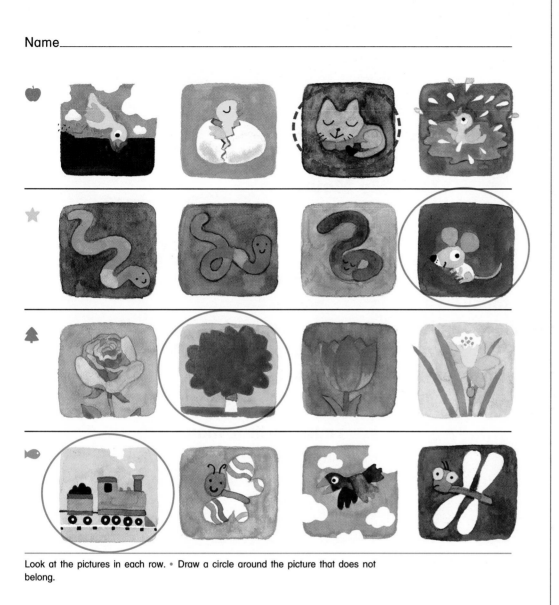

Look at the pictures in each row. • Draw a circle around the picture that does not belong.

Pupil Edition, page 105

PRACTICE BOOK, page 105

Meeting Individual Needs for Comprehension

EASY	ON-LEVEL	CHALLENGE	LANGUAGE SUPPORT
Have children cut out butterfly shapes of different sizes, and color and decorate them. When they are finished, ask how children could sort them (color, size, tails, shape, and so on). Invite children to sort by one of the attributes they have listed.	**Explain** that you want to make a category called *Farm Animals*. Show children pictures of different animals, and ask if each would belong in that category. Make a group of pictures that show farm animals.	**Show** children photographs of ducks and chicks. Compare the pictures to the drawings in the book. Ask how they are the same and how they are different.	**Ask** each child to choose an animal that might live on a farm. Ask each child to describe the animal, using as many details as possible. Then talk about how the animals are alike and how they are different.

105

Develop Phonological Awareness

Listen

Iggy the Iguana
a poem

I Miss My Mouse
a poem

Is Iggy Iguana in his cage?
Or is he out today?
If Iggy Iguana is running
    around,
I won't come in to play.

I hid my mouse inside my
    house.
I don't remember where.
I'm not sure what I did
    with him,
So Mom is on a chair.

I miss my little mousey,
And I have some big regrets.
Just where could I have
    put him?
Oh, how could I forget?

Big Book of Phonics Rhymes and Poems, pages 25, 26–27

Objective: Focus on Word Rhythm

IDENTIFY THE ACTION WORD Have children sit in a circle. Read the poem "Iggy the Iguana." Point out that sometimes an action word tells how something moves. Then reread the poem and have children identify the action word *running*.

MOVE TO THE SYLLABLES Have children stand. Say the word *running*, pausing between syllables. Demonstrate the action of running in rhythm to the syllables by lifting one leg on *run*, and the other leg on *-ning*. Repeat rhythmically. Invite children to join in.

TRY MORE ACTION WORDS Introduce more action words ending in *-ing*. Have children do the action rhythmically by syllables. Then invite children to suggest and demonstrate other actions words.

> **jumping   swaying   wiggling**

Objective: Listen for /i/

LISTEN FOR INITIAL /I/ Read the poem "Iggy the Iguana," emphasizing and segmenting the initial /i/ sound. Have children say the /i/ sound. Then say the words *Iggy* and *itch*. Ask if the words begin with the same sound. Invite children to demonstrate what they do if they have an itch.

Say other words and have children pretend they have an itch if they hear /i/ at the beginning of the word.

if	log	insect	net	it

LISTEN FOR MEDIAL /i/ Read the poem "I Miss My Mouse," emphasizing the words with the medial /i/ sound. Have children say the /i/ sound.

Reread the poem, pausing after each line. Have children name the words that have the medial /i/ sound.

LISTEN FOR /I/ Have children sit in a line. Set a box at one end and give a picture of an iguana to the child at the other end. Tell children the iguana is Iggy. Then say words and have children pass Iggy toward his box each time they hear a word that has the /i/ sound.

big	insect	dip	got	wish

Read Together

From Phonemic Awareness to Phonics

Objective: Identify /I/ *I, i*

IDENTIFY THE LETTERS
Display the Big Book of Phonics Rhymes and Poems, pages 25 and 26–27. Point to the letters and identify them. Say the sound the letters stand for.

REREAD THE POEMS Reread the poems. Point to each word, emphasizing those with the /i/ sound.

FIND WORDS WITH *I, i* Have children look for words with *I* or *i* in the poems. Provide self-stick dots to place under the letters.

Ii

I Miss My Mouse

I hid my mouse
Inside my house.
I don't remember where.
I'm not sure
What I did with him,
So mom is on a chair.

I miss my little mousey,
And I have some big regrets.
Just where could I have put him?
Oh, how could I forget?

26   27

Big Book of Phonics Rhymes and Poems, pages 26–27

TESTED
OBJECTIVES

Children will:

- identify and use /i/ *I, i*
- write letters *I, i*

MATERIALS

- letter cards from the Word Play Book

TEACHING TIP

INSTRUCTIONAL Have children form a small circle; then say, "Let's make the circle a little bit bigger." Ask everyone to take a small step back. Keep repeating this, and invite children to join in on the phrase *little bit bigger*. At some point, ask children to notice that the sound in the middle of all three of these words is the same. Emphasize the /i/ sound as you continue until the circle is as big as you can make it.

ALTERNATE TEACHING STRATEGY

LETTER */i/i*

For a different approach to teaching this skill, see page T32.

▶ **Visual/Auditory/ Kinesthetic**

Review /i/ i

TEACH

Identify and Use /i/ I, i

Tell children they will review the sound /i/ and write letters *I, i*. Write the letters on the chalkboard. Then ask them to name the sound that is the same in the following words: *Sid is a big dog. Is Min a big cat?* Write *i___* on one side of the chalkboard and *___i___* on the other, and list each word under its correct heading. Invite volunteers to underline each letter *i*.

Write I, i

Say the following words, and have children hold up their *i* letter cards and point to the side of the chalkboard where the word belongs: *sit, is, pit, tin, lid, in, it, dim*. Write the word, drawing a blank line where the *i* belongs. Ask volunteers to write the missing *I, i*.

PRACTICE

Complete the Pupil Edition Page

Read the directions on page 106 of the Pupil Edition, and make sure children clearly understand what they are being asked to do. Identify each picture, and complete the first item together. Then work through the page with children or have them complete the page independently.

ASSESS/CLOSE

Identify and Use I, i

Say the following sentences, and have children write the letter *i* when they hear a word that begins with *i* or has *i* in the middle: "Her new pin is made of tin. His pet pig is big." Read the sentences again. Ask children to circle one of their letter *i*'s for each word that begins with *i*.

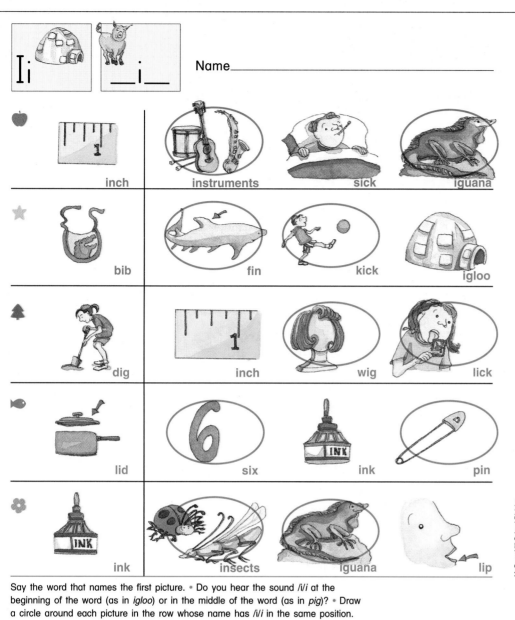

Ii 🌳 igloo / pig __i__

Name _____

Say the word that names the first picture. • Do you hear the sound /i/i at the beginning of the word (as in *igloo*) or in the middle of the word (as in *pig*)? • Draw a circle around each picture in the row whose name has /i/i in the same position.

Row 1: inch | instruments | sick | iguana
Row 2: bib | fin | kick | igloo
Row 3: dig | inch | wig | lick
Row 4: lid | six | ink | pin
Row 5: ink | insects | iguana | lip

106 Unit 2 Review /i/i

McGraw-Hill School Division

Pupil Edition, page 106

ADDITIONAL PHONICS RESOURCES

Practice Book, *page 106*
Phonics Workbook

McGraw-Hill School
TECHNOLOGY

Phonics CD-ROM

Activities for practice with Initial and Medial Letters

PRACTICE BOOK, page 106

Meeting Individual Needs for Phonics

EASY	ON-LEVEL	CHALLENGE	LANGUAGE SUPPORT
Display the following word cards on the chalkboard ledge: *did, Sid, in, dim, it, is, Min.* Read the words aloud, and ask children to repeat each word after you. Have children sort the word cards to show initial and medial *i* words.	**Display** word cards that show initial and medial /i/ *I, i* on the chalkboard ledge. Have children use two-color counters and make a row that shows the same pattern of *i* words by using one color for initial *i* words and the second color for medial *i* words.	**Give** children two cards that show i___ and ___i___. Point out that each card shows a different place for /i/ *i*. Then give children a stack of *i* word cards, and ask them to read and sort the words into two piles.	**Teach** children the following chant, and have them repeat it several times, first saying the *i* words louder than the other words and then saying the *i* words more softly: *sit, sit, sat/ did, did, dad/ pit, pit, pat.*

106

Teacher Read Aloud

Listen

Mary Had a Little Lamb
by Sarah Josepha Hale

Mary had a little lamb,
Its fleece was white as snow;
And everywhere that Mary went,
The lamb was sure to go.

It followed her to school one day,
That was against the rule;
It made the children laugh and play
To see a lamb at school.

And so the teacher turned it out,
But still it lingered near,
And waited patiently about
Till Mary did appear.

"Why does the lamb love Mary so?"
The eager children cry.
"Why, Mary loves the lamb, you
   know,"
The teacher did reply.

Selection also appears on page T7.

Oral Comprehension

LISTENING AND SPEAKING Ask children if they have ever seen a lamb or a picture of a lamb. Invite them to describe what it looked like. Then tell children that you are going to read a familiar poem about a lamb and a little girl.

After you read the poem, make a list of words that describe the lamb. Ask: *"What color was the lamb? How did the fleece feel?"*

Activity Have children retell the story of the poem. Then invite small groups of children to act out the poem as you reread it. Using paper plates, glue, cotton balls, and magic markers, have children create masks of lamb faces.

107A *Sid Said*

Real-Life Reading

Can you point to each part of Mary's little lamb?

wool

tail

leg

ear

eye

nose

mouth

hoof

14

15

Big Book of Real-Life Reading, pages 14–15

Objective: Diagram

READ THE PAGE Ask children if they have pets and what their names are. Remind children of the pet that Mary had in the poem "Mary Had a Little Lamb." Explain that children will see a diagram of a lamb. A diagram can show a picture of something that has labels for its different parts. Then read the text and discuss the picture.

ANSWER THE QUESTION Read each word again, tracking print from left to right. Then volunteers point to the body part. Ask: *How many legs does a lamb have? How many ears?*

Cross Curricular: Science

LABELING PET PICTURES
Provide pictures of common pets, such as cats, dogs, hamsters, and bunnies. Draw the following pictures on small stick-on notes: ears, eyes, nose, mouth, leg, tail. Children attach the stick-on

notes to the correct body part. You may wish to have them use the Big Book of Real-Life Reading for reference.

OBJECTIVES

Children will:

- **identify and read the high-frequency word** *said*

....

MATERIALS

- **word cards from the Word Play Book**

TEACHING TIP

Make an experience chart of a recent class trip or experience. Record children's descriptions of the experience, including *said (child's name)*. ("We went to the zoo," said Paul.) Have children match their word card to the word *said*.

Introduce High-Frequency Words: *said*

PREPARE

Listen to Words   Explain to children that they will be learning a new word: *said*. Say the following sentence: *"Where is my lamb?" said Mary*. Say the sentence again, and ask children to raise a finger when they hear the word *said*. Repeat with the sentence: *"Here it is!" said the teacher*.

TEACH

Model Reading the Word in Context   Give a word card to each child, and read the word. Reread the sentences, and have children raise their word cards when they hear the word.

Identify the Word   Write the sentences above on the chalkboard. Track print and read each sentence. Children hold up their word card when they hear the word *said*. Then ask volunteers to point to and underline the word *said* in the sentences.

PRACTICE

Complete the Pupil Edition Page   Read the directions on page 107 to the children, and make sure they clearly understand what they are asked to do. Complete the first item together. Then work through the page with children or have them complete the page independently.

ASSESS/CLOSE

Review the Page   Review children's work, and note children who are experiencing difficulty or need additional practice.

Name _____

said

🍎 Dan <u>said</u>, "I am Dan."

⭐ Nan <u>said</u>, "I am Nan."

🌲 Dad <u>said</u>, "I am Dad."

🐟 Sam <u>said</u>, "I am Sam."

Read the sentences. • Then draw a line under the word *said* in each sentence.

Pupil Edition, page 107

**HIGH-FREQUENCY
WORDS**
For a different approach
to teaching this skill, see
page T27.

▶ **Visual/Auditory/
Kinesthetic**

Practice 107

Name _____

🍎 Dad <u>said</u>, "Dan!"

☆ Dan <u>said</u>, "Nan!"

🔔 I <u>said</u>, "Dad!"

Read the sentence. Then draw a line under the word *said*.

3 Unit 2
Introduce High-Frequency Words: *said*

At Home: Play "Simon Said." Take turns giving the
directions "Simon said ____." Have the child do what
"Simon said"!

107

PRACTICE BOOK, page 107

Meeting Individual Needs for Vocabulary

EASY	ON-LEVEL	CHALLENGE	LANGUAGE SUPPORT
Say a short phrase, such as "It is cold outside." Ask children to repeat what you said. Have them hold up the word card when they say the word *said*.	**Role-play** a conversation. Supply a topic or question such as, "What is your favorite color?" Then write the word *said* on chart paper and rephrase the conversation, saying: I said ____. You said ____. Have children continue the activity, working in pairs.	**Display** some cartoons and talk about why speech bubbles are used. Have children draw a picture of Mary with a speech bubble showing something she might say. Then children share their drawings, saying: Mary said, "____."	**Read** a classroom picture book that uses the word *said*. Point to the word as you read, and have children repeat some phrases that use the word.

Develop Phonological Awareness

Listen

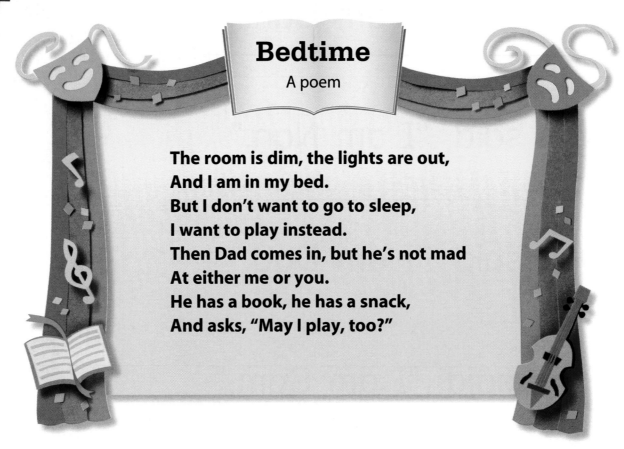

Bedtime
A poem

The room is dim, the lights are out,
And I am in my bed.
But I don't want to go to sleep,
I want to play instead.
Then Dad comes in, but he's not mad
At either me or you.
He has a book, he has a snack,
And asks, "May I play, too?"

Objective: Focus on Rhythm

READ THE POEM Darken the room and gather children in a circle. Then read the poem "Bedtime." Invite children to share stories of favorite bedtime routines.

MARCH TO SHOW RHYTHM Invite children to stand and march in place. Count aloud to keep them moving together in a steady rhythm and pace. Then have children sit. Explain that words in poems can be spoken in a steady beat. Then read "Bedtime" in a steady, rhythmic cadence, stressing the meter and beat of each sentence. Ask children to stand and march to the beat as you reread the poem.

MARCH TO A TEMPO Reread the poem several times. Continue to stress the rhythm, but increase or decrease the speed at which you read. Children march in rhythm and tempo.

Objective: Listen to Blending Short *i*

LISTEN TO THE SOUNDS Read the poem "Bedtime" aloud to children. Reread the first line, stressing the word *dim*. Explain that *dim* means there is very little light. Then model how to segment each sound in the word. Have children repeat. Help children determine that *dim* has three sounds.

$$/d/-/i/-/m/$$

BLEND SOUNDS Invite three volunteers to the front of the classroom. Assign each a sound in the word *dim*. Have children say their sound, starting with the one at the left. After practicing several times, give each a flashlight. Remind children that *dim* means "very little light." Have the three children turn their lights on. Then ask them to say their sounds in order as they turn off their lights. Repeat several times.

BLEND MORE WORDS Have children use the flashlights as prompts to blend other words.

did   Sid   Dan   Sam

Read Together

From Phonemic Awareness to Phonics

Objective: Identify Word Endings

LISTEN FOR A RHYMING WORD Read the first line of the poem "Bedtime," inviting children to listen for a word that rhymes with *Tim*. Write the words *dim* and *Tim* on the board.

dim   Tim

IDENTIFY THE LETTERS Invite a volunteer to underline the letters in the words that are the same. Identify the letters and say the sounds the letters stand for.

NAME RHYMING WORDS Invite children to suggest rhyming words. Write them on the board, circling the ending letters *im*.

him   Jim   Kim   rim   Tim

NAME OTHER RHYMING WORDS Have children suggest rhyming words for *Sid, Min, dam, mad,* and *Dan*. Work on one rhyming family at a time. Write their responses on the board, circling the end letters.

OBJECTIVES

Children will:

- identify and blend /i/*i* and /a/*a* words
- read and write short *i* and *a* words
- review m/*m*, /s/*s*, /d/*d*, /n/*n*

....

MATERIALS

- letter cards from the Word Building Book

TEACHING TIP

INSTRUCTIONAL Say the following sentence: *Sam is sad.* Ask children to hold up their *a* letter cards when they hear a word that has the /a/ sound. Say the sentence again. Ask children to hold up their *i* letter cards when they hear a word that has the /i/ sound.

ALTERNATE TEACHING STRATEGY
....

BLENDING SHORT *i*

For a different approach to teaching this skill, see Unit 2, page T32.

▶ **Visual/Auditory/ Kinesthetic**

Review Blending with short *i*, *a*

 **TEACH**

Identify *i*, *a* as Symbols for /i/, /a/
Tell children they will learn to read and write short *i* and *a* words.

- Display the *i* and *a* letter cards and say /i/ and /a/. Have children repeat the sounds /i/ and /a/ as you point to the letter cards.

BLENDING Model and Guide Practice
- Place a *d* card after the *i* card and after the *a* card. Blend the sounds together and have children repeat after you: _id and _ad.

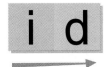 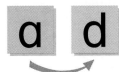 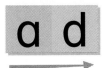

- Place another *d* letter card before the *i*, *d* cards. Place an *m* letter card before the *a*, *d* cards. Blend the sounds in the word to read *did*. Have children repeat after you. Follow the same procedure for *mad*.

Use the Word in Context
- Have children use *did* in a sentence, perhaps a question, such as: *Did you enjoy the story? Did you hear the song?* Have children use *mad* in a sentence, as well.

Repeat the Procedure
- Use the following words to continue modeling and for guided practice with short *i* and *a*: *dim, Sid, Sam, Nan dam, Min, in.*

PRACTICE

Complete the Pupil Edition Page
Read the directions on page 108 to the children, and make sure they clearly understand what they are being asked to do. Identify each picture, and complete the first item together. Work through the page with children, or have them complete the page independently.

ASSESS/CLOSE

Build Short *i* Words
Observe children as they complete page 108. Give children letter cards *m, s, d,* and *n* and ask them to build four short *i* words.

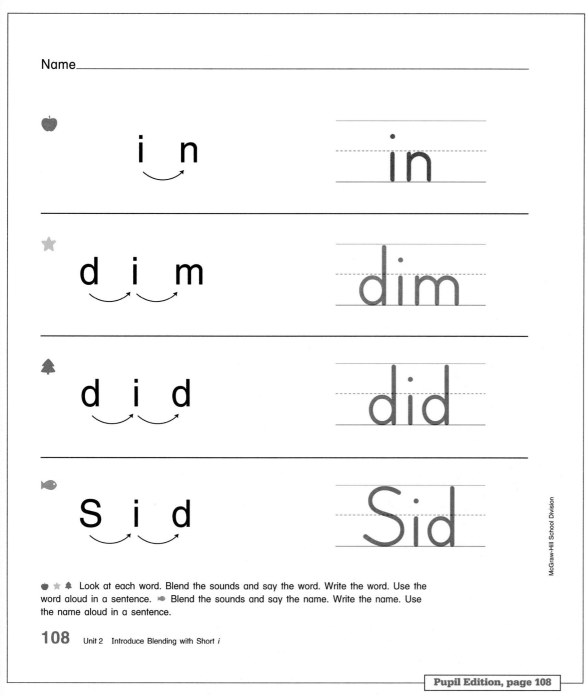

Name

🍎 i   n   in

⭐ d   i   m   dim

🌲 d   i   d   did

🐟 S   i   d   Sid

🍎 ⭐ 🌲 Look at each word. Blend the sounds and say the word. Write the word. Use the word aloud in a sentence. 🐟 Blend the sounds and say the name. Write the name. Use the name aloud in a sentence.

108   Unit 2   Introduce Blending with Short *i*

McGraw-Hill School Division

Pupil Edition, page 108

ADDITIONAL PHONICS RESOURCES

Practice Book, *page 108*
Phonics Workbook

McGraw-Hill School
TECHNOLOGY

🔵 Phonics CD-ROM
Activities for practice with Blending and Segmenting

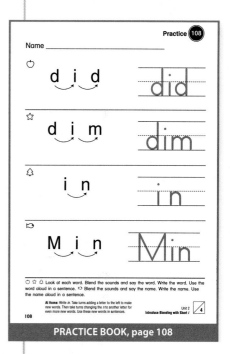

PRACTICE BOOK, page 108

Meeting Individual Needs for Phonics

EASY	ON-LEVEL	CHALLENGE	LANGUAGE SUPPORT
Display word cards: *dim, Nan, did, Sam, Sid.* Then call out a word and ask a volunteer to take that word card. Continue until all the word cards have been taken. Then ask children to read their words and return them to the chalkboard ledge. Repeat one or two times.	**Have** children repeat after you and blend letter sounds to read the following word cards aloud: *did, Man, dim, Sid, Min, Dan, in.* Display all the cards and ask questions, such as: *Which word rhymes with Sid? Which word rhymes with Min? Which word rhymes with Dan?*	**Write** the following words on the chalkboard: *Nan, sad, Dad, man, in, Sid, Min, dim.* Have children work in small groups and make up a story that uses at least three of the words. Record the stories and invite children to perform them.	**To** reinforce recognition of short *a* and *i*, write the following names on the chalkboard: *Nan, Dan, Dad, Sid, Min.* Have children repeat as you blend sounds to read the names aloud. Ask children if they know other names with the sound /a/ or /i/.

108

Guided Instruction

BEFORE READING

PREVIEW AND PREDICT Display the title page. Take a brief **picture walk** through the first three spreads, focusing on the illustrations.

- What are the children doing?

- What do you think will happen in the story?

- Do you think the story will be realistic or make-believe?

SET PURPOSES Ask children what they might want to find out as they read the story, for example, to discover what the children will paint.

Sid Said

TEACHING TIP

To put the book together:

1. Tear out the story page.

2. Fold the pages on the lines.

3. Fold each section on fold line.

4. Assemble book.

INSTRUCTIONAL Before beginning the story, review color words. Use crayons to identify colors and match to objects in the classroom.

Min said, "That is ."

3

Sid said, "That is ."

2

Sam said, "That is ."

4

Guided Instruction

DURING READING

☑ **Blending with Short *i***

☑ **Classify and Categorize**

☑ **Concepts of Print**

☑ **High-Frequency Words: *said***

(1) **CONCEPTS OF PRINT** Model how to track print. Read the title on page 1, and then have children repeat the words after you.

(2) **BLENDING WITH SHORT *i*** Model: *Let's blend together the sounds the letters stand for to read the first word on page 2: S-i-d. Sid.*

(3) **HIGH-FREQUENCY WORDS** Point to the word *said* on page 3, and have children read it with you as they track print.

(4) **CONCEPTS OF PRINT** Frame the quotation marks on page 4 and identify them. Explain that these marks show that someone is speaking. Ask: *Who is speaking?* (Sam)

109/110B

Guided Instruction

DURING READING

5 **STORY DETAILS** After you read the text on page 5 and discuss the picture, ask children to tell what has happened so far in the story.

6 **CLASSIFY AND CATEGORIZE** After you read the text on page 6, ask children how the words that follow "that is" on each page are alike.

7 **MAKE PREDICTIONS** Ask children what they think will happen next.

8 **STORY DETAILS** Ask children to describe the picture that the friends created, using color words.

Sid said, "That is 🌥️."

5

Sam said, "That is 🔵."

7

Min said, "That is  ."

6

That is ⬛ , ⬛ , ⬛ , ⬛ , ⬛ , and ⬛ .

8

Guided Instruction

AFTER READING

RETURN TO PREDICTIONS AND PURPOSES
Remind children of the predictions they made before reading. Did what they predict actually happen? Were their questions answered? Revisit the story as necessary.

RETELL THE STORY Have children work in pairs and take turns retelling the story.

LITERARY RESPONSE In their journals have children write about a friend that they like to play with. Have them draw a picture of something that they and their friend enjoy doing together.

CENTER Activity

Cross Curricular: Art

CLASS MURAL Provide containers of tempera paint and mural paper. Have small groups work together to make a class mural. You may first wish to brainstorm and decide on a theme, such as the forest, a park, or a farm.

▶ **Spatial/Interpersonal**

OBJECTIVES

Children will:

- classify and categorize to understand a story

....

MATERIALS

- *Sid Said*

TEACHING TIP

INSTRUCTIONAL Help children to classify and categorize classroom books. Think of categories together, and help children decide where certain books belong.

Introduce Classify and Categorize

PREPARE

Think About the Story
Ask children to recall the story *Sid Said*. Ask the children to name other colors that might have been used in the story.

TEACH

Classify and Categorize Objects
Reread the story together. Then have them name the art medium that the children are using. (paints) Make a picture or word list of other items that belong in the category of *Things to Draw With*. Point out that we can sort objects, animals, plants, and so on into different groups.

PRACTICE

Complete the Pupil Edition Page
Read the directions on page 111 to the children, and make sure they clearly understand what they are asked to do. Identify each picture, and complete the first item together. Then work through the page with children or have them complete the page independently.

ASSESS/CLOSE

Review the Page
Review children's work, and note children who are experiencing difficulty.

Name_____

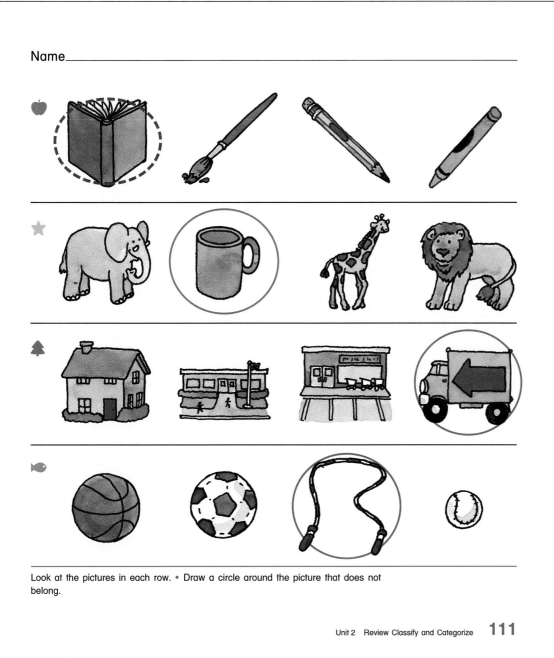

Look at the pictures in each row. • Draw a circle around the picture that does not belong.

Unit 2   Review Classify and Categorize   **111**

ALTERNATE TEACHING STRATEGY

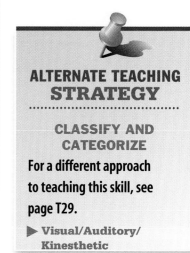

CLASSIFY AND CATEGORIZE

For a different approach to teaching this skill, see page T29.

▶ **Visual/Auditory/ Kinesthetic**

PRACTICE BOOK, page 111

Meeting Individual Needs for Comprehension

EASY	ON-LEVEL	CHALLENGE	LANGUAGE SUPPORT
Provide children with a can of buttons. Have them sort the buttons by shape, size, color, or other categories.	**Make** a picture or word list of items in your classroom. Have children categorize the items into living and non-living categories.	**Have** children think of ways that the children in the story are alike and different: boys or girls, hair color, glasses, and so on. You may wish to make a chart to show the information.	**Give** children a carton of blocks. Give children a few categories for sorting. Then invite children to think of their own categories.

111

Develop Phonological Awareness

Listen

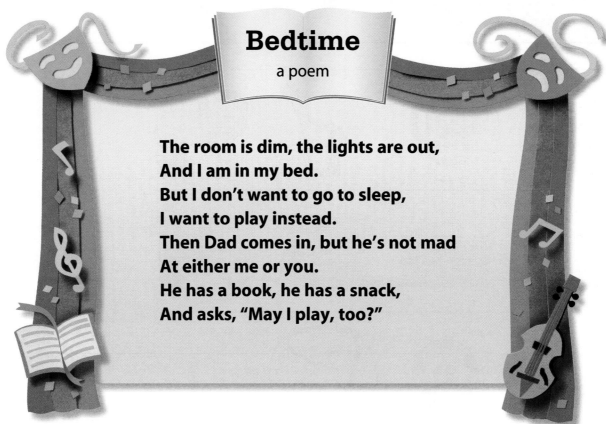

Bedtime
a poem

The room is dim, the lights are out,
And I am in my bed.
But I don't want to go to sleep,
I want to play instead.
Then Dad comes in, but he's not mad
At either me or you.
He has a book, he has a snack,
And asks, "May I play, too?"

Objective: Focus on Syllables

IDENTIFY SYLLABLES Read the poem "Bedtime." Ask: *What did Dad bring into the bedroom?* (book, snack) Ask children to place a hand under their chin as they say the words *book* and *snack*. Ask how many times their chin moved. Explain that *book* and *snack* each have one syllable. Repeat with the word *wagon*.

> book   snack   wag-on

COUNT SYLLABLES Gather a box of toys whose names contain one or two syllables. Have children select a toy. Have each child name the toy and identify the number of syllables.

> bear   whistle   ball   marble

RELATE NUMERALS TO SYLLABLES Write *1* or *2* dots on index cards. Give each child one card. Children take turns finding a toy whose name has the number of syllables shown on the card.

Objective: Blending Short *a* and *i*

LISTEN FOR SOUNDS Read the poem "Bedtime." Say the word *dim* and repeat it, segmenting each sound. Introduce the word *dam*, explaining it is a place that holds water. Sound out *dam*. Ask children how *dim* and *dam* are the same and how they are different. Help children determine that the beginning and ending sounds are the same, but the middle sound is different.

> **dim—/d/-/i/-/m/   dam—/d/-/a/-/m/**

CHANGE SOUNDS Say the sentence: *My name is Sid*, segmenting the sounds in the name *Sid*. Model how to blend the sounds to identify the word. Have children repeat the sentence. Then tell children that you will say a new sentence. Ask children to listen carefully. Then say: *I am not sad*, segmenting each sound in the word *sad*. Have children blend the sounds and repeat the sen-

tence. Then say the words *Sid* and *sad*, segmenting each sound. Point out that the middle sounds in *Sid* and *sad* are different.

> **My name is /S/-/i/-/d/.**
> **I am not /s/-/a/-/d/.**

BLEND WORDS Continue the activity with the sentences below.

> **I can't find /d/-/a/-/d/.**
> **Where /d/-/i/-/d/ he go?**

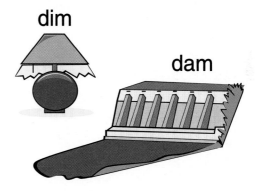

dim

dam

Read Together

From Phonemic Awareness to Phonics

Objective: Identify Word Endings

IDENTIFY THE LETTERS Write the words *dim* and *dam* on the chalkboard. Frame the letters *im* in the word *dim* and identify them. Say the sounds the letters stand for. Then frame the letters *am* in the word *dam* and identify them. Say the sounds the letters stand for.

> **dim   dam**

LISTEN FOR RHYMING WORDS Say words that end with *im* or *am*. Children respond with

the word *dim* or *dam* to identify the rhyming word. Write the word in the correct column and invite a volunteer to circle the ending letters.

> **dim: Kim Tim him Jim**
> **dam: ham jam Pam ram**

FIND A MATCH Write the words above on index cards. Mix them up and give one card to each child. Have children walk around the room to find a partner that has a matching word ending.

OBJECTIVES

Children will:

- identify and blend /a/*a*, /i/*i* words
- read and write short *i, a* words
- review /m/*m*, /s/*s*, /d/*d*, /n/*n*

....

MATERIALS

- Letter cards from the Word Building Book

TEACHING TIP

INSTRUCTIONAL Give each child a pretend name tag with one of the following names: *Nan, Dan, Sam, Sid, Min.* Make up sentences that direct specific characters by name to pick up a book, clap hands, and so on. Ask children to repeat their pretend names.

ALTERNATE TEACHING STRATEGY
....

BLENDING SHORT *a, i*
For a different approach to teaching this skill, see Unit 1, page T32, and Unit 2, page T32.

▶ **Visual/Auditory/ Kinesthetic**

Review Blending with short *i, a*

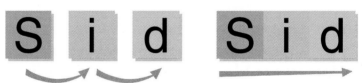

TEACH

Identify *a, i* as Symbols for /a/, /i/
Tell children they will continue to read words with *a* and *i*.

- Display the *i* letter card and say /i/. Have children repeat the sound /i/ after you as you point to the *i* card.

BLENDING Model and Guide Practice
- Place a *d* card after the *i* card. Point to each and blend sounds together to say _*id*. Have children repeat after you.

- Place a uppercase *S* letter card before the *id*. Blend the sounds in the words as you track print with the finger and read *Sid*.

$$\text{S} \quad \text{i} \quad \text{d} \qquad \text{S} \quad \text{i} \quad \text{d}$$

Use the Words in Context
- Have children begin a sentence saying *Sid is sad because . . .* Ask them to imagine Sid as a pet or a character from a story.

Repeat the Procedure
- Use the following words to continue modeling and for guided practice with short *i, a*: *Sam, Nan, dim, Min, did, dad, man.*

PRACTICE

Complete the Pupil Edition Page
Read the directions on page 112 to the children, and make sure they clearly understand what they are being asked to do. Identify each picture, and complete the first item together. Then work through the page with children, or have them complete the page independently.

ASSESS/CLOSE

Build Short *a, i* Words
Observe children as they complete page 112. Give children letter cards *m, s, d, n.* Ask them to build two short *a* and two short *i* words.

Name

🍎 S i d   Sid

⭐ d i m   dim

🌲 m a n   man

🐟 s a d   sad

🍎 Look at the name. Blend the sounds and say the name. Write the name. Use the name aloud in a sentence. ⭐🌲🐟 Look at each word. Blend the sounds and say the word. Write the word. Use the word aloud in a sentence.

112 Unit 2   Introduce Blending with Short *i, a*

McGraw-Hill School Division

Pupil Edition, page 112

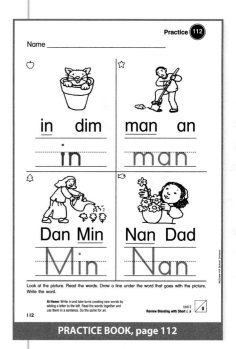

Practice 112

Name

in dim	man an
in	man
Dan Min	Nan Dad
Min	Nan

Look at the picture. Read the words. Draw a line under the word that goes with the picture. Write the word.

At Home: Write *in* and take turns creating new words by adding a letter to the left. Read the words together and use them in a sentence. Do the same for *an*.

112   Unit 2
Review Blending with Short *i, a*   8

PRACTICE BOOK, page 112

Meeting Individual Needs for Phonics

EASY	ON-LEVEL	CHALLENGE	LANGUAGE SUPPORT
List the following words on the chalkboard: *did, dim, dam.* Ask children to select the word that completes a sentence. Say, for example: *With the curtains closed, the room is very (dim). The water flowed over the (dam).* Have children repeat each word after you.	**Give** each child one of the following word cards: *Dad, sad, mad, in, dam, dim.* Ask children to draw a picture that shows what the word means. Have children label their picture with the word and share it with the class.	**Invite** children to identify the nonsense short *a* or *i* word. Write words such as the following on the chalkboard: *mad, sad, dad, nad; did, dim, sim, Sid.* Have them read each word aloud; then ask them to identify the nonsense word. (*nad, sim*)	**Help** children distinguish between the /a/ and /i/ sounds by having them repeat after you as you chant pairs of short *a* and *i* words that are similar, emphasizing the difference in the vowel sound. For example: *did, dad; dam, dim; Sid, sad; Min, man.*

112

Reread the Decodable Story

Sid Said

☑ **Initial and Medial** *i*
☑ **High-Frequency Word:** *said*
☑ **Concepts of Print**
☑ **Use Illustrations**

Sid Said

Guided Reading

SET PURPOSES Tell children that when they read the story again they can find out more about what happened. Explain that you want them to look for words that have the letter *i*. Remind them that they know the word *said* and will see it again in this story.

REREAD THE BOOK As you guide children through the story, address specific problems they may have had during the first read. Use the following prompts to guide the lesson:

- **USE ILLUSTRATIONS** Ask children how the small pictures in this story help them to read the sentence.

- **CONCEPTS OF PRINT** After reading page 8, model tracking print from left to right to the end of the first line. Demonstrate the return sweep to the second line.

RETURN TO PURPOSES Ask children if they found out more about what happened in the story. Ask if they found any words

that begin with *i*, or that have the middle *i*. Ask if anyone saw the word *said*.

LITERARY RESPONSE Ask children to choose some colors from the story and write about and draw a rainbow.

- Ask children to describe the colors of their rainbows.

- Ask children to compare the colors of their drawings to the colors used in the story.

INFORMAL ASSESSMENT

HIGH-FREQUENCY WORD: *said*

HOW TO ASSESS
Take a walk through the story with the children. Ask them to point to the word *said* each time they see it.

FOLLOW UP
If children have difficulty identifying the word *said*, point to each word on the page and ask, *Is this word said?*

 Read the Patterned Book

Come In!

☑ **Short /i/** *i*
☑ **Classify and Categorize**
☑ **High-Frequency Word:** *said*
☑ **Concepts of Print**

Guided Reading

PREVIEW AND PREDICT Read the title and the author's and the illustrator's names. Take a **picture walk** through pages 2–4, paying attention to what children see in Pig's house. Have children make predictions about what they think will happen in the story.

SET PURPOSES Have children decide what they want to find out from the story and predict what the animals are going to do. Tell them that the story contains words with short *i*.

READ THE BOOK Use the following prompts while the children are reading or after they have read independently. Remind them to run their fingers under each word as they read.

Pages 2–3: Point to the word that begins with *s. We know this word. Let's read it together:* said. *High-Frequency Words*

Point to the quotation marks. *What do these marks tell you?* (A character is saying the words.) *Concepts of Print*

Pages 4–5: *What animals do you see in Pig's house?* (rooster, rabbit, dog, pig) *How are these animals alike and different?* (They are all animals. They are all different sizes.) *Classify and Categorize*

Pages 6–7: Point to the word *in. The word* in *begins with the /i/ sound. Let's read it together:* in. *Can you find another word with the /i/ sound?* (lit) *Phonics*

RETURN TO PREDICTIONS AND PURPOSES Ask children if they found out what they needed to know from the story. Check to see if their predictions were correct.

LITERARY RESPONSE The following questions will help focus children's responses:

• Why did the animals get on each other's backs?

• Think of a time when you solved a problem. Write about it in your journal and draw a picture.

LANGUAGE SUPPORT

ESL Show pictures of the animals in the story. Have children identify them and share what they know about these animals. Then reread the story, and have children read the story with a partner.

CENTER Activity

Cross Curricular: Math

WHO'S FIRST Write numbers on index cards. Have children retell the story to a partner, using numbers to show how many animals are in each picture. You may wish to have children make craft-stick puppets and act out the story, using the numbers.

▶ **Spatial/Logical**

OBJECTIVES

Children will:

- **identify and read the high-frequency word** *said*

MATERIALS

- word cards from the Word Play Book
- *Sid Said*

Review *said, I, is*

PREPARE

Listen to Words Explain to children that they will be reviewing the word *said*.

Say the following phrase, using children's names: Steven said ___. Ask that child to complete the phrase.

TEACH

Model Reading the Word in Context Have children reread the decodable book. Ask children to listen for the word *said*.

Identify the Word Have children look at their word cards, and ask them to look for the word in sentences. Have children read the sentences and track print. Have volunteers put a self-stick note below the word *said*. Have children move the stick-on note from page to page.

Review High-Frequency Words Give children word cards for the following words: *said, the, a, my, that, I, and, is*. Then say the words, and have children hold up the appropriate word cards.

PRACTICE

Complete the Pupil Edition Page Read the directions on page 113 to the children, and make sure they clearly understand what they are asked to do. Complete the first item together. Then work through the page with children or have them complete the page independently.

ASSESS/CLOSE

Review the Page Review children's work, and note children who are experiencing difficulty or need additional practice.

Name _____

 Nan said, "Sam <u>is</u> sad."

⭐ Sam <u>said</u>, "Am I sad?"

🌲 "<u>I</u> am ," said Sam.

Read each sentence. ● Draw a line under the word *is*. ⭐ Draw a line under the word *said*. 🌲 Draw a line under the word *I*.

Unit 2   Review *said, I, is*   **113**

Pupil Edition, page 113

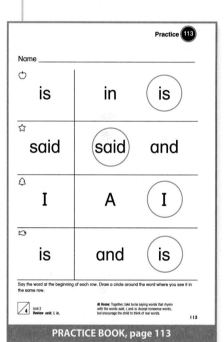

PRACTICE BOOK, page 113

Meeting Individual Needs for Vocabulary

EASY	ON-LEVEL	CHALLENGE	LANGUAGE SUPPORT
Write the word *said* on the chalkboard and read it together. Have children count and say the number of letters in the word. Then children use the word in sentences.	**Give** children letter cards for *s, a, i,* and *i*. Write each letter on the chalkboard, and have children find the matching letter. Then read the word, and complete this phrase: This morning, our teacher said "___."	**Write** the following poem: I said yes, You said no. I said stop, You said __. Children complete with a rhyming word. Then write similar poems together.	**Read** classroom books that use the word *said*. Emphasize the word, and have children point to the character that is speaking.

**GRAMMAR/SPELLING
CONNECTIONS**
Model subject-verb
agreement, complete
sentences, and correct
tense so that students
may gain increasing con-
trol of grammar when
speaking and writing.

Interactive Writing

Write a New Story

Prewrite

LOOK AT THE STORY PATTERN Revisit
The Chick and the Duckling, noting the dialogue pattern used in the story. As you read,
have children join in on *Me, too.* Talk about
other things that the Chick and Duckling
could do together. Make a list with words
and pictures.

Draft

WRITE A CLASS STORY Explain that
children are going to write a new story about
the Chick and the Duckling. Choose one of
the ideas from the list.

- Begin by deciding what the Chick and the
  Duckling will do. Incorporate the dialogue
  pattern from the story. Write dialogue on
  sentence strips.

- Give pairs of children a sentence strip and
  have them illustrate the page.

Publish

CREATE THE BOOK Share the illustrations. Then have children help you transpose
the text from the sentence strips to each
matching page. Make sure the sequence is
correct, and reread the story.

Presentation Ideas

MAKE PUPPETS Have children make puppets from craft sticks. They can use markers to draw on the sticks, or cut out figures from construction paper and tape them to the sticks.

▶ **Representing/Viewing**

PUT ON A PUPPET SHOW Have partners act out the new story. Encourage them to include dialogue that follows the story pattern.

▶ **Speaking/Listening**

COMMUNICATION TIPS

- **Speaking** Remind children to speak clearly and loudly when they are performing for others.

- **Listening** Remind children to listen attentively and quietly while puppet shows are being performed. Have them say what they enjoyed about each show.

TECHNOLOGY TIP

Using a computer, children may wish to input the phrase: *Me, too.* Help children identify the correct keys to type.

LANGUAGE SUPPORT

ESL Show pictures of chicks and ducklings, and have children identify each. Then show pictures of hens and ducks, and talk about how the animals are alike and different.

Meeting Individual Needs for Writing

EASY	ON-LEVEL	CHALLENGE
Draw Pictures Have children draw a favorite part of the story. Then help them label the picture *Me, too*.	**Journal Entry** Ask children to choose one of the characters from the story, and write about how the character might feel at the end of the story. Remind children to sound out words as they write.	**Create a Character** Have children create a new character for the book. Ask them to decide who the character is, his or her name, and what the character does with Chick and Duckling. Help children write and illustrate the new part of the story.

Is Sam Mad?

Children will read and listen to a variety of stories about friends learning from each other as they work and play together.

**Decodable Story,
pages 121–122**

**Listening
Library
Audiocassette**

**Patterned Books,
page 125B**

by Ian Paul
illustrated by Susan Lexa

Tweedy's Toys
by Constance Andrea Keremes

**Teacher Read Aloud,
page 119A**

The **ABC** Street Fair

Written By Constance Keremes
Illustrated By Lindy Burnett

**Listening
Library
Audiocassette**

**ABC Big Book,
pages 115A–115B**

Pamela Duncan Edwards • Henry Cole

WARTHOGS in the Kitchen
A Sloppy Counting Book

**Listening
Library
Audiocasse**

**Literature Big Book,
pages 117A–117B**

Pupil Edition,
pages 114–125

Big Book of Real-Life Reading,
page 8

Big Book of Phonics Rhymes and
Poems, pages 14–15, 16, 33, 34–35

 **Listening**
Library
Audiocassette

ADDITIONAL RESOURCES

Practice Book,
pages 114–125

- **Phonics Kit**
- **Language Support Book**
- **Alternate Teaching Strategies,**
  pages T24–T33

McGraw-Hill School
TECHNOLOGY

Phonics CD-ROM Provides
extra phonics support.

interNET CONNECTION Research & Inquiry Ideas.

Visit www.mhschool.com

Is Sam Mad?

READING AND LANGUAGE ARTS

- **Phonological Awareness**

- **Phonics** review /d/*d*; /s/*s*; /m/*m*; blending with short *i, a*

- **Comprehension**

- **Vocabulary**

- **Beginning Reading Concepts**

- **Listening, Speaking, Viewing, Representing**

- **Cross Curriculum**

- **Writing**

DAY 1

The ABC Street Fair
Written By Constance Keremes
Illustrated By Lindy Burnett

Focus on Reading Skills

Develop Phonological Awareness, 114G–114H
"Dinosaurs for Dinner" and "Molly" *Big Book of Phonics Rhymes and Poems,* 14–15, 33

 **Review Initial /d/*d*, /s/*s*, /m/*m*,** 114I–114
Practice Book, 114
Phonics/Phonemic Awareness Practice Book

Phonics CD-ROM

Read the Literature

 Read *The ABC Street Fair* Big Book, 115A–115B
Shared Reading

Build Skills

☑ Shapes and Numbers, 115C–115
Practice Book, 115

 Activity Language Arts, 115B

 Writing Prompt: Write about your favorite page in *The ABC Street Fair.*

Journal Writing, 115B
Letter Formation, 114I

DAY 2

WARTHOGS in the Kitchen
A Sloppy Counting Book
Pamela Duncan Edwards • Henry Cole
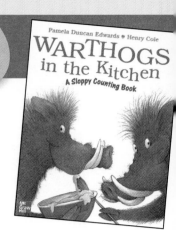

Focus on Reading Skills

Develop Phonological Awareness, 116A–116B
"The Red Balloon" and "Where Is Tim?" *Big Book of Phonics Rhymes and Poems,* 16, 34

 **Review Final /d/*d*, /m/*m*,** 116C–116
Practice Book, 116
Phonics/Phonemic Awareness Practice Book

Phonics CD-ROM

Read the Literature, 117A–117B

 **Read** *Warthogs in the Kitchen* Big Book
Shared Reading

Build Skills

☑ Story Details, 117C–117
Practice Book, 117

 Activity Math, 117B

 Writing Prompt: Write about a neat thing to do with a friend.

Journal Writing, 117B
Letter Formation, 116C

☑ = **Skill Assessed in Unit Test**

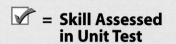

DAY 3

Tweedy's Toys

Focus on Reading Skills

Develop Phonological Awareness,
118A–118B
"Dinosaurs for Dinner" and "The Red Balloon" *Big Book of Phonics Rhymes and Poems,* 14–16

**Review /d/d, /m/m, /s/s,** 118C–118
Practice Book, 118
Phonics/Phonemic Awareness Practice Book

 CD-ROM

Read the Literature

Read "Tweedy's Toys" Teacher Read Aloud, 119A–119B
Shared Reading

Read the Big Book of Real-Life Reading, 8–9
☑ Diagrams

Build Skills

☑ High-Frequency Words: *and, I, is, said,* 119C–119
Practice Book, 119

 **Language Arts/Art,** 119B

 Writing Prompt: Draw a picture of your favorite way to travel. It can be by foot, train, car, or any other way. Tell why you like that way of travel.

DAY 4

Is Sam Mad?

Focus on Reading Skills

Develop Phonological Awareness,
120A–120B
"Lost and Found"

Review Blending with Short *i, a,*
120C–120
Practice Book, 120
Phonics/Phonemic Awareness Practice Book

 **CD-ROM**

Read the Literature

Read "Is Sam Mad?" Decodable Story,
121/122A–121/122D

☑ Review *d, s, m, i;* Blending
☑ Classify and Categorize
☑ High-Frequency Words: *said*
☑ Concepts of Print

Build Skills

☑ Classify and Categorize,
123A–123
Practice Book, 123

 Math, 121/122D

 **Writing Prompt:** Look at the title page. Write about a time when you were mad.

Letter Formation
Practice Book, 121–122

DAY 5

Building
Is Sam Mad?
Ian Paul
Illustrated by Susan Lexa

Focus on Reading Skills

Develop Phonological Awareness,
124A–124B
"Lost and Found"

Review Blending with Short *i, a,*
124C–124
Practice Book, 124
Phonics/Phonemic Awareness Practice Book

 **CD-ROM**

Read the Literature

Reread "Is Sam Mad?" Decodable Story, 125A

Read "Building" Patterned Book, 125B
Guided Reading
☑ Review *d, s, m, i;* Blending
☑ Classify and Categorize
☑ High-Frequency Words: *said*
☑ Concepts of Print

Build Skills

☑ High-Frequency Words: *and, I, is, said,* 125C–125
Practice Book, 125

 125B

 Writing Prompt: Write about something you learned while playing or working with friends.

Interactive Writing, 126A–126B

Develop Phonological Awareness

Listen

Dinosaurs for Dinner

Six Silly Seals

If dinosaurs came for dinner,
I'd give them all a treat.
Dinosaurs for dinner!
What do dinosaurs eat?
A ton of mashed potatoes?
A dump truck full of dates?
A dandelion salad served
on dinosaur-sized plates?
Dinosaurs for dinner!
It could be so divine.
Dinosaurs for dinner!
The pleasure would be mine.

Six silly seals
Can wiggle in the sea.
Six silly seals
Are silly as can be.
Six silly seals
Can sail without a boat.
They hold onto a whale's tail,
And across the sea they float.

Big Book of Phonics Rhymes and Poems, pages 14–15, 48

Objective: Review Initial /d/

IDENTIFY INITIAL D Read the title, "Dinosaurs for Dinner." Ask: "<u>Who</u> is coming? What meal are they coming for?" When children respond, ask what sound they hear at the beginning of *dinosaurs*. Pronounce the sound /d/ and have children say it with you. Then repeat the procedure with *dinner*.

Read the poem aloud and have children listen for the words that begin with /d/.

dinosaurs dinner do dump dandelion divine

MAKE A DINOSAUR MENU Ask children if they can think of other silly things that the dinosaurs might eat for dinner. Explain that the dinosaurs eat only things that begin with /d/. Model a sentence for children to use: "If dinosaurs came for dinner, I'd give them a desk." Encourage children to exaggerate the words beginning with /d/.

Objective: Review Initial /s/

READ THE POEM Read aloud the poem "Six Silly Seals." As you read, draw out the initial /s/ sounds. Have children tell who the poem is about. Ask, "What sound do you hear at the beginning of *six? Silly? Seals?* Let's say these words together...*s-s-six s-s-silly s-s-seals.*" Reread the poem and ask children if they hear any other words that begin with the /s/ sound.

> **sea   sail**

USE THE POEM Provide opportunities for children to say and hear the initial /s/ sound by posing questions such as:

- How many seals are there? (six)
- How are the seals described? (silly)
- Where do they wiggle? (in the sea)
- What does a boat do? (sail)

Read Together

From Phonemic Awareness to Phonics

Objective: Review Initial /m/ *M, m*

IDENTIFY THE LETTER Tell children that the letter *m* stands for the sound /m/. Show children the Phonics Rhyme poem and indicate the *m* in the upper right corner. Identify *m* and have children repeat the sound with you.

READ THE POEM Ask children to listen for the /m/ sound as you read the poem. Point to each word as you read, drawing out the words beginning with /m/.

SHOW THE LETTERS Give children an index card with the letter *m* on it. Explain that you will read the poem and they should hold up their card whenever you come to a word that begins with *m*. Remind children that the *m's* might be capital or small letters. Read the poem slowly, line by line, exaggerating the words that begin with /m/.

Molly

Molly is our milk cow.
She moos with all her might.
She gives us lots of milk to drink
Morning, noon, and night.

Molly is our milk cow.
She eats grass every day.
She grazes in the meadow
And watches as we play.

33

Big Book of Phonics Rhymes and Poems, page 33

114H

OBJECTIVES

Children will:

- identify and write /d/*D,d*, /s/*S,s*, /m/*M,m*

- discriminate among initial letters *d, s,* and *m*

·····································

MATERIALS

- letter cards from the Word Building Book

TEACHING TIP

INSTRUCTIONAL Ask children if they know a name that begins with /d/. Write the names on the chalkboard. Repeat the question for names that begin with /s/ and /m/. Remind children that people's names always begin with a capital letter, and encourage them to talk about the shapes of *D, S,* and *M.*

ALTERNATE TEACHING STRATEGY

·····································

INITIAL /d/*d*, /s/*s*, /m/*m*

For a different approach to teaching this skill, see pages T24, T28, T30.

▶ **Visual/Auditory/ Kinesthetic**

Review Initial /d/ *d*, /s/ *s*, /m/ *m*

TEACH

Discriminate among /d/*D,d*, /s/*S,s*, and /m/*M,m*

Tell children they will review the sounds /d/, /s/, and /m/ and the letters *d, s,* and *m* that stand for the sounds. Write the letters on the chalkboard, and have children say their sounds. Ask them to hold up their *d, s,* or *m* letter cards when they hear words that begin with /d/, /s/, and /m/, and read this pretend postcard: *Dear Mom, Camp is such fun. We see the sun each day. The days go by so fast. Can you and Dad come to see me on Sunday?*

Write and Use *D,d, S,s,* and *M,m*

Write the pretend postcard on the chalkboard. Read it aloud as you track print with your hand, and have children write *D,d, S,s,* or *M,m* when they recognize one of these initial letters. Invite volunteers to identify the letters and to underline the words that begin with them.

PRACTICE

Complete the Pupil Edition Page

Read the directions on page 114 of the Pupil Edition, and make sure children clearly understand what they are being asked to do. Identify each picture, and complete the first item together. Then work through the page with children or have them complete the page independently.

ASSESS/CLOSE

Identify and Use *D,d, S,s, M,m*

Have children write *D, S, M* on three squares of paper and *d, s, m* on three more squares. On the chalkboard write this sentence: *Did Min see Sam do his math?* Read the question, and ask children to show the pattern of initial /d/, /s/, and /m/ words with their paper squares.

Name_____

Dd Ss Mm

money   seesaw   dinosaur

Mm   Ss   Dd

seal   mouse   dishes

Ss   Mm   Dd

Say the name of each picture. • Then write the letter for the sound you hear at the beginning of the picture name.

114   Unit 2   Review Initial /d/d, /s/s, /m/m

McGraw-Hill School Division

Pupil Edition, page 114

ADDITIONAL PHONICS RESOURCES

Practice Book, *page 114*
Phonics Workbook

McGraw-Hill School
TECHNOLOGY

Phonics **CD-ROM**
Activities for practice with Initial Letters

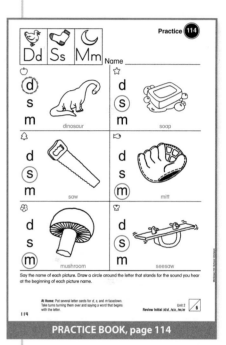

PRACTICE BOOK, page 114

Meeting Individual Needs for Phonics

EASY	ON-LEVEL	CHALLENGE	LANGUAGE SUPPORT
Give children three crayons and a Letter Wheel divided into six sections, with both forms of *d, s, m,* printed on it, one per section. Ask children to color the two sections that show different forms of the same letter. Children then identify the letter and the sound.	**Show** children pictures of things whose names begin with *d, s,* and *m,* and ask them to write letters on self-stick notes with which to label the pictures. Examples: *dog, doll, sack, 6, map, mop.*	**Ask** children to think of things to eat that begin with *d, s, m,* for example: *donut, dessert, dates; salad, soup, sandwich; milk, macaroni, mango.* Invite them to make up a menu for a meal, choosing a food item from each letter group.	**Have** children sort word cards that show words beginning in *d, s,* and *m.* Give them words that show both capital and lowercase forms. Say *Dan, Sue, Max, dad, sad, mad,* and ask them to hold up a word card that begins with the same letter.

114

OBJECTIVES

- match letter cards with letters in the story
- use letters to recognize key words in the story

LANGUAGE SUPPORT

ESL Have children work in pairs to do ABC activities. Pair ESL children with children who are fluent in English. Encourage children to work together.

Read the Big Book

Before Reading

Develop Oral Language
Read "The Alphabet Chant" with the children on pages 6–7 in the Big Book of Phonics Rhymes and Poems. Remind children that they have read a story about a family who goes to a street fair. Ask how the story begins and how it ends.

Set Purposes
Explain to children that as they reread the story, they will use letters to name key words. They will also match letter cards with the letters in the book. Distribute two or three capital and lowercase letters to each child. As you read the story, children holding the letter in the story stand up and name the letter. Tell children that they will also use the illustrations to learn more about the story.

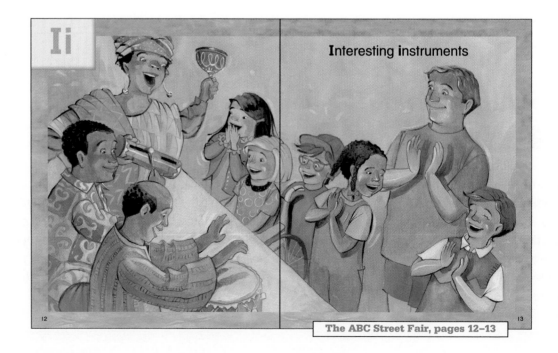

The ABC Street Fair, pages 12–13

During Reading

Read Together

- As you point to the letter, have children holding the letter cards stand up and identify them. Run your finger under each word in the story as you read. Have children repeat the words after you. *Concepts of Print*

- As you read the story, stop before you read some of the key words. After the letter is identified, ask volunteers to say the word. Then have children say the word with you. *Phonics*

- After you read page 14, ask children to predict what could happen if the juggler takes his eyes off the balls. *Make Predictions*

- After you read page 29, ask children what might be inside the boxes. *Use Illustrations/Make Inferences*

The ABC Street Fair, page 30

After Reading

Literary Response

JOURNAL WRITING Ask children to draw a picture of what might be in the boxes on page 29.

ORAL RESPONSE Ask questions such as:

- *Do you think the same thing is in each box?*

- *What else might be in one of the boxes?*

ABC Activity

Provide trays of salt or sand and have children practice writing letters. Point to letters in the Big Book, and have children name and write them.

CENTER Activity

Cross Curricular: Language Arts

FOOD ORDER Make alphabet cards with pictures of foods. Label the food with the letter that matches the initial sound. Have pairs of children name the letters and put the cards in ABC order.

▶ **Logical/Kinestetic**

 OBJECTIVES

Children will:

- identify shapes
- review numbers 1–10

MATERIALS

- *The ABC Street Fair*
- paper shapes
- number cards 1–10

TEACHING TIP

INSTRUCTIONAL Watch for children who are not developmentally ready to identify and count shapes. Break down tasks for these children, having them sort shapes without counting or count shapes that have previously been identified and sorted.

Review Shapes and Numbers

PREPARE

Name the Shape

Draw a circle, a square, a triangle, and a rectangle on the chalkboard. Play a game by giving clues to name a shape, such as: *I'm thinking of a shape with four sides. It has two long sides and two short sides.* Volunteers point to the correct shape and name it.

TEACH

Recognize and Count Shapes

Draw a circle, a triangle, a rectangle, and a square on chart paper. Then take a picture walk through the Big Book *The ABC Street Fair*. Ask volunteers to find items that have these shapes. Each time an item is found, the child makes a tally mark under the corresponding shape on the chart paper. Stop before you have more than 10 of one shape, and count to find the total for each.

PRACTICE

Count Groups and Color Shapes

Read the directions on page 115 to the children, and make sure they clearly understand what they are being asked to do. Identify each picture, and complete the first item together. Then work through the page with children, or have them complete the page independently.

ASSESS/CLOSE

Review the Page

Check children's work on the Pupil Edition page. Note areas where children need extra help.

Name _____

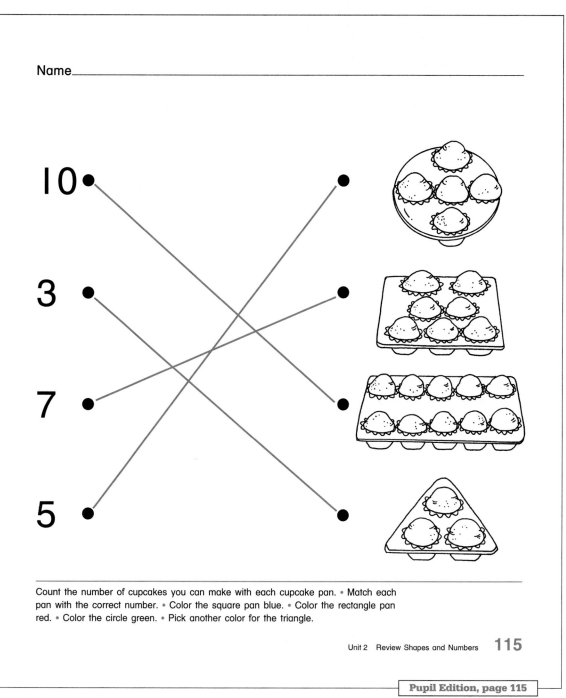

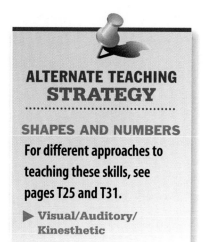
Count the number of cupcakes you can make with each cupcake pan. • Match each pan with the correct number. • Color the square pan blue. • Color the rectangle pan red. • Color the circle green. • Pick another color for the triangle.

Unit 2   Review Shapes and Numbers   **115**

Pupil Edition, page 115

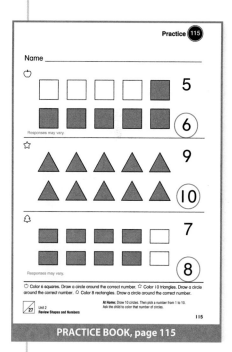

PRACTICE BOOK, page 115

Meeting Individual Needs for Beginning Reading Concepts

EASY	ON-LEVEL	CHALLENGE	LANGUAGE SUPPORT
Provide number cards 1–10, and paper shapes. Ask a child to choose a card and name the number. Then he or she counts out that number of shapes. Ask the child to name each shape.	**Cut** out paper shapes and hide them in the classroom. Invite small groups of children to go on a Shape Hunt. Give them a few minutes to look for the shapes and collect them. Then each child counts to find how many of each shape he or she collected.	**Draw** halves of shapes on chart paper. Then invite children to complete the shapes according to your directions, such as: *How can you complete this shape to make a triangle?* Discuss the results.	**Counting** songs and poems are an invaluable aid to help children develop counting skills. Children will also enjoy finger plays that involve counting.

Develop Phonological Awareness

Listen

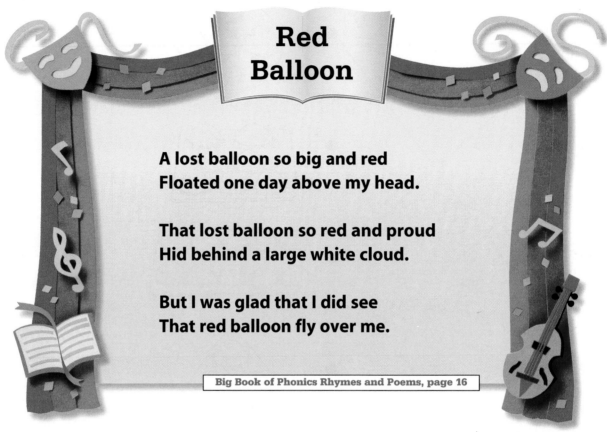

Red Balloon

A lost balloon so big and red
Floated one day above my head.

That lost balloon so red and proud
Hid behind a large white cloud.

But I was glad that I did see
That red balloon fly over me.

Big Book of Phonics Rhymes and Poems, page 16

Objective: Review Final /d/

IDENTIFY FINAL D Read aloud the poem, exaggerating the final /d/ sound in *red, floated, head, and, proud, hid, behind, cloud, glad,* and *did.* Ask children what color the balloon is. Ask: "What sound do you hear at the end of *red*?" Have children repeat the /d/ with you.

SEGMENT WORDS Work with children to segment final /d/ words. For example, say, "r-e-d." As you pronounce the word, emphasize the final d. Have children repeat the word after you. Other words to segment are:

> h-i-d   d-i-d   a-n-d

REREAD THE POEM Read the poem again and ask children to listen for other words that end in /d/. As a child identifies a word, have the class pronounce it, emphasizing the /d/ ending. Repeat until all the words are identified.

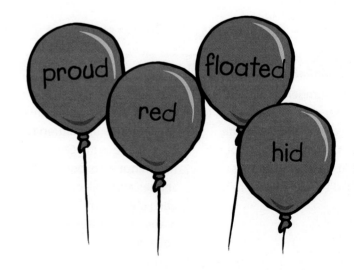

Objective: Review Initial /d/

PLAY A GUESSING GAME Extend children's understanding of final /d/ by playing this game. Say, "I'm thinking of something that ends with /d/. It's something that you sleep in. What is it?" When children guess, have them repeat the answer with you emphasizing the final /d/ sound. Continue play using clues such as these, but always beginning by mentioning that the word ends in the sound of /d/:

- It is part of your body. (head)
- It is something you write on. (pad)
- It is another word for "father." (dad)
- It is what you eat. (food)

USING FINAL /D/ Ask children to look for things in the classroom that are red. When a child finds something, he or she should say, "I see something red." Ask another child to say, "What is red?" Encourage children to pronounce and listen for the final /d/ sound.

Read Together

From Phonemic Awareness to Phonics

Objective: Review Final /m/*m*

IDENTIFY THE LETTER Review with children that the letter *m* stands for the sound /m/. As you display the Phonics Rhyme poem, point to the letters in the upper right corner. Tell children that the letter is *m*, and say its sound. Have children repeat the sound with you. Explain that the /m/ sound can occur at the end of words. Give the example:

> **Tim, Tim!**

READ THE POEM Read the poem aloud. With a pointer, tap each word. Draw out the words with final /m/.

MATCH THE SOUNDS AND LETTERS As you read the poem again, call on volunteers to come up and point to the letter *m* in the words that end with the /m/ sound.

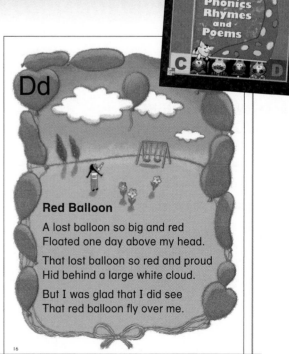

Dd

Red Balloon

A lost balloon so big and red
Floated one day above my head.

That lost balloon so red and proud
Hid behind a large white cloud.

But I was glad that I did see
That red balloon fly over me.

16

Big Book of Phonics Rhymes and Poems, page 16

Review Final /d/d,/m/m

OBJECTIVES

Children will:

- identify and discriminate between /d/ *d* and /m/ *m*
- write and use letters *d* and *m*

MATERIALS

- letter cards from the Word Play Book

TEACHING TIP

INSTRUCTIONAL Give children assorted tactile letters *d* and *m*. Ask them to sort to show the same letter. Encourage children to describe the shape of each letter. Then say several words that end in *d* or *m*, such as *bad, good, hid, room, hum, jam*. Invite children to hold up the letter that shows the final /d/ or /m/ sound.

ALTERNATE TEACHING STRATEGY

FINAL /d/*d*, /m/*m*

For a different approach to teaching this skill, see page T24.

▶ **Visual/Auditory/ Kinesthetic**

TEACH

Identify and Discriminate Between /d/d and /m/m

Tell children they will review the sounds /d/ and /m/, and write the letters *d* and *m*. Have children repeat the /d/ and /m/ sounds after you as you write the letters. Say: "Sam had a ham." Ask children to repeat the sentence and to hold up the letter card that shows if a word ends in /d/ or /m/. Write the sentence on the chalkboard. Point to each word silently. Ask children to hold up a card that matches the word's last letter.

Write *d, m*

Write ____*d* on one side of the chalkboard and ____*m* on the other side. Show the following word cards one at a time, and ask children to point to the side of the chalkboard where they belong: *dad, dim, am, did, Tim, mad*. Write the word below its correct heading, and draw a circle around the last letter. Have children write *d* or *m* for each word.

PRACTICE

Complete the Pupil Edition Page

Read the directions on page 116 of the Pupil Edition, and make sure children clearly understand what they are being asked to do. Identify each picture, and complete the first item together. Then work through the page with children or have them complete the page independently.

ASSESS/CLOSE

Identify and Use *d, m*

Have children write letters *d* and *m* on blank cards. Give clues and ask children to think of a word that ends with *d* or *m*, for example: *This is a musical instrument that goes "boom, boom."* (drum) *This is something you do with a book.* (read) Children say the word and hold up the letter.

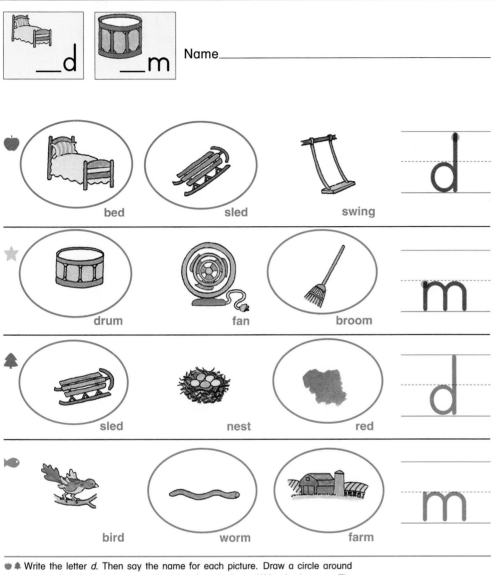

Name_____

bed   sled   swing   **d**

drum   fan   broom   **m**

sled   nest   red   **d**

bird   worm   farm   **m**

🍎 🌲 Write the letter *d*. Then say the name for each picture. Draw a circle around each picture that has the same ending sound as *bed*. ⭐ 🐟 Write the letter *m*. Then say the name for each picture. Draw a circle around each picture that has the same ending sound as *drum*.

116   Unit 2   Review Final /d/d and /m/m

McGraw-Hill School Division

Pupil Edition, page 116

Say the name of each picture. Draw a circle around the letter that stands for the sound you hear at the end of each picture name.

At Home: Play "Rhyme Time." Take turns saying words that end with *d* and *m*. The other person says a word that rhymes.

116   Review Final /d/d, /m/m   Unit 2

PRACTICE BOOK, page 116

Meeting Individual Needs for Phonics

EASY	ON-LEVEL	CHALLENGE	LANGUAGE SUPPORT
Form a circle and play "Pass the Hat." Put pictures of objects whose names end in *m* and *d* into a hat. Children pass the hat as they sing a song. Raise your hand and the person with the hat pulls out a picture and identifies whether the name of the object ends in *d* or *m*.	**Give** children paper strips with this incomplete sentence: *Da_ and Mo_ ha_ a meal of ha_ and ja_.* Say the sentence, "Dad and Mom had a meal of ham and jam." Have children write the missing letters on their strips, and read the sentence aloud.	**Say** a word that ends in *d* or *m*. Invite volunteers to say words, including people's names, that end in the same letter. Remind children to think of words that rhyme, such as *bad, dad, had, mad* or *dim, him, Jim, Kim*.	**Play** a variation of "Simon Says." Demonstrate gestures for: be mad; be sad; be glad; hum; drum. Tell children to follow directions only if you first say *Simon says*…Otherwise, ask them to show the letter card that matches the final *d* or *m* they hear in your directions.

OBJECTIVES

- review words with final /d/*d*
- review words with initial /s/*s*
- story details
- classify and categorize

....

MATERIALS

- Literature Big Book: *Warthogs in the Kitchen*

TEACHING TIP

Gather easy-to-read children's cookbooks for the learning center. Include actual cooking utensils such as measuring cups and spoons. A children's cooking video or CD-ROM can also be shown.

Read the Big Book

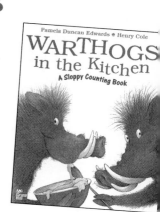

Before Reading

DEVELOP ORAL LANGUAGE Invite children to learn and pantomime with you a new verse for the teapot song they sang earlier during the second reading of the Literature Big Book:

I'm a little warthog
short and stout.
Here are my tusks. Here is my snout.
When I get in the kitchen
see me bake.
Stir and sift
to make cupcakes!

Have children recall the story they read about warthogs in a kitchen. Display the Literature Big Book and read the title with children. Ask them to recall what the book was about.

Set Purposes   Have children think about their purpose for reading the Big Book again. For example, they might reread to find out what happens first, next, and last.

3

Three cake makers read the book to check how.

8

4

Four scoops of sugar should go in now.

Warthogs in the Kitchen, pages 8–9   9

117A   *Is Sam Mad?*

During Reading

Warthogs in the Kitchen, page 13

Read Together As this is a counting book, you may wish to pause before any numerals, allowing time for children to shout them out as you read.

- As you read, emphasize how you move your finger from left to right and word for word, down to page. *Concepts of Print*

- As you read, have children identify any words they see with either final /d/*d* or initial /s/*s* when appropriate. *Phonemic Awareness*

- Remind children that the book is called a "sloppy counting book." Pause throughout the reading and have children find story details in either words or pictures that show the warthogs are sloppy. *Story Details*

- On pages that clearly illustrate the kitchen, have children find objects to match various categories. For example: *Find something that stirs. Find something that you can eat. Find something that pours. Classify and Categorize*

- At the conclusion of the story, provide the following inquiry question: *The warthogs had fun baking. Have you ever helped bake something? What kinds of things would you like to learn about cooking?*

After Reading

Literary Response Discuss with children their favorite parts of the story. Then repeat the inquiry question: *What kinds of things would you like to learn about cooking?* Have children record their responses in their journals.

ORAL RESPONSE Have children share their writing with the class.

Cross Curricular: Math

HOW MUCH? Provide children with various measuring instruments, both for dry and liquid measure. Have available a box of dry cereal. Have children estimate, or guess, how many pieces of dry cereal it will take to fill the various containers. Then have them actually fill the containers. Data can be recorded in a picture and number chart.

▶ **Logical/Mathematical**

OBJECTIVES

Children will:

- use story details to understand a story

MATERIALS

- *Warthogs in the Kitchen*

TEACHING TIP

INSTRUCTIONAL Provide counters. As you come to each number in the Big Book, ask children to show the corresponding number with their counters.

Review Story Details

PREPARE

Discuss Story Details

Review the story *Warthogs in the Kitchen* with children. Ask the children to describe what the warthogs' cupcakes look like, using as many details as possible.

TEACH

Review Details to Understand the Story

Turn to the page with the numeral 3 on it. Read the text and have children tell how the number relates to that part of the story. Discuss the kind of book the warthogs are reading. Have children explain why the warthogs are reading this book. Draw children's attention to other details about the story provided in the text and illustration. For example, *What are the warthogs called in the text? What cooking tools do they have ready?*

PRACTICE

Complete the Pupil Edition Page

Read the directions on page 117 to the children, and make sure they clearly understand what they are asked to do. Identify each picture, and complete the first item together. Then work through the page with children or have them complete the page independently.

ASSESS/CLOSE

Review the Page

Review children's work and make note of any children who need additional help.

Name_____

Think about the story "Warthogs in the Kitchen." • In each row, circle the pictures
that show something from the story.

Pupil Edition, page 117

y

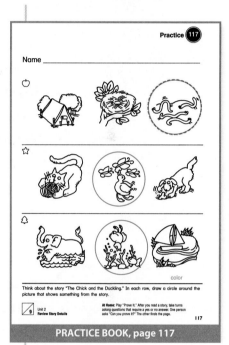
ALTERNATE TEACHING
STRATEGY
....
STORY DETAILS
For a different approach
to teaching this skill, see
page T26.

▶ **Visual/Auditory/
Kinesthetic**

Meeting Individual Needs for Comprehension

EASY	ON-LEVEL	CHALLENGE	LANGUAGE SUPPORT
Have children take turns telling about what they think is the funniest part of the story. Encourage children to give details that help explain why they think something is funny. Remind children that the details can come from both the text and the illustrations.	**Have** children use the story to review the ingredients needed for making cupcakes. As children identify items, write them on a poster pad. Ask children to offer details about each ingredient. For example, what happens when the warthogs pour the sugar?	**Have** children draw their own pictures of a special animal, real or make-believe. Then have children dictate several details about the animal. Invite children to share their pictures and details with the class.	**Work** with children to describe a warthog. Direct children to the illustrations in the story. Ask questions such as: *What is a warthog's fur like? What is its face like? How many paws does it have?* Explain that children are using details to create these descriptions.

117

Develop Phonological Awareness

Listen

Dinosaurs for Dinner
a poem

Red Balloon
a poem

If dinosaurs came for
   dinner,
I'd give them all a treat.
Dinosaurs for dinner!
What do dinosaurs eat?
A ton of mashed potatoes?
A dump truck full of dates?
A dandelion salad served
   on dinosaur-sized plates?
Dinosaurs for dinner!
It could be so divine.
Dinosaurs for dinner!
The pleasure would be mine.

A lost balloon so big and red
Floated one day above my
   head.
That lost balloon so red and
   proud
Hid behind a large white cloud.
But I was glad that I did see
That red balloon fly over me.

Big Book of Phonics Rhymes and Poems, pages 14–15, 16

Objective: Focus on Word Length

READ THE POEM Read the poem "Dinosaurs for Dinner." Invite children to join in on familiar words.

LISTEN FOR THE LONGER WORD Say the words *dogs* and *dinosaurs*. Repeat the words, clapping for each syllable. Ask children which word is longer. Using letter cards, show the word *dogs*. Then show the word *dinosaurs*, lining up the letter cards under the ones that spell *dog*. Invite children to count and compare the number of letter cards to check their answer as to which word is longer.

IDENTIFY THE LONGER WORDS Repeat the activity with other word pairs.

potatoes/dates	book/picture
television/table	football/bat

Objective: Listen for /d/, /m/, and /s/

LISTEN FOR /D/ Reread the poem "The Red Balloon," focusing on the words with the initial and final /d/ sound. Have children repeat the /d/ sound. Say words from the poem which begin or end with /d/. Have children repeat the words, emphasizing the /d/ sound.

> red floated day head
> proud hid behind

LISTEN FOR /M/ AND /S/ Repeat the activity, focusing on words with the initial /s/ sound.

> so see

Using "Dinosaurs for Dinner," repeat the activity. This time focus on words with initial and final /m/.

> came mashed them mine

LISTEN FOR THE MISSING SOUNDS Read a line from either poem, leaving off an initial or final /d/, /s/, or /m/ from one of the words. Have children name the incomplete word and the missing sound.

> A lost balloon __o big and
> red; so /s/

From Phonemic Awareness to Phonics

Read Together

Objective: Identify /s/S, s

IDENTIFY THE LETTERS
Display the Big Book of Phonics Rhymes and Poems, pages 14 and 15. Show sound the letters stand for.

REREAD THE POEM Reread the poem. Point to each word, emphasizing those with /s/.

FIND WORDS WITH s Ask volunteers to frame words in the poem with s. Say each word.

Dd

Dinosaurs for Dinner

If dinosaurs came for dinner,
I'd give them all a treat.

Dinosaurs for dinner!
What do dinosaurs eat?

A ton of mashed potatoes?
A dump truck full of dates?

A dandelion salad served
On dinosaur-sized plates?

Dinosaurs for dinner!
It could be so divine.

Dinosaurs for dinner!
The pleasure would be mine.

Big Book of Phonics Rhymes and Poems, pages 14–15

OBJECTIVES

Children will:

- identify letters *D, d, M, m, S, s*

- identify and discriminate among /d/D, d, /m/M, m, and s/S, s

- write and use letters *D, d, M, m,* and *S, s*

....

MATERIALS

- letter cards from the Word Play Book

ALTERNATE TEACHING STRATEGY

....

LETTERS /d/d, /m/m, /s/s

For a different approach to teaching this skill, see pages T24, T28, T30.

▶ **Visual/Auditory/ Kinesthetic**

Review /d/d, /m/m, /s/s

TEACH

Identify and Discriminate Among /d/D, d, /s/S, s and /m/M, m

Tell children they will review the sound /d/, /s/, and /m/. Write the letters *D, d, S, s,* and *M, m* on different sections of the chalkboard, and have children repeat the sounds as you point to the letters. Display the word cards *Dad, sad, mad,* and read each word aloud as you point to it. Ask children to identify the fist letter of each word and place the word card on the ledge right below it. Point out that all three words end with the letter *d.*

Write and Use D, d, S, s, M, m

Point to the letter pairs *D, d, S, s,* and *M, m* on the chalkboard. Give each child three index cards and have them write the capital form of the letter on one side and the lowercase form on the other side. Then ask children to show the card that matches the first letter of the following word cards: *Min, dim, man, Sam, Dan, said.* Using the word cards *dim, Sam,* and *said,* ask children to show the card that matches the last letter of each word.

PRACTICE

Complete the Pupil Edition Page

Read the directions on page 118 to children, and make sure they clearly understand what they are being asked to do. Identify each picture, and complete the first item together. Then work through the page with children, or have them complete the page independently.

ASSESS/CLOSE

Identify and Use D, d, S, s, M, m

On the chalkboard make five columns with these headings: *d_, _d, m_, __m, s__.* Read the following words and have children say which column the word belongs in: *Sam, did, man.* Point out that two of the words can go in two columns. (did, Sam)

Name_____

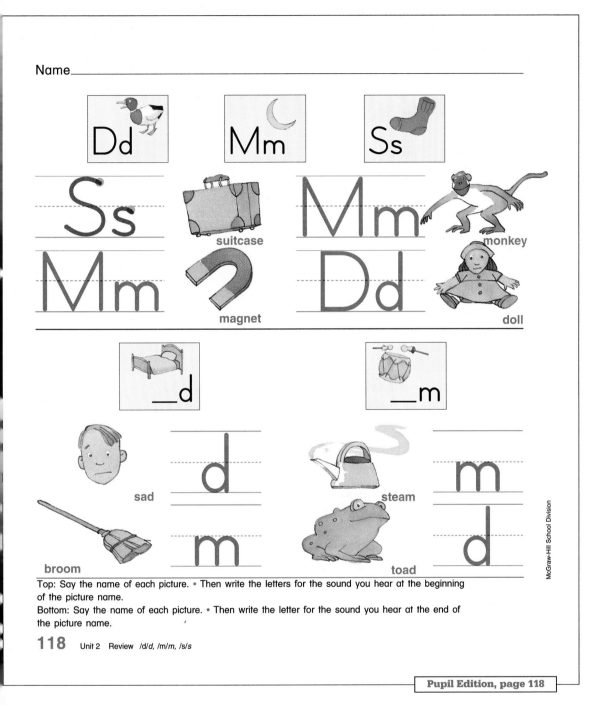

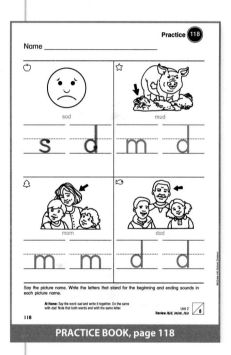

Top: Say the name of each picture. • Then write the letters for the sound you hear at the beginning of the picture name.

Bottom: Say the name of each picture. • Then write the letter for the sound you hear at the end of the picture name.

118 Unit 2 Review /d/d, /m/m, /s/s

Pupil Edition, page 118

ADDITIONAL PHONICS RESOURCES

Practice Book, *page 118*
Phonics Workbook

McGraw-Hill School
TECHNOLOGY

Phonics CD-ROM

Activities for practice with initial letters

PRACTICE BOOK, page 118

Meeting Individual Needs for Phonics

EASY	ON-LEVEL	CHALLENGE	LANGUAGE SUPPORT
Give children pictures of objects whose names begin with *d, m,* or *s,* such as *sad, duck, mop, man, dish, seal.* Ask them to name each object and then sort them into three groups of *d, m,* and *s* objects.	**Give** each child a word card with a word that begins in *d, s,* or *m* or end in *d* or *m.* Ask children to write a *d, s,* or *m* letter card that matches the first or last letter of their word. Ask children to read the card aloud and to name the *d, s,* or *m* letter and tell its position.	**Play** "categories" and ask children to name places, food, articles of clothing, classroom objects, animals, and so on that begin with the letters *d, m,* or *s.* Keep a running list of all the words the children can think of.	**Identify** objects in the room, such as *door, desk, map, mat, sink, soap.* Ask children to repeat the names after you. Then have them hold up the letter card that shows the first letter of each word. Children can write letter labels on stick-on notes to attach to the objects.

118

Teacher Read Aloud

Listen

Tweedy's Toys

By Constance Andrea Keremes

Tucked away in a forgotten corner of a very big, very busy city was a tiny toy shop. Tweedy's Toys was the name of the shop. It was owned by a little old man named Mr. Tweedy.

Early each morning, Mr. Tweedy would shuffle down the stairs from the loft where he lived above the shop. Munching the last of his breakfast toast, he would set about opening up the shop for business. First he polished the long glass counter until it shone like a mirror. Mr. Tweedy always smiled at his reflection.

"Hello there, handsome," he chuckled.

Then Mr. Tweedy shook out his feather duster and dusted all the toys along the rows and rows of shelves in the shop. Boxed games and bouncing balls, baby dolls and bobbing boats—they all got a wipe and a wink from Mr. Tweedy, who loved and cared for his toys as if they were his own little children.

Of all his many toys, the one that Mr. Tweedy liked best was the model train that he kept in his shop window.

Continued on page T2

Oral Comprehension

LISTENING AND SPEAKING Ask children to pay close attention to the order in which things happen in "Tweedy's Toys" as you reread the story. Have children focus on the beginning, middle, and end of the story by asking questions such as these: *How did Mr. Tweedy feel at the beginning of the story? What happened when he saw the star? Where did the little train go?*

Activity Invite children to create a Big Book version of the story. Write a sentence telling about each major event on poster-sized paper. Assign each group a "page" of the book and have them illustrate that part of the story. Have children create a cover and bind the finished pages together.

▶ **Spatial/Interpersonal**

Real-Life Reading

Funnel

Engine

Wheels

Can you name the pa[rts]
of the train?

Door

Car

BIG BOOK OF
REAL
LIFE
READING

Big Book of Real-Life Reading, pages 8–9

Objective: Following Directions

REVIEW THE PAGE Elicit from children ideas on how they might use a diagram to show the parts of a familiar object at home, in school, or at the playground. Ask children to name different diagrams they might have seen.

FOLLOW-UP ACTIVITY Have children choose one favorite toy or object. Then have them make a drawing of the object, and label each of its parts. Make a large model diagram for them of an object in your classroom that children know and enjoy.

CENTER Activity

Cross Curricular: Language Arts/Art

Show children pictures of trains moving through different environments. Have them:

• draw a picture of a train

• make a list of what they like best about trains

▶ **Logical/Interpersonal**

119B

OBJECTIVES

Children will:

- review high-frequency words *and, I, is, said*

....

MATERIALS

- word cards from the *Word Play* book
- *Is Sam Mad?*

TEACHING TIP

INSTRUCTIONAL Tell children that *I* is sometimes a word all by itself and is sometimes a letter in other words. Write the word *said* on the chalkboard and have a volunteer point out the *i*. Mention that the word *I* is always a capital letter.

Review *I, and, is, said*

PREPARE

Listen to Words   Explain to children that they will be reviewing the words *and, I, is,* and *said*. Read the following sentences aloud and have children listen carefully.

1. *The little train huffed <u>and</u> puffed.*

2. *<u>I</u> like this story.*

3. *The children <u>said</u>, "That engine <u>is</u> great."*

Tell children that you will read the sentences again. Ask children to raise their hands when they hear a high-frequency word. Mention that a sentence might have more than one of these words.

TEACH

Model Reading the Word in Context   Distribute the word cards with the high-frequency words so that each child has a set. Hold up the cards, one at a time, and pronounce the word. Ask children to listen for the words as you reread the sentences. Have children hold up their hands when they hear the appropriate words.

Identify the Word   Write the three sentences on the chalkboard. Reread the sentences, pointing to each word as you read. Have children hold up the correct word card when they hear and see each high-frequency word. Call on volunteers to come up and circle the words in the sentences.

Write the Word   Have children write or trace the word *and*.

PRACTICE

Complete the Pupil Edition Page   Read the directions on page 119 to children, and make sure they clearly understand what they are asked to do. Complete the first item together. Then work through the page with children or have them complete the page independently.

ASSESS/CLOSE

Review the Page   Review children's work on page 119 and note any children who are experiencing difficulty.

Name_____

🍎 said   is   (and)   I

⭐ and   (I)   said   is

🌲 said   and   (is)   I

🐟 is   I   and   (said)

Read the words. ⬤ Draw a circle around the word *and*. ⭐ Draw a circle around the word *I*. ♠ Draw a circle around the word *is*. ➤ Draw a circle around the word *said*.

Unit 2   Review High-Frequency Words: *and, I, is, said*   **119**

Pupil Edition, page 119

ALTERNATE TEACHING
STRATEGY

HIGH-FREQUENCY
WORDS
For a different approach
to teaching this skill, see
page T27.

▶ **Visual/Auditory/
Kinesthetic**

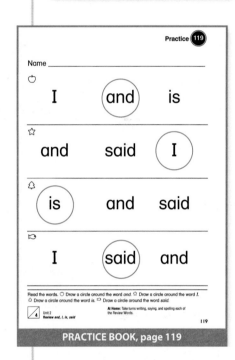

PRACTICE BOOK, page 119

Meeting Individual Needs for Vocabulary

EASY	ON-LEVEL	CHALLENGE	LANGUAGE SUPPORT
Have children dictate sentences that begin with *I*. Model some examples such as: *I am a girl. I am six*. Write each child's sentence on a sentence strip. Then have children take turns repeating their sentences to the class. Ask children to point to the word *I*.	**Provide** pictures of familiar animals. Write on the chalkboard: *This is a (cat). The (cat) said, "(Meow)."* Help children identify each animal, then ask them what the animals said. Complete the sentences for each picture. Ask children to identify the words *is* and *said*.	**Invite** children to make up a sentence using each of the high-frequency words. Record children's sentences on a tape recorder. Play the tape and have children hold up the correct word card when they hear a high-frequency word.	**Write** the following list of pairs on the chalkboard: *sock and shoe; left and right; mom and dad; hammer and nails; peanut butter and jelly*. Read the pairs aloud and have children repeat them. Call on children to come up and point to the word *and* in each pair.

119

Develop Phonological Awareness

Listen

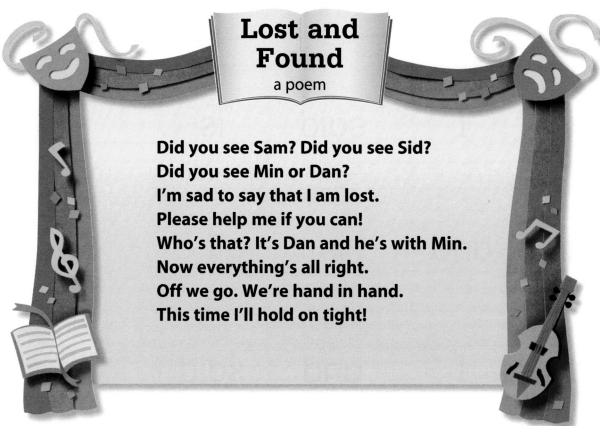

Lost and Found
a poem

Did you see Sam? Did you see Sid?
Did you see Min or Dan?
I'm sad to say that I am lost.
Please help me if you can!
Who's that? It's Dan and he's with Min.
Now everything's all right.
Off we go. We're hand in hand.
This time I'll hold on tight!

Objective: Focus on Listening

LISTEN FOR NAMES Tell children that you will read a poem that names four children. Encourage children to listen for those names. Then read "Lost and Found." Have children tell the names.

Sam   Sid   Min   Dan

PLAY A GAME Have children sit in a circle and invite them to play a listening game. Choose a volunteer to leave the group and go to a place where the child can not hear or see the class. Then instruct one child in the group to say *Dan*. Tell the other children to say *Min*. Ask the volunteer to return to the group. Children say their assigned name repeatedly while the volunteer walks among the children listening for the different name.

CHANGE THE NAMES Repeat the activity several times, changing the names that are spoken.

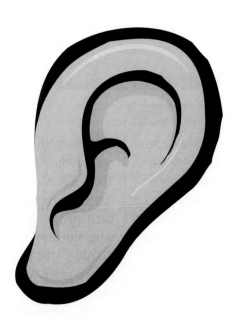

Objective: Blending Short *i* with /m/, /s/, and /d/

LISTEN FOR THE SEGMENTED WORD Invite children to listen as you read the poem "Lost and Found." Explain that you will read one word in a funny way. Then read the poem and segment the sounds in the word *did* each time it appears. Have children determine that *did* was read differently.

/d/-/i/-/d/

BLEND SOUNDS Divide children into four groups. Assign each group one of the following sounds: /i/, /m/, /s/, or /d/. Point to each group several times so they can practice saying their sound. Have the /i/ and /d/ groups blend the word *did*. Point to the groups, slowly at first, and then increasing the speed until the word flows smoothly. Have children identify the word *did*.

BLEND MORE WORDS Repeat the activity with the words *dim* and *Sid*.

/d/ /i/ /m/

From Phonemic Awareness to Phonics

Objective: Identify Word Endings

LISTEN FOR RHYMING WORDS Read the poem "Lost and Found." Ask children what name in the poem rhymes with the word *hid*. Write *hid* and *Sid* on the chalkboard. Then say *Jim, jet, him* and ask children to identify the rhyming words. Write *Jim* and *him* on the chalkboard.

hid Sid Jim him

IDENTIFY THE LETTERS Ask volunteers to circle the letters in each word pair that are the same.

Identify the letters and have children say the sounds the letters stand for.

NAME OTHER RHYMING WORDS Invite children to name other words which rhyme with each word pair. Write their responses on the chalkboard in the correct group and circle the ending letters to show they are the same.

dim Kim Tim rim
lid did kid rid

PHONICS AND DECODING

Review Blending with short *i*

Children will:

- identify and blend /i/ *i* words
- read and write short *i* words
- review /m/ *m*, /s/ *s*, /d/ *d*

· ·

MATERIALS

- letter cards from the Word Play Book

TEACHING TIP

INSTRUCTIONAL To produce a quick review of short *a* and short *i*, say the following words: *Nan, Sid, in, Dad, did, man.* First ask children to hold up their *i* letter cards when they hear a word with the sound /i/. Then ask them to hold up their *a* letter cards when they hear a word with the sound /a/.

ALTERNATE TEACHING STRATEGY

· ·

BLENDING SHORT *i*

For a different approach to teaching this skill, see page T32.

▶ **Visual/Auditory/ Kinesthetic**

TEACH

Identify *i* as a Symbol for /i/

Tell children that today they will be reading and writing words with *i*.

- Display the *i* letter card and say /i/. Have children repeat the sound /i/ after you as you point to the *i* card.

BLENDING Model and Guide Practice

- Place an *m* card after the *i* card. Blend the sounds together and have children repeat after you: *im*.

- Place a *d* letter card before the *i, m* cards. Blend the sounds in the word to read *dim*. Have children repeat after you.

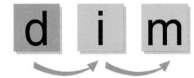 

Use the Word in Context

Have children use *dim* in a sentence, perhaps describing a setting in a familiar story. Give a simple definition, such as *hard to see, dark*.

Repeat the Procedure

- Use the following words to continue modeling and for guided practice with short *i*: *Min, in, dim, did, Sid*.

PRACTICE

Complete the Pupil Edition Page

Read the direction on page 120 to children, and make sure they clearly understand what they are being asked to do. Identify each picture, and complete the first item together. Then work through the page with children, or have them complete the page independently.

ASSESS/CLOSE

Write Short *i* Words

Observe children as they complete page 120. Ask them to choose a short *i* word that begins with *s, m,* or *d,* and write it two times.

Name _____

🍎 d i d did

⭐ S i d Sid

🌲 s a d sad

🐟 D a d Dad

🍎 🌲 Blend the sounds and say the word. Write the word. Use the word aloud in a sentence. ⭐ 🐟 Blend the sounds and say the name. Write the name. Use the name aloud in a sentence.

120 Unit 2 Review Blending with Short *i, a*

McGraw-Hill School Division

Pupil Edition, page 120

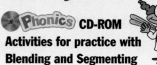

ADDITIONAL PHONICS RESOURCES

Practice Book, *page 120*
Phonics Workbook

McGraw-Hill School
TECHNOLOGY

💿 **Phonics** CD-ROM

Activities for practice with Blending and Segmenting

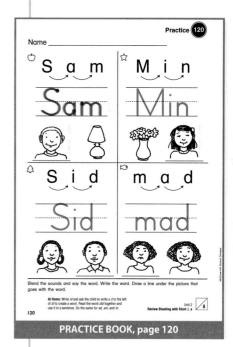

PRACTICE BOOK, page 120

Meeting Individual Needs for Phonics

EASY	ON-LEVEL	CHALLENGE	LANGUAGE SUPPORT
Write *s, m, d* on one part of the chalkboard and *i* on another part. Have children use their letter cards to form the words you write that use these letters, such as: *did, Sid, dim*. Ask them to repeat the words as you track print with your finger.	**On** the chalkboard ledge, display letter cards to show the first two letters of a word, such as *di_*. Invite children to use the letter cards *m, s, d*, and *i* to copy what they see and then complete the word. Ask them to blend sounds to read the words aloud.	**Ask** children to write the word you are saying by listening very closely and blending the sounds in their heads. Pronounce each letter sound very distinctly, and say: *did, Min, dim, Sid, sad, Sam*. Check to see that children have correctly written the six words.	**To** reinforce short *i* and *a* words, write these sentences: *Nan is in. Is Sid sad?* Have children read the first sentence. Ask volunteers to draw a circle around the short *a* word, and draw lines under the short *i* words. Repeat with the second sentence.

120

Guided Instruction

BEFORE READING

PREVIEW AND PREDICT Display the title page. Take a brief **picture walk** through the first three spreads, focusing on the illustrations.

- Why do you think Sam is mad?

- What do you think will happen in the story?

- Do you think the story will be realistic or make-believe?

SET PURPOSES Discuss with the children what they might want to find out as they read the story. For example, they might read to discover what Sam is doing or if he will continue to feel mad.

TEACHING TIP

To put the book together:

1. Tear out the story pages.

2. Cut along dotted line.

3. Fold each section on fold line.

4. Assemble book.

INSTRUCTIONAL Say the word *mad*. Then ask children to say as many rhyming words as they can think of. You may wish to make a word list.

Is Sam Mad?

Sid said that I am mad.

3

McGraw-Hill School Division

Nan said that I am mad.

2

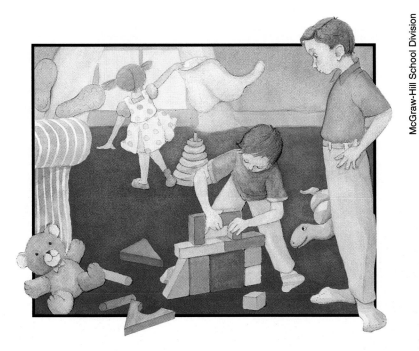

McGraw-Hill School Division

Dan said that I am mad.

4

Guided Instruction

DURING READING

☑ **Blending with Short *i***

☑ **Classify and Categorize**

☑ **Concepts of Print**

① **CONCEPTS OF PRINT** Model how to run your finger from left to right under each word as you read. Read the story title, and then have children repeat the words after you as they track the print.

② **HIGH-FREQUENCY WORDS** Point to the first word on page 2 and read it aloud. Have children read it with you, tracking print as they do so. Repeat with the word *said*.

③ **BLENDING WITH SHORT *i*** Model: *Look at page 3. Let's blend the sounds of the letters together to read the first word. S-i-d. Sid.*

④ **CONCEPTS OF PRINT** After you read the text on page 4 and discuss the illustration, ask children: *How many words are in this sentence?* (6) Frame the period and identify it.

LANGUAGE SUPPORT

ESL Invite volunteers to demonstrate various facial expressions, such as *mad, happy, sad, surprised,* and *worried* and have the rest of the class identify the various expressions being portrayed.

Guided Instruction

DURING READING

5 **CLASSIFY AND CATEGORIZE** After you read the text and look at the picture on page 5, ask children how the blocks are alike and how they are different. Have them describe how they could sort the blocks.

6 **MAKE PREDICTIONS** After reading page 6, ask children what they think will happen next.

7 **CONCEPTS OF PRINT** Frame the question mark on page 7, and identify it. Have children reread the text, using the proper inflection at the end of the sentence.

8 **MAKE INFERENCES** Ask children why Sam is happy. (Possible answer: He built the tower again by himself.)

INFORMAL ASSESSMENT

BLENDING WITH SHORT *i*

HOW TO ASSESS
Have children point to the first word on page 3 and read the word. (Sid)

FOLLOW UP
Continue to model the blending of sounds in short *i* words for children who are having difficulty.

Min said that I am mad.

5

Am I mad?

7

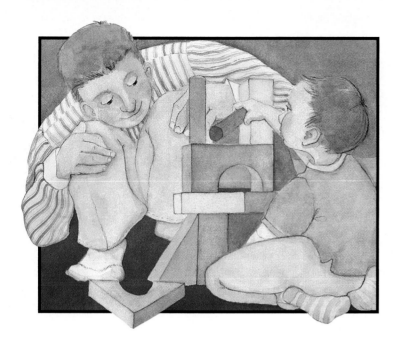

Dad said that I am mad.

6

I am Sam and I am .

8

Guided Instruction

AFTER READING

RETURN TO PREDICTIONS AND PURPOSES
Remind children of their predictions and questions. Ask if their questions were answered. Revisit the story as necessary.

RETELL THE STORY Have volunteers act out the events of the story.

LITERARY RESPONSE Have children write about something they would like to build with blocks and draw a picture of the item.

CENTER Activity

Cross Curricular: Math

BLOCK SORTING Set out a variety of blocks, such as blocks made of different materials, or blocks of different colors. Make picture direction cards that show children how to sort the blocks.

▶ **Logical/Mathematical**

Introduce Classify and Categorize

OBJECTIVES

Children will:

- classify and categorize to understand a story

MATERIALS

- *Is Sam Mad?*

TEACHING TIP

INSTRUCTIONAL Review exclamation points, question marks, and periods. Identify each mark of punctuation, and explain what each one means. Have children look for examples in classroom books.

PREPARE

Discuss Story Details Ask children to recall the story *Is Sam Mad?* Ask children who the characters are, and what Sam is doing. Ask children to describe the blocks that Sam is using.

TEACH

Classify and Categorize Story Details Reread the story together. Talk about the blocks Sam is using, and how they are alike and different. Discuss categories for the blocks: square, round, different colors, and so on. Then have children talk about other things that belong in the category of *Things to Build With.*

PRACTICE

Complete the Pupil Edition Page Read the directions on page 123 to the children, and make sure they clearly understand what they are asked to do. Identify each picture, and complete the first item together. Then work through the page with children or have them complete the page independently.

ASSESS/CLOSE

Review the Page Review children's work, and note children who are experiencing difficulty.

> Things to build with
>
> hammer
>
> nails
>
> wood

Name _____

Look at the pictures in each row. • Draw a circle around the picture that does not belong.

ALTERNATE TEACHING STRATEGY

CLASSIFY AND CATEGORIZE

For a different approach to teaching this skill, see page T29.

▶ **Visual/Auditory/ Kinesthetic**

PRACTICE BOOK, page 123

Meeting Individual Needs for Comprehension

EASY	ON-LEVEL	CHALLENGE	LANGUAGE SUPPORT
Cut out picture of toys from magazines and catalogs. Have children think of ways to classify the toys: things with wheels, things to build with, stuffed animals, dolls, and so on.	**Collect** various items from your classroom. Ask children how you could sort the items. Encourage them to think of different categories.	**Play** "Guess My Rule." Collect a tray with classroom items on it. Then take a few items and sort them into two groups (possibly "Things to Write with" and "Things You Don't Write with.") Ask children to guess your rule for sorting. Have children play on their own.	**Continue** to provide children with opportunities to sort and classify items as the *same* and *different*. Begin with items that are similar except for characteristics such as color or shape. Have children continue to verbalize as they sort.

123

Develop Phonological Awareness

Listen

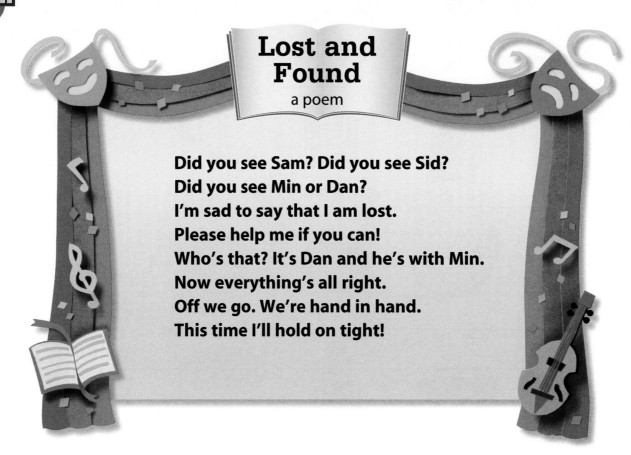

Lost and Found
a poem

Did you see Sam? Did you see Sid?
Did you see Min or Dan?
I'm sad to say that I am lost.
Please help me if you can!
Who's that? It's Dan and he's with Min.
Now everything's all right.
Off we go. We're hand in hand.
This time I'll hold on tight!

Objective: Identify Word Length

FORM GROUPS Read the poem "Lost and Found." Repeat the poem several times substituting children's names. As their name is read, children stand and move to form a group. Each rereading will create a group of four.

> **Did you see Carlos?**

SHOW NAMES WITH CUBES In advance write children's names on sentence cards. Provide children with their name cards and a handful of connecting cubes. Have children place a cube on each letter of their name and then join the cubes together. Invite children to compare the length of their cubes to see whose name is the longest, the shortest, or the same.

ORDER NAMES Regroup children so that all those with the same number of letters in their names stand together. Have children identify the child with the longest and shortest name(s) in the class.

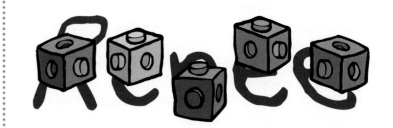

Objective: Blending Short *i* and *a* with /m/, /s/, /d/, and /n/

LISTEN FOR NAMES Read the poem "Lost and Found," suggesting children listen carefully to all the names. Have children recall the names.

> **Sam   Sid   Min   Dan**

BLEND A NAME Invite three children to work together blending sounds to form a name. Explain that you will whisper one sound of a name into each child's ear. Tell them they must work together to blend the sounds to identify the name. Beginning on the left, whisper one sound for the name *Min* into each child's ear. Point to each child and have them say their sound. Repeat several times and increase the speed until children can clearly hear the name *Min*.

> **/m/-/i/-/n/**

BLEND OTHER NAMES Invite different volunteers to blend other names.

> **Sam   Sid   Dan**

Read Together

From Phonemic Awareness to Phonics

Objective: Identify Word Endings

LISTEN FOR RHYMING WORDS Read the poem "Lost and Found," inviting children to listen for a word that rhymes with the name *Dan*. Write the words *Dan* and *can* on index cards.

> **Dan can**

IDENTIFY THE LETTERS Circle the letters in the words that are the same. Identify the letters and say the sounds. Then write the rhyming pairs *jam- ham* and *pan-*

man in separate columns on the board. Circle the ending letters.

NAME OTHER RHYMING WORDS Give the index cards to two volunteers. Ask them to tell how the words are alike. Identify the letters that are the same and say the sound each stands for. Then invite other children to name words that rhyme. Write each suggestion on an index card and give it to the child that said the word. Invite the child to join the line.

USE THE OTHER NAMES Write *Sid*, *Min*, and *Dan* on index cards. Repeat the previous activity, working with one name at a time. Give clues, if necessary, so that all children have suggested a rhyming word and joined a line.

OBJECTIVES

Children will:

- identify and blend /a/*a*, /i/*i* words
- read and write short *a*, *i* words
- review /m/*m*, /s/*s*, /d/*d*, /n/*n*

....

MATERIALS

- letter cards from the *Word Building Book*

TEACHING TIP

INSTRUCTIONAL You may have children in your class from other regions or cultural groups who pronounce short *a* or *i* differently from the other children. This is sometimes apparent when blending sounds aloud. Point out that there are variations because we come from many different places. Demonstrate respect for differences in accents.

ALTERNATE TEACHING STRATEGY
....

BLENDING SHORT *a*, *i*

For a different approach to teaching this skill, see Unit 1, page T32; Unit 2, page T32.

▶ **Visual/Auditory/ Kinesthetic**

Review Blending with short *a, i*

TEACH

Identify *a, i* as Symbols for /a/, /i/

Tell children they will continue to read words with *a* and *i*.

- Display the *a* letter card and say /a/. Have children repeat the sound /a/ after you as you point to the *a* card.

BLENDING Model and Guide Practice

- Place a *d* card after the *a* card. Point to each and blend sounds together to say *ad*. Have children repeat after you.

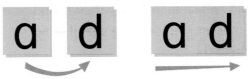

- Place an *m* letter card before the _*ad*. Blend the sounds in the word as you track print with your finger and read *mad*.

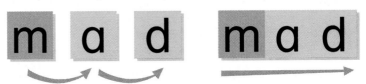

Use the Words in Context

- Have children use *mad* in a sentence.

Repeat the Procedure

- Use the following words to continue modeling and for guided practice with short *a, i: Dan, Sam, man, dim, dam, did, Min.*

PRACTICE

Complete the Pupil Edition Page

Read aloud the directions on page 124. Identify each picture and complete the first item together. Then work through the page with children, or have them complete the page independently.

ASSESS/CLOSE

Write Short *a, i* Words

Observe children as they complete the page. Ask them to write two short *a* words and two short *i* words.

Name

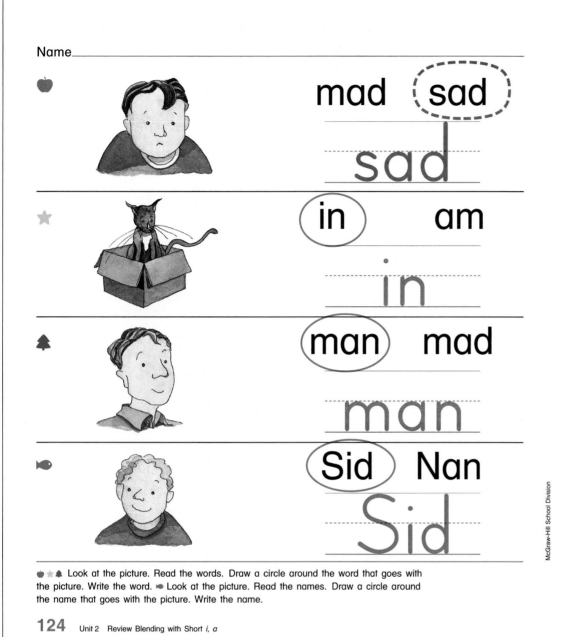

mad (sad)

sad

(in) am

in

(man) mad

man

(Sid) Nan

Sid

McGraw-Hill School Division

● ★ ▲ Look at the picture. Read the words. Draw a circle around the word that goes with the picture. Write the word. ➟ Look at the picture. Read the names. Draw a circle around the name that goes with the picture. Write the name.

124 Unit 2 Review Blending with Short *i, a*

Pupil Edition, page 124

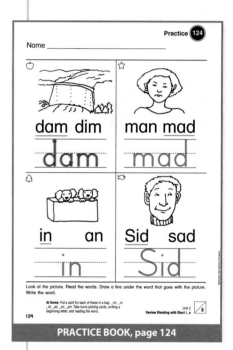

PRACTICE BOOK, page 124

Meeting Individual Needs for Phonics

EASY	ON-LEVEL	CHALLENGE	LANGUAGE SUPPORT
On the chalkboard write: *dad, dim*. Ask children to say a word that begins the same way and write it: *did*.	**Have** children work in pairs to write two words that are different by only one letter, such as *dim, did; dim, dam*. Give each pair several letter cards *a, i, m, s, d, n* and two blank 3-letter word strips. Children blend sounds to read aloud the words they write.	**Give** some groups of children the following word cards, in random order: *Nan, man, Dan, dad, mad, sad*; give other groups the following word cards: *sad, Sam, dam, dim, did, Sid*. Ask groups to arrange the words in order so that each new word changes by only one letter.	**Reinforce** ESL children's ability to discriminate between /m/ and /n/ by having them stretch initial and final sounds of words, such as: *mmmad, dimmm, Nnnnan, Dannn*.

Reread the Decodable Story

Is Sam Mad?

☑ **Initial and Final** *d, s, m, i*
☑ **High-Frequency Words:** *and, I, is, said*
☑ **Use Illustrations**
☑ **Concepts of Print**

Is Sam Mad?

Guided Reading

SET PURPOSES Tell children that when they read the story again, they can find out more about what happened. Explain that you also want them to look for and read words that have the letters *d, s, m,* and *i.* Remind them that they know the words *and, I, is,* and *said,* and will see them again in this story.

REREAD THE BOOK As you guide children through the story, address specific problems they may have had during the first read. Use the following prompts to guide the lesson:

• **CONCEPTS OF PRINT** Ask children to find words that begin with a capital letter. Ask them to find lowercase letters that match the capital letters.

• **USE ILLUSTRATIONS** Ask what word the rebus picture on page 8 stands for. (happy)

RETURN TO PURPOSES Ask children if they found out more about what happened in the story. Ask if they found any words that have the letters *d, s, m,* or *i.* Ask who found the words *and, I, is,* or *said.*

LITERARY RESPONSE Ask children to write and draw a picture of how they look when they are angry.

• Talk about ways to help deal with anger, such as talking to a grownup, taking some time to be alone, and so on.

INFORMAL ASSESSMENT

CONCEPTS OF PRINT

HOW TO ASSESS
Write the names in the story: Sid, Nan, Dan, Min, Sam. Have children identify each capital letter.

FOLLOW UP
If children have difficulty, refer them to the alphabet chart. Point to the capital letters and talk about how they differ from the lowercase letters.

Read the Patterned Book

Self-Selected Reading

UNIT SKILLS REVIEW

☑ **Phonics**

☑ **Comprehension**

☑ **High-Frequency Words**

Help children self-select a Patterned Book to read and apply phonics and comprehension skills.

Guided Reading

SET PURPOSES Tell children that they will be reading one of the four patterned books. Ask children to read to find the pattern in the story they select.

READ THE BOOK You may want to use the following prompts to guide the children as they are reading. Remind children to run their fingers under each word in the sentence as they read.

Tell children that if they see a word they don't know, they should look at the first letter and make the beginning sound. They can blend together the sounds of the word to read it. *Phonics and Decoding*

Ask children to recall the details in the story they selected to help them understand it better. Tell them to think about who was in the story and what happened. *Story Details*

Point out that the children will be seeing some familiar words in the story. Ask them to try to remember where they have seen the words before. *High-Frequency Words*

Model how to run your finger from left to right under each word as you read. Ask children to read the titles as they track print. *Concepts of Print*

RETURN TO PURPOSES Ask children to share the patterns they found in the stories they selected. Discuss similarities and differences in the patterns. Give prompts such as: *How many words were in your pattern? Can you make up a new sentence with your pattern?*

LITERARY RESPONSE Pair children with partners and tell them they will talk to each other about the books they read. Help focus the children's thinking and discussion by asking questions such as: *How were the characters alike in each story? How were they different from one another?* Have children share what they have learned after comparing their stories.

☑ **Phonics and Decoding**

- Initial /d/d, /s/s, /m/m, /i/i
- Final /d/d, /n/n
- Medial /i/i
- Blending with Short *a, i*

☑ **Comprehension**

- Story Details
- Classify and Categorize

☑ **Vocabulary**

- High-Frequency Words: *and, I, is, said*

Cross Curricular: Social Studies

BUILD A CITY Provide a set of building blocks. Let children work as partners to build a city together. Tell them to discuss what kinds of buildings they need. Encourage them to share ideas with their partners and to listen to the ideas of each other as they work together.

▶ **Interpersonal**

OBJECTIVES

Children will:

- review high-frequency words *and, I, is, said*

....

MATERIALS

- word cards from the *Word Play* book
- *Is Sam Mad?*

TEACHING TIP

MANAGEMENT If children are unable to complete the worksheet on their own, you may wish to assign them to work with a partner.

Review I, and, is, said

PREPARE

Listen to Words

Read aloud the following sentences stressing the underlined high-frequency words. Use the suggested motions given in parentheses. Ask children to listen to the sentences and then repeat each high-frequency word with you after the sentence is finished.

1. *The blocks are big and little.* (*hands open wide, hands close together*)

2. *I like blocks.* (*point to self*)

3. *This is my favorite block shape.* (*make a triangle with fingers*)

4. *The children said the blocks are fun.* (*point to class*)

TEACH

Model Reading the Word in Context

Read the decodable story in the Pupil Edition. Ask children to listen for and identify the high-frequency words.

Identify the Words

Give each child a set of word cards for the high-frequency words. Identify one of the words and then read aloud a sentence from the story with that word. Point to the words as you read. Ask children to hold up the correct word card. After reviewing each of the high-frequency words in this way, have children take out their own copies of the story. Read each sentence again and ask volunteers to identify the word in the sentence. You might have children place a different colored stick-on note (yellow for *and*, pink for *I*, and so on) under each high-frequency word in their book.

Write the Word

Have children write the word *and*.

Review High-Frequency Words

Hold up a word card for each high-frequency word and have children pronounce the word.

PRACTICE

Complete the Pupil Edition Page

Read the directions on page 125 to the children, and make sure they clearly understand what they are asked to do. Complete the first item together. Then work through the page with children or have them complete the page independently.

ASSESS/CLOSE

Review the Page

Review children's work on page 125 and note any children who need additional support.

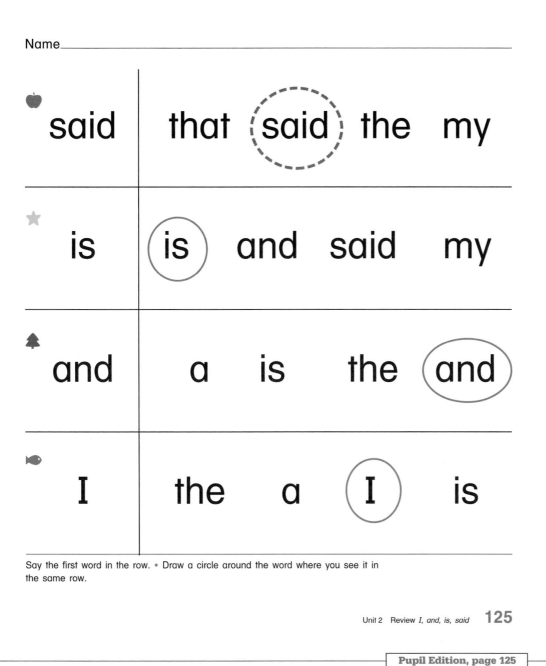

Name_____

🍎 said | that (said) the my

⭐ is | (is) and said my

🌲 and | a is the (and)

🐟 I | the a (I) is

Say the first word in the row. • Draw a circle around the word where you see it in the same row.

Unit 2 Review *I, and, is, said* **125**

Pupil Edition, page 125

ALTERNATE TEACHING STRATEGY

HIGH-FREQUENCY WORDS

For a different approach to teaching the skill, see page T27.

▶ **Visual/Auditory/ Kinesthetic**

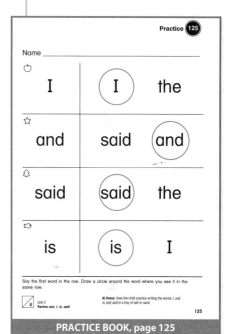

Practice 125

Name _____

🔄 I | (I) the

☆ and | said (and)

🔔 said | (said) the

🔄 is | (is) I

Say the first word in the row. Draw a circle around the word where you see it in the same row.

4 Unit 2
Review *and, I, is, said*

At Home: Have the child practice writing the words *I, and, is,* and *said* in a tray of salt or sand.

125

PRACTICE BOOK, page 125

Meeting Individual Needs for Vocabulary

EASY	ON-LEVEL	CHALLENGE	LANGUAGE SUPPORT
Have children draw pictures of themselves and a friend or family member. Label each child's picture, "My Friend and I." Have children share their pictures with the class and identify the words *my, and,* and *I.*	**Write** each of these sentence beginnings on large pieces of paper: *Nan said; Sid said; Dan said; Min said; Dad said*. Tack up the papers around the room. Ask children to find the word *said* somewhere in the room and then repeat the whole sentence from the story.	**Have** children choose a classroom book and look for the high-frequency words in the story. Children can indicate the words with stick-on notes. Read aloud the sentences in which the words appear.	**Give** children practice in subject/verb agreement using the pronoun *I* and the verb *is.* Have children repeat these sentences with you paying attention to *I am* and *is: I am happy. He is happy. I am mad. She is mad. I am tired. The boy is tired. I am tall. The dog is short.*

125

Interactive Writing

Write a Class Book

Prewrite

IDENTIFYING LETTERS OF THE ALPHABET Reread the story *The ABC Street Fair* and ask children to match the letters with the pictures they see. Ask questions such as: *What picture do you see on this page? What is the first letter in the word* apples*? Does anyone have a name that begins with this letter?* Then ask children if they have ever been to a street fair, and what it was like. Then ask children to suppose that their class was going to have a fair. Make a list of items to sell.

Draft

WRITE A CLASS STORY Look at the list that children made, and ask if they want to change any items. Explain that they are going to write a story about the items to sell at the Class Fair.

- Begin by naming each item on the list, and determining the beginning sound. Have children help you write the initial sound for each item. Continue through the list, labelling a separate sheet of paper for each item.

- Give each child a page to illustrate.

Publish

CREATE THE BOOK After the pages are illustrated, ask a volunteer to make a cover and then assemble the pages to make a book. Make sure the pages are in alphabetical order. Reread the story together.

Presentation Ideas

REREAD THE STORY Invite pairs of children to read the class book together. Children may wish to add dialogue and characters.

▶ **Speaking/Listening**

ACT OUT THE STORY Have small groups act out going to the class fair and buying some of the items. Use classroom items as props. Children may also use model pennies to buy items.

▶ **Representing**

Meeting Individual Needs for Writing

EASY	ON-LEVEL	CHALLENGE
Write Pages Invite children to write additional pages for the book. Children can choose different items to sell. Help them label the pages and illustrate them.	**Draw Pictures** Ask children to draw a picture of something they would like to buy from the Class Fair. Have them label their pictures.	**Write a Story** Have groups of children write a short story about attending a different type of fair. Help them label their pictures, following the pattern of the ABC book. Have children share their books.

Wrap Up
the Theme

All Kinds of Friends
*When we work and play together,
we learn more about ourselves.*

REVIEW THE THEME Read the theme statement to children. Discuss things they have recently learned about themselves as they have worked and played together.

READ THE POEM Read the poem "Making Friends" aloud. Let pairs of girls act out the poem as you reread it. Then read it again, changing "new girl" to "new boy." Ask the boys to act it out this time.

> **MAKING FRIENDS**
>
> **when I was in kindergarten
> this new girl came in our class one day
> and the teacher told her to sit beside me
> and I didn't know what to say
> so I wriggled my nose and made my bunny face**
>
> **and she laughed
> then she puffed out her cheeks
> and she made a funny face
> and I laughed
> so then
> we were friends.**
>
> *Eloise Greenfield*

AUDIO

**Student
Listening
Library**

DISCUSS THE POEM Ask children to share some of their experiences with making new friends in kindergarten. Talk about how their experiences and the experiences in the poem are similar.

LOOKING AT GENRE: FANTASY The Literature Big Books *Warthogs in the Kitchen* and *Chick and the Duckling* are fantasy stories. Remind children of another fantasy story, *Peanut Butter and Jelly*, from the previous unit. Compare the characters in each story and discuss how fantasies allow animals to talk, to work, and to play together like people.

Research *and* Inquiry

Theme Project: Give the Presentation

GROUP Help children present their Wild Animal Murals to the class. Ask children to explain what they have learned about the animal.

Draw Conclusions Lead children in a discussion about things the animals have in common. Children should also see that animals have individual differences—the foods they eat, how they eat, and how they look.

Ask More Questions Now that children have reviewed information about different animals, they will most likely come up with other things they would like to know. Through additional information gathering, children can find the answers to questions such as:

• *Why do giraffes sleep?*

• *Do lions live with their family members?*

HIGH-FREQUENCY WORDS

GROUP Place several objects in a box. Invite two children to take out one object each and hold them up for everyone to see. Ask a third child to hold the *and* word card and stand between the two children holding the objects. Invite the class to "read," for example: *a toy truck* **and** *a cap*.

Unit Review

Dan and Dad
and

Dad, Dan, and I
I

I am Sam!
is

Sid Said
said

Is Sam Mad?
review: *and, I, is, said*

☑ SKILLS & STRATEGIES

Phonics and Decoding
☑ Initial /d/*d*, /s/*s*, /m/*m*, /i/*i*
☑ Final d/*d*, /m/*m*
☑ Medial /i/*i*
☑ Blending with Short *a, i*

Comprehension
☑ Story Details
☑ Classify and Categorize

Vocabulary
☑ High-Frequency Words: *and, I, is, said*

Beginning Reading Concepts
☑ Numbers
☑ Shapes: Circle, Triangle, Square, Rectangle

McGRAW-HILL READING

UNIT Assessment

UNIT 2 ASSESSMENT

Assessment
Follow-Up

Use the results of the informal and formal assessment opportunities in the unit to help you make decisions about future instruction.

SKILLS AND STRATEGIES	Alternate Teaching Strategies
Phonics and Decoding	
Initial /d/d, /s/s, /m/m, //i/i	T24, T28, T30, T32
Final /d/d, /m/m	T24, T30
Medial /i/i	T32
Blending with Short i, a	T32
Comprehension	
Story Details	T26
Classify and Categorize	T29
Vocabulary	
High-frequency words; and, I, is, said, my, that	T27
Beginning Reading Concepts	
Numbers	T25
Shapes: Circle, Triangle, Square, Rectangle	T31
Writing	
Letter Formation	T34

McGraw-Hill School
TECHNOLOGY

 CD-ROM Provides extra phonics support.

 Research & Inquiry Ideas.
Visit www.mhschool.com

Cover Illustration: Mary Jane Begin

The publisher gratefully acknowledges permission to reprint the following copyrighted material:

"Aekyung's Dream" by Min Paek. Copyright © 1978, 1988 by Children's Book Press.

"Amazing Grace" by Mary Hoffman. Text copyright © 1991 by Mary Hoffman. Illustrations copyright © 1991 by Caroline Binch. Used by permission of Dial Books for Young Readers.

"Annie's Pet" by Barbara Brenner. Text copyright © 1989 by Bank Street College of Education. Used by permission of Bantam Books, a division of Bantam Doubleday Dell Publishing Group, Inc.

ANY KIND OF DOG by Lynn Whisnant Reiser. Copyright © 1992 by Lynn Whisnant Reiser. Reprinted by permission of William Morrow & Company.

THE APPLE PIE TREE by Zoe Hall. Text copyright ©1996 by Zoe Hall. Illustrations copyright ©1996 by Shari Halpern. Reproduced by permission of Scholastic Inc.

"Beehive" from A CHILDREN'S SEASONAL TREASURY compiled by Betty Jones. Copyright © 1971 by Dover Publishing, Inc. Reprinted by permission of Dover Publishing, Inc.

THE CHICK AND THE DUCKLING by Mirra Ginsburg. Text copyright © 1972 by Mirra Ginsburg. Illustration copyright © 1972 by Jose Aruego. Reprinted by permission of Simon & Schuster Children's Publishing Division.

"Cinderella" is primarily based on the version by Charles Perrault, in THE BLUE FAIRY BOOK, edited by A. Lang (1889) and incorporates elements of the Brothers Grimm version, translated by L. Crane (1886), as well as details from the retelling by F. Baker and A. Thorndike in EVERYDAY CLASSICS: THIRD READERS (1920).

"Clay" from A SONG I SANG TO YOU by Myra Cohn Livingston. Copyright © 1958, 1959, 1965, 1967, 1969, 1984 by Myra Cohn Livingston. Used by permission of Marian Reiner for the author.

"The Clever Turtle" retold by Margaret H. Lippert from CHILDREN'S ANTHOLOGY. Copyright © 1988 by Macmillan Publishing Company, a division of Macmillan Inc.

THE EARTH AND I by Frank Asch. Copyright © 1994 by Frank Asch. Reprinted by permission of Harcourt Brace & Company.

THE ENORMOUS CARROT by Vladimir Vagin. Copyright © 1998 by Vladimir Vagin. Reproduced by permission of Scholastic Inc.

"Every Time I Climb a Tree" from FAR AND FEW by David McCord. Copyright © 1929, 1931, 1952 by David McCord. Reprinted by permission of Little, Brown & Company.

"50 Simple Things Kids Can Do to Save the Earth" from 50 SIMPLE THINGS KIDS CAN DO TO SAVE THE EARTH by The EarthWorks Group. Copyright © 1990 by John Javna.

"Five Little Seeds" from THIS LITTLE PUFFIN compiled by Elizabeth Matterson. Copyright © 1969 by Puffin Books. Reproduced by permission of Penguin Books. Reprinted by permission.

FLOWER GARDEN by Eve Bunting. Text copyright ©1994 by Eve Bunting, illustrations copyright ©1994 by Kathryn Hewitt. Reprinted by permission of Harcourt Brace & Company.

"The Hare and the Tortoise" from THE FABLES OF AESOP by Aesop, retold by Joseph Jacobs (c. 1900).

"Helping" from WHERE THE SIDEWALK ENDS by Shel Silverstein. Copyright © 1974 by Evil Eye Music, Inc. Reprinted by permission of HarperCollins Publishers.

"Hill of Fire" from HILL OF FIRE by Thomas P. Lewis. Text copyright © 1971 by Thomas P. Lewis. Used by permission of Harper & Row Publishers, Inc.

"How Many Spots Does a Leopard Have?" from HOW MANY SPOTS DOES A LEOPARD HAVE AND OTHER STORIES by Julius Lester. Copyright © 1989 by Julius Lester. Reprinted by permission of Scholastic Inc.

"It Could Always Be Worse" by Margot Zemach. Copyright © 1976 by Margot Zemach. Reprinted by permission of Farrar, Straus & Giroux, Inc.

"A Kite" from READ-ALOUD RHYMES FOR THE VERY YOUNG. Copyright © 1986 by Alfred A. Knopf, Inc.

"Learning" from POETRY PLACE ANTHOLOGY by M. Lucille Ford. Copyright © 1983 by Instructor Publications, Inc.

"The Legend of the Bluebonnet" by Tomie dePaola. Copyright © 1983 by Tomie dePaola. Used by permission of The Putnam Publishing Group.

"Little Brown Rabbit" from THIS LITTLE PUFFIN compiled by Elizabeth Matterson. Copyright © 1969 by Puffin Books. Reprinted by permission of Penguin Books Ltd.

"The Little Red Hen" from WHAT YOUR KINDERGARTNER NEEDS TO KNOW edited by E. D. Hirsch, Jr., and John Holdren. Copyright © 1996 by The Core Knowledge Foundation. Used by permission of Delta Books, a division of Bantam Doubleday Dell Publishing Group, Inc.

"The Little Turtle" from COLLECTED POEMS by Vachel Lindsay. Copyright © 1920 by Macmillan Publishing Co., Inc., renewed 1948 by Elizabeth C. Lindsay.

"Making Friends" from NATHANIEL TALKING by Eloise Greenfield. Text copyright © 1988 by Eloise Greenfield. Illustrations copyright © by Jan Spivey Gilchrist. Used by permission of Writers and Readers Publishing, Inc., for Black Butterfly Children's Books.

"Mary Had a Little Lamb" from WHAT YOUR KINDERGARTNER NEEDS TO KNOW edited by E. D. Hirsch, Jr., and John Holdren. Copyright © 1996 by The Core Knowledge Foundation. Used by permission of Delta Books, a division of Bantam Doubleday Dell Publishing Group, Inc.

"Morning Verse" from THE KINDERGARTEN SERIES. Copyright ©1983 by Wynstone Press. Reprinted by permission of Wynstone Press.

NATURE SPY by Shelley Rotner and Ken Kreisler. Text copyright © 1992 by Shelley Rotner and Ken Kreisler. Illustrations copyright © 1992 by Shelley Rotner. Reprinted by permission of Simon & Schuster Children's Publishing Division.

PEANUT BUTTER AND JELLY by Nadine Bernard Westcott. Copyright ©1987 by Nadine Bernard Westcott. Reprinted by permission of Dutton Children's Books, a division of Penguin Books USA Inc.

PRETEND YOU'RE A CAT by Jean Marzollo, illustrated by Jerry Pinkney. Text copyright © 1990 by Jean Marzollo. Paintings copyright © 1990 by Jerry Pinkney. Reprinted by permission of Dial Books for Young Readers, a division of Penguin Putnam Inc.

"Shell" from WORLDS I KNOW AND OTHER POEMS by Myra Cohn Livingston. Copyright © 1985 by Myra Cohn Livingston. Reprinted by permission of Margaret K. McElderry Books, an imprint of Simon & Schuster Children's Publishing Division.

Acknowledgments

SHOW AND TELL DAY by Anne Rockwell. Text copyright © 1997 by Anne Rockwell. Illustrations copyright © 1997 by Lizzy Rockwell. Reprinted by permission of HarperCollins Publishers.

"The Squeaky Old Bed" from CROCODILE! CROCODILE! STORIES TOLD AROUND THE WORLD by Barbara Baumgartner. Text copyright © 1994 by Barbara Baumgartner. Illustrations copyright © by Judith Moffatt. Used by permission of Dorling Kindersley.

"The Three Little Pigs" by Joseph Jacobs from TOMIE DEPAOLA'S FAVORITE NURSERY TALES. Illustrations copyright © 1986 by Tomie dePaola. Used by permission of the Putnam Publishing Group.

"Tommy" from BRONZEVILLE BOYS AND GIRLS by Gwendolyn Brooks. Copyright © 1956 by Gwendolyn Brooks Blakely.

"The Town Mouse and the Country Mouse" retold and illustrated by Lorinda Bryan Cauley. Copyright © 1984 by Lorinda Bryan Cauley. Used by permission of G.P. Putnam's Sons.

Untitled from JUNE IS A TUNE THAT JUMPS ON A STAIR by Sarah Wilson. Copyright © 1992 by Sarah Wilson. Used by permission of Simon & Schuster Books for Young Readers.

"The Velveteen Rabbit; or, How Toys Become Real" from WHAT YOUR KINDERGARTNER NEEDS TO KNOW edited by E. D. Hirsch, Jr., and John Holdren. Copyright © 1996 by The Core Knowledge Foundation. Used by permission of Delta Books, a division of Bantam Doubleday Dell Publishing Group, Inc.

WARTHOGS IN THE KITCHEN by Pamela Duncan Edwards. Text ©1998 by Pamela Duncan Edwards. Illustrations ©1998 by Henry Cole. Reprinted by Hyperion Books for Children.

"Whistling" from RAINY RAINY SATURDAY by Jack Prelutsky. Copyright © 1980 by Jack Prelutsky. Used by permission of William Morrow & Company.

WHITE RABBIT'S COLOR BOOK by Alan Baker. Copyright © 1994 by Alan Baker. Reprinted by permission of Larousse Kingfisher Chambers, Inc.

"Winnie the Pooh" from WINNIE-THE-POOH by A. A. Milne. Copyright © 1926 by E.P. Dutton, renewed 1954 by A. A. Milne.

"Winter Days in the Big Woods" from LITTLE HOUSE IN THE BIG WOODS by Laura Ingalls Wilder. Copyright © 1932 by Laura Ingalls Wilder, renewed 1959 by Roger L. MacBride. Illustrations copyright © 1994 by Reneé Graef. Used by permission of HarperCollins Publishers.

"Wonderful World" from POETRY PLACE ANTHOLOGY by Eva Grant. Copyright © 1983 by Instructor Publications, Inc.

"Yesterday's Paper" by Mabel Watts from READ-ALOUD RHYMES FOR THE VERY YOUNG. Copyright © 1986 by Alfred A. Knopf, Inc.

Contents

Tweedy's Toys

By Constance Andrea Keremes

Tucked away in a forgotten corner of a very big, very busy city was a tiny toy shop. Tweedy's Toys was the name of the shop. It was owned by a little old man named Mr. Tweedy.

Early each morning, Mr. Tweedy would shuffle down the stairs from the loft where he lived above the shop. Munching the last of his breakfast toast, he would set about opening up the shop for business. First he polished the long glass counter until it shone like a mirror. Mr. Tweedy always smiled at his reflection.

"Hello there, handsome," he chuckled.

Then Mr. Tweedy shook out his feather duster and dusted all the toys along the rows and rows of shelves in the shop. Boxed games and bouncing balls, baby dolls and bobbing boats—they all got a wipe and a wink from Mr. Tweedy, who loved and cared for his toys as if they were his own little children.

Of all his many toys, the one that Mr. Tweedy liked best was the model train that he kept in his shop window. The train had been in the window since the very first day that Mr. Tweedy had opened his store, some fifty years ago. Although the train was now very old, it was still a splendid one, with a shiny black engine that had a funnel that puffed out real smoke. Round and round a track the train clacked, pulling a car piled high with toys.

"Off you go, little friend," said Mr. Tweedy as he flipped the switch that started the train. "Maybe today, maybe today someone will stop in."

Mr. Tweedy sighed and looked out the window. How quiet the street was. Nothing but boarded-up shops and empty apartments where people had not lived for years and years. Once, long ago when Mr. Tweedy was a young man, the street had been a busy, bustling place. There were dozens of shops back then, each one with a peppermint-striped awning and a big plate glass window displaying everything from shoes to sausages. And the people! So many people. Mr. Tweedy shook his head, remembering. How fine it was to greet all the people as they went from one shop to the next.

"Lots of how-de-dos and handshakes in those days," said Mr. Tweedy. "And lots of children, too. Boys and girls with their noses pressed up close against my window for a better look at my little train."

He smiled softly. "Seems like we laughed all the day long."

Mr. Tweedy dabbed a tear, feeling lonely. It had been a long time since a boy or girl had visited his shop. People just did not stop his way anymore. Bigger stores with flashy lights had opened up in other parts of the city. Soon people were rushing to the new stores. And soon the little shops on Mr. Tweedy's street went out of business.

Now only Mr. Tweedy was left. Each morning as he switched on the model train, he wished that someone might remember his little shop of toys. But of course, no one ever did. And then poor Mr. Tweedy would wait until the clock struck six and quietly lock up the shop for the night.

One night, as Mr. Tweedy slipped in his key to lock the front door of the shop, something silvery bright caught his eye. It was a little star winking down at him from the sky. Now stars as bright and sassy as that little fellow were a rare sight in a big city of skyscrapers and smokestacks. Mr. Tweedy forgot all about locking the door, and dashed outside for a better look.

"A wishing star!" he said, his eyes wide. "I haven't seen the like since I was a boy."

He stretched his fingers up, up, as though he might pluck the star right from the sky and put it in his pocket.

"Have you a bit of magic for me?" asked Mr. Tweedy. "A friend or two is all I ask for—someone to visit me here in my little shop."

Mr. Tweedy looked hopefully at the star. But as he did so, a sudden gust of wind swept a great puff of clouds across the sky. The tiny star disappeared.

"Gone!" Mr. Tweedy shook his head. "I guess that means I won't be getting my wish after all."

Without bothering to lock up the shop, he went sadly to bed. No sooner had Mr. Tweedy fallen asleep, then the clouds parted and out popped the little star. The star twinkled, and a silvery spark of

Read Aloud

light found its way to the toy shop. That tiny bit of light had only just come to rest on the toy train when something remarkable occurred.

Chug-chug-chug-chug! Choo Choo! The train came to life with a shudder and shake that nearly knocked its car of toys off the track. As much as the train would have liked to spend the night playing with all the toys in the shop, he knew that he had an important job to do. He knew that his owner, Mr. Tweedy, was lonely and needed some friends to cheer him up.

The little train huffed and puffed, and nearly burst his funnel thinking of how he might help. And then, with a great circle of smoke he sang out:

"Clickety Clack! No time to waste, I've got a job to do.

Clickety Clack! Away I go to find a friend or two."

It was lucky indeed that Mr. Tweedy had left the door open, for the train chugged once, twice around his track and then flew up, up, into the night sky. Far below him lay the great city, a bustling place even late at night. Sleek skyscrapers twinkled with lights bright as stars, while taxis and buses whizzed down the avenues like shiny bugs.

But not everyone in the city was awake. Some apartment buildings lay dark and silent, their occupants fast asleep. The little train puffed to one such apartment and flew in an open window straight to the bedroom where Maria Díaz lay sleeping. Maria was a grown-up dreaming grown-up dreams about buses to catch, bills to pay, and sometimes, about her grandsons, Luis and Anthony. But when the little train circled her head, she began dreaming of being a girl once again.

There she stood, all of eight years old, pigtails bobbing as she pressed her freckled face to the window of Tweedy's toy shop for a glimpse at the model train and her favorite toy: the doll with the pigtails just like her own.

"Look, Papa," she clapped her hands in delight, turning to her father. "See how the little doll rides atop the train."

She could still hear the train's whistle as she woke up. "What a strange dream," thought Maria. "I haven't thought of that in years. How lovely it would be to take my grandsons to see it. Perhaps tomorrow. . ." And then she yawned and fell back asleep.

Meanwhile, the little train chugged his way all over the city, visiting the bedrooms of grown-ups who had played in Tweedy's toy shop when they were children. Over on the West Side, Michael Wong nearly tumbled out of bed as his dreams turned to toy trains and twirling tops. "Trains and toys. Just the things to share with my niece Anna."

And on the East Side, Edie Edsel choo-chooed in her sleep, dreaming of the model train that held the tiny picture book about faraway places. " How I would like to share that book with my children," said Edie when she woke up.

And so it went, all the night long, grown-ups dreaming of their childhood days at Tweedy's. Each one awakened in the dark to think how nice it would be to see the old shop again. Just as the stars slipped from the sky, the little train puffed back to the toy shop and settled back behind the window.

The next day, which was Saturday, a line of adults and children traveled to a long forgotten part of the city. By car, by bus, on bike, and on foot, they all made their way to Tweedy's Toys.

Mr. Tweedy was astounded when he came downstairs to his shop and found a line of people outside the door. And then the handshakes and how-de-dos filled the morning as everyone got to know each other once again.

"We should never have stayed away so long," the visitors told Mr. Tweedy.

"Such a fine neighborhood this used to be," Michael Wong said.

"We can fix it up again—let's all write to City Hall to see what we can do!" said Edie Edsel.

Mr. Tweedy could only nod his head in delight, too happy for words.

And all the while the old and new friends laughed and played together, the little train puffed merrily around his track:

"Clickety-clack, clickety clack!

Now what do you think of that?"

The Legend of Bluebonnet

an old tale of Texas
retold and illustrated by Tomie dePaola

"Great Spirits,
the land is dying. Your People are dying, too,"
the long line of dancers sang.
"Tell us what we have done to anger you.
End this drought. Save your People.
Tell us what we must do so you will send the rain
that will bring back life."

For three days,
the dancers danced to the sound of the drums,
and for three days, the People called Comanche
watched and waited.
And even though the hard winter was over,
no healing rains came.

Drought and famine are hardest
on the very young and very old.

Among the few children left
was a small girl named She-Who-Is-Alone.
She sat by herself watching the dancers.
In her lap was a doll made from buckskin—a war-
    rior doll.
The eyes, nose and mouth were painted on
with the juice of berries. It wore beaded leggings
and a belt of polished bone.
On its head were brilliant blue feathers
from the bird who cries "Jay-jay-jay."
She loved her doll very much.

"Soon," She-Who-Is-Alone said to her doll,
"the shaman will go off alone to the top of the hill
to listen for the words of the Great Spirits.
Then, we will know what to do so that once more
the rains will come and the Earth will be green
    and alive.
The buffalo will be plentiful
and the People will be rich again."

As she talked, she thought of the mother who
    made
the doll, of the father who brought the blue
    feathers.
She thought of the grandfather and the
    grandmother

she had never known. They were all like shadows.
It seemed long ago that they had died from the
    famine.
The People had named her and cared for her.
The warrior doll was the only thing she had left
from those distant days.

"The sun is setting," the runner called
as he ran through the camp. "The shaman is
    returning."
The People gathered in a circle and the shaman
    spoke.

"I have heard the words of the Great Spirits,"
    he said.
"The People have become selfish.
For years, they have taken from the Earth
without giving anything back.
The Great Spirits say the People must sacrifice.
We must make a burnt offering
of the most valued possession among us.
The ashes of this offering shall then be scattered to
the four points of the Earth, the Home of the
    Winds.
When this sacrifice is made,
drought and famine will cease.
Life will be restored to the Earth and to the
    People!"

The People sang a song of thanks to the Great
    Spirits
for telling them what they must do.

"I'm sure it is not my new bow
that the Great Spirits want," a warrior said.
"Or my special blanket," a woman added,
as everyone went to their tipis to talk and
    think over
what the Great Spirits had asked.

Everyone, that is, except She-Who-Is-Alone.
She held her doll tightly to her heart.
"You," she said, looking at the doll.
"You are my most valued possession.
It is you the Great Spirits want."
And she knew what she must do.

As the council fires died out
and the tipi flaps began to close,
the small girl returned to the tipi,
where she slept, to wait.

The night outside was still except for the distant
    sound
of the night bird with the red wings.
Soon everyone in the tipi was asleep, except
    She-Who-Is-Alone.
Under the ashes of the tipi fire one stick still
    glowed.
She took it and quietly crept out into the night.

She ran to the place on the hill
where the Great Spirits had spoken to the shaman.
Stars filled the sky, but there was no moon.
"O Great Spirits," She-Who-Is-Alone said,
"here is my warrior doll. It is the only thing I have
from my family who died in this famine.
It is my most valued possession. Please accept it."

Then, gathering twigs,
she started a fire with the glowing firestick.
The small girl watched
as the twigs began to catch and burn.

She thought of her grandmother and grandfather,
her mother and father and all the People—
their suffering, their hunger.
And before she could change her mind,
she thrust the doll into the fire.

She watched until the flames died down
and the ashes had grown cold.

Then, scooping up a handful, She-Who-Is-Alone
scattered the ashes to the Home of the Winds,
the North and the East, the South and the West.

And there she fell asleep
until the first light of the
morning sun woke her.
She looked out over the hill,
and stretching out from all sides, where the ashes
    had fallen,
the ground was covered with flowers—beautiful
    flowers,
as blue as the feathers in the hair of the doll,
as blue as the feathers of the bird who cries "
    Jay-jay-jay."

When the People came out of their tipis,
they could scarcely believe their eyes.
They gathered on the hill with She-Who-Is-Alone
to look at the miraculous sight.
There was no doubt about it,
the flowers were a sign of forgiveness
from the Great Spirits.

And as the People sang
and danced their thanks to the Great Spirits,
a warm rain began to fall
and the land began to live again.
From that day on,
the little girl was known by another name—
"One-Who-Dearly-Loved-Her-People."

And every spring,
the Great Spirits remember the sacrifice of a
    little girl
and fill the hills and valleys of the land, now
    called Texas,
with the beautiful blue flowers.

Even to this very day.

The Town Mouse and the Country Mouse

retold and illustrated by Lorinda Bryan Cauley

The Country Mouse lived by himself in a snug little hole in an old log in a field of wild flowers.

One day he decided to invite his cousin the Town Mouse for a visit, and he sent him a letter.

When his cousin arrived, the Country Mouse could hardly wait to show him around. They went for a walk, and on the way they gathered a basket of acorns.

They picked some wild wheat stalks.

They stopped by the river and sat on the bank, cooling their feet.

And on the way home for supper, they picked some wild flowers for the house.

The Country Mouse settled his cousin in an easy chair with a cup of fresh mint tea and then went about preparing the best country supper he had to offer.

He made a delicious soup of barley and corn.

He simmered a root stew seasoned with thyme.

Then he made a rich nutcake for dessert, which he would serve hot from the oven.

The Town Mouse watched in amazement. He had never seen anyone work so hard.

But when they sat down to eat, the Town Mouse only picked and nibbled at the food on his plate. Finally, turning up his long nose, he said, "I cannot understand, Cousin, how you can work so hard and put up with food such as this. Why, you live no better than the ants and work twice as hard."

"It may be simple food," said the Country Mouse, "but there is plenty of it. And there is nothing I enjoy more than gathering everything fresh from the fields and cooking a hot supper."

"I should die of boredom," the Town Mouse complained. "I never have to work for my supper, and in my life there is hardly ever a dull moment."

"I can't imagine any other life," answered the Country Mouse.

"In that case, dear Cousin, come back to town with me and see what you have been missing."

So, out of curiosity, the Country Mouse agreed to go. Off they went, scampering across fields while avoiding the cows and down a dirt lane, edged with bright flowers, until at last they reached the cobblestones leading into town.

The streetlights flickered eerily, and with each horse and carriage that clip-clopped by, the Country Mouse trembled with fear.

At last they reached a row of elegant town houses, their windows glowing in lamplight. "This is where I live," said the Town Mouse. The Country Mouse had to admit that it looked warm and inviting.

They went inside and crept past the ticktock of the grandfather clock in the hall and into the living room. The Town Mouse led his cousin to a small entrance hole behind the wood basket next to the fireplace.

Once inside, the Town Mouse it a candle and started a fire. The Country Mouse looked around the room. It was so much grander than his little hole in the old log. Why, his cousin's bed was covered with a fine silk handkerchief as a bedspread.

They had been traveling all day, and the Country Mouse was tired and hungry. So he was surprised when his cousin started to go back through the entrance hole. "Could we have something to eat before you show me around?" he asked timidly.

"But of course," said his cousin. "That is where we are going. To have a feast of a supper."

They went through the living room and into the dining room and there on a large table was the remains of a fine supper. The Country Mouse's eyes were wide with astonishment. He had never seen so much food all at once, nor so many kinds.

"Help yourself," invited the Town Mouse. "Whatever you like is yours for the taking."

The Country Mouse scampered across the starched white linen and stared at the dishes. Creamy puddings, cheeses, biscuits and chocolate candies. Cakes, jellies, fresh fruit and nuts!

It all looked and smelled delicious. He hardly knew where to begin.

He took a sip from a tall, sparkling glass and thought, "This is heaven. Maybe I have been wrong to have wasted my life in the country."

He had just started nibbling on a piece of strawberry cake when suddenly the dining room doors flew open and two servants came in to clear away the dishes.

The two mice scampered off the table and hid beneath it. When they heard the doors close again, the Town Mouse coaxed his cousin back onto the table to eat what was left.

But they had hardly taken two bites when the doors opened again and a small girl in her nightdress ran in to look for her doll, which had fallen under the table. This time the Town Mouse hid behind the jug of cream and the Country Mouse crouched in terror behind the butter dish. But she didn't see them.

As soon as the girl was gone, the Town Mouse began to eat again. But the Country Mouse stood listening. "Come on," said his cousin. "Relax and enjoy this delicious cheese."

But before the Country Mouse could even taste it, he heard barking and growling outside the door. "Wha-, what's that?" he stammered.

"It is only the dogs of the house," answered the Town Mouse. "Don't worry. They're not allowed in the dining room." And with that, the doors burst open and in bounded two roaring dogs. This time the mice scampered down the side of the table, out of the room, and back to the hole in the living room just in the nick of time.

"Cousin, you may live in luxury here, but I'd rather eat my simple supper in the country than a feast like this in fear for my life. I'm going home right away," said the Country Mouse.

"Yes, I suppose that the hectic life of the town is not for everybody, but it's what makes me happy. If you ever need a little excitement in your life, you can come for another visit," replied his cousin.

"And any time you want a little peace and quiet and healthy food, come and visit me in the country," said the Country Mouse.

Then off he went to his snug little home in the fields, whistling a tune and looking forward to a good book by the fire and a mug of hot barley-corn soup.

Mary Had a Little Lamb
from the poem by Sarah Josepha Hale

Mary had a little lamb,
Its fleece was white as snow;
And everywhere that Mary went,
The lamb was sure to go.

It followed her to school one day,
That was against the rule;
It made the children laugh and play
To see a lamb at school.

And so the teacher turned it out,
But still it lingered near,
And waited patiently about
Till Mary did appear.

"Why does the lamb love Mary so?"
The eager children cry.
"Why, Mary loves the lamb, you know,"
The teacher did reply.

Practice 66

Dd Name _____

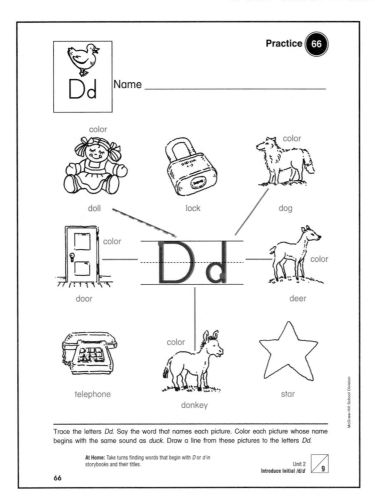

color — doll
lock
color — dog
color — door
D d
color — deer
telephone
color — donkey
star

Trace the letters *Dd*. Say the word that names each picture. Color each picture whose name begins with the same sound as *duck*. Draw a line from these pictures to the letters *Dd*.

At Home: Take turns finding words that begin with *D* or *d* in storybooks and their titles.

Unit 2
Introduce Initial /d/d 9

66

Practice 67

Name _____

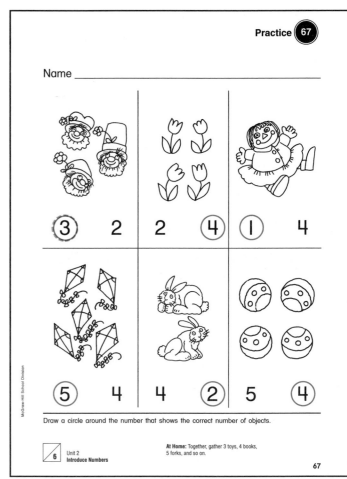

③ 2 | 2 ④ 1 | 4
⑤ 4 | 4 ② 5 | ④

Draw a circle around the number that shows the correct number of objects.

6 Unit 2
Introduce Numbers

At Home: Together, gather 3 toys, 4 books, 5 forks, and so on.

67

Practice 68

_d Name _____

color
happy | sad | **d**
color
lid | pig | **d**
cow | sled | **d**
color

Say the name of the pictures in each row. Color the picture whose name has the same ending sound as *bed*. Write the letter *d*.

At Home: Write *sad* and read it together. Change *s* to *d* to form a new word. Then change *dad* to *mad*.

Unit 2
Introduce Final /d/d 6

68

Practice 69

Name _____

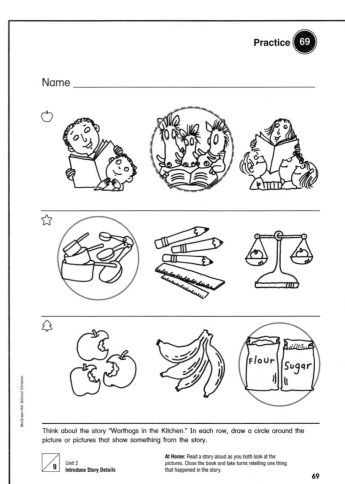

Think about the story "Warthogs in the Kitchen." In each row, draw a circle around the picture or pictures that show something from the story.

9 Unit 2
Introduce Story Details

At Home: Read a story aloud as you both look at the pictures. Close the book and take turns retelling one thing that happened in the story.

69

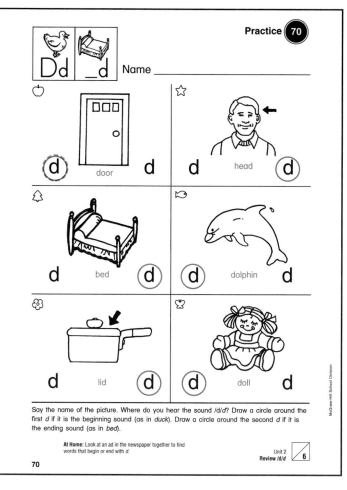

Practice 70

Dd | _d   Name _____

Say the name of the picture. Where do you hear the sound /d/d? Draw a circle around the first d if it is the beginning sound (as in *duck*). Draw a circle around the second d if it is the ending sound (as in *bed*).

At Home: Look at an ad in the newspaper together to find words that begin or end with d.

Unit 2
Review /d/d 6

70

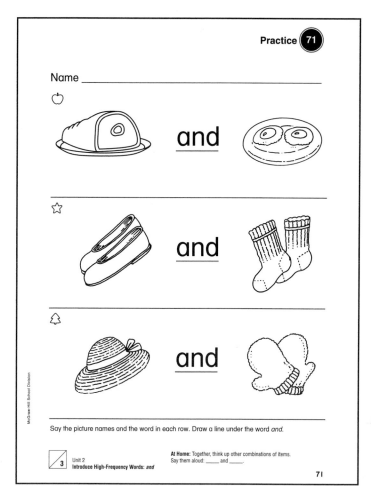

Practice 71

Name _____

and

and

and

Say the picture names and the word in each row. Draw a line under the word *and*.

3 Unit 2
Introduce High-Frequency Words: *and*

At Home: Together, think up other combinations of items. Say them aloud: _____ and _____.

71

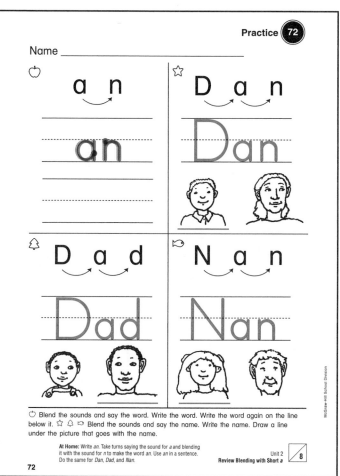

Practice 72

Name _____

a n → an

D a n → Dan

D a d → Dad

N a n → Nan

Blend the sounds and say the word. Write the word. Write the word again on the line below it. Blend the sounds and say the name. Write the name. Draw a line under the picture that goes with the name.

At Home: Write an. Take turns saying the sound for a and blending it with the sound for n to make the word an. Use an in a sentence. Do the same for Dan, Dad, and Nan.

Unit 2
Review Blending with Short a 8

72

Practice 73

Dd   Name _____

D D D D

D D D D

D D D D

D D D D

Trace and write capital D. Start at the dot.

4 Unit 2
Handwriting: D

At Home: Together, take a stick and practice writing D in the ground, in the sand, or in another soft surface, such as clay.

73

Dan and Dad • PRACTICE

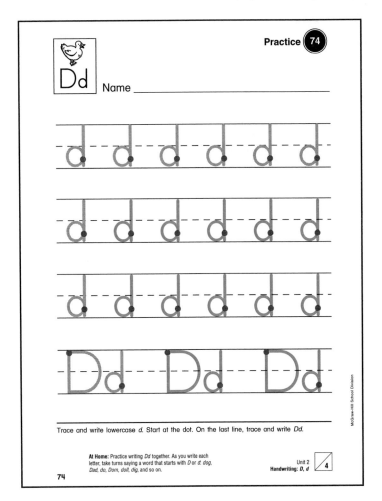

Practice 74

Dd Name _____

Trace and write lowercase d. Start at the dot. On the last line, trace and write Dd.

At Home: Practice writing Dd together. As you write each letter, take turns saying a word that starts with D or d: dog, Dad, do, Dom, doll, dig, and so on.

Unit 2
Handwriting: D, d 4

74

Practice 75

Name _____

Think about the story "Dan and Dad." In each row, draw a circle around the picture that shows something from the story.

Unit 2
Review Story Details 9

At Home: Read a story aloud. Then say things that did and things that did not occur. The child then checks the book to make sure.

75

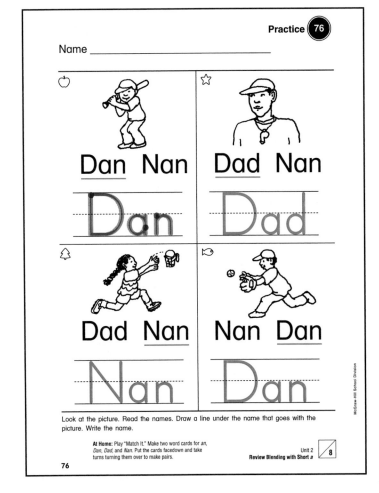

Practice 76

Name _____

Dan Nan   Dad Nan

Dan   Dad

Dad Nan   Nan Dan

Nan   Dan

Look at the picture. Read the names. Draw a line under the name that goes with the picture. Write the name.

At Home: Play "Match It." Make two word cards for an, Dan, Dad, and Nan. Put the cards facedown and take turns turning them over to make pairs.

Unit 2
Review Blending with Short a 8

76

Practice 77

Name _____

my   and

a   and

my   and

Read each word and say the picture names. Draw a circle around the word and. Draw a line under the word my. Draw two lines under the word a. Draw a circle around the word and. Draw a line under the word my. Draw a picture of two things that belong to you.

Unit 2
Review and, my, a 3

At Home: Play "Pair Up." You say a ___. The child says and ___, completing the pair.

77

T10 Annotated Workbooks

Dad, Dan, and I • PRACTICE

Name _____

color — lamp, sailboat

color — peanut, sandwich

color — sun, kite

color — seven, nine

Write the letters Ss. Say the word that names each picture. Color the picture whose name begins with the same sound as sock.

At Home: Each of you put your hand in a sock to make a sock puppet. Take turns having the sock say words that begin with s.

Unit 2
Introduce Initial /s/s
8

78

Name _____

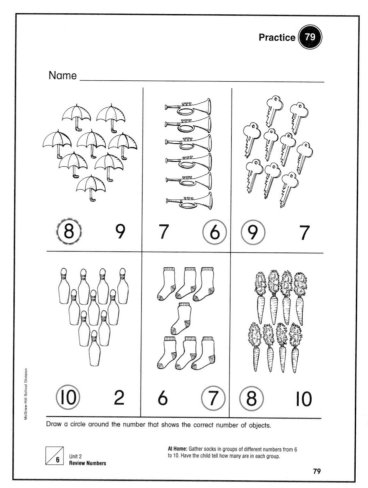

8 9 | 7 6 | 9 7

10 2 | 6 7 | 8 10

Draw a circle around the number that shows the correct number of objects.

6 Unit 2
Review Numbers

At Home: Gather socks in groups of different numbers from 6 to 10. Have the child tell how many are in each group.

79

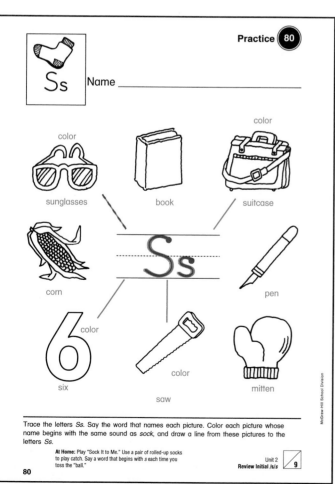

Name _____

color — sunglasses, book, color — suitcase

corn, Ss, pen

six, color — saw, color — mitten

Trace the letters Ss. Say the word that names each picture. Color each picture whose name begins with the same sound as sock, and draw a line from these pictures to the letters Ss.

At Home: Play "Sock It to Me." Use a pair of rolled-up socks to play catch. Say a word that begins with s each time you toss the "ball."

Unit 2
Review Initial /s/s
9

80

Name _____

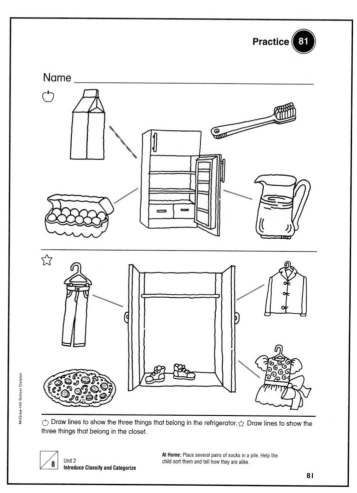

Draw lines to show the three things that belong in the refrigerator. ☆ Draw lines to show the three things that belong in the closet.

8 Unit 2
Introduce Classify and Categorize

At Home: Place several pairs of socks in a pile. Help the child sort them and tell how they are alike.

81

T11

Dad, Dan, and I • PRACTICE

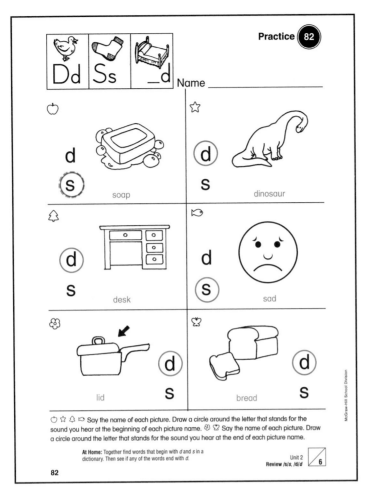

d s — soap

d s — dinosaur

d s — desk

d s — sad

d s — lid

d s — bread

Say the name of each picture. Draw a circle around the letter that stands for the sound you hear at the beginning of each picture name. Say the name of each picture. Draw a circle around the letter that stands for the sound you hear at the end of each picture name.

At Home: Together find words that begin with *d* and *s* in a dictionary. Then see if any of the words end with *d*.

Unit 2
Review /s/s, /d/d 6

82

Practice 83

Name _____

I

I

I

I

Read the sentence by saying the word and telling about the picture. Draw a circle around the word *I*. Draw a picture of yourself doing something to help out after the word *I*. Then draw a circle around the word *I*.

5 Unit 2
Introduce High-Frequency Words: *I*

At Home: Make a list of things your child does to help out at home. Have your child circle the word *I* and draw a picture of his or her favorite thing to do.

83

Practice 84

Name _____

N a n

Nan

D a d

Dad

s a d

sad

D a n

Dan

Blend the sounds and say the word. Write the word. Draw a line under the picture that goes with the word.

At Home: Write *Nan*. Take turns saying the sound for *N* and blending it with the sound for *a* and the sound for *n* to make the word *Nan*. Use the word *Nan* in a sentence. Do the same for *Dad*, *sad*, and *Dan*.

Unit 2
Review Blending with Short *a* 8

84

Practice 85

Ss Name _____

S S S S

S S S S

S S S S

S S S S

Trace and write capital *S*. Start at the dot.

4 Unit 2
Handwriting: *S*

At Home: As you write *S* together, try to guide the child to make the upper and lower curves equal.

85

Practice 86

Ss

Name _____

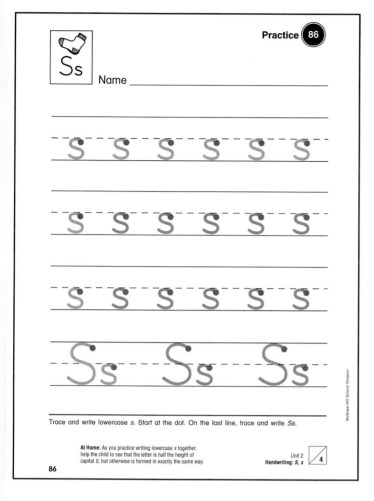

S S S S S S

S S S S S S

S S S S S S

Ss Ss Ss

Trace and write lowercase *s*. Start at the dot. On the last line, trace and write *Ss*.

At Home: As you practice writing lowercase *s* together, help the child to see that the letter is half the height of capital *S*, but otherwise is formed in exactly the same way.

Unit 2
Handwriting: S, s 4

86

Practice 87

Name _____

Draw lines to show the three things that belong in the classroom. Draw lines to show the three things that belong in the garden.

8 Unit 2
Review Classify and Categorize

At Home: Play "Categories." Name three things that belong together. Ask your child to name one more.

87

Practice 88

Name _____

sad   an

sad

Dad   Dan

Dan

Dad   Nan

Nan

Dad   sad

Dad

Look at the picture. Read the words. Draw a line under the word that goes with the picture. Write the word.

At Home: Add two cards with the word *sad* to your card set of the words *an*, *Dan*, *Dad*, and *Nan*. Use all the cards to make pairs as you play "Match It."

Unit 2
Review Blending with Short a 8

88

Practice 89

Name _____

and

my   and

I ♡ my ☐ .

Say each word and the picture names. Draw a circle around the word *and*. Draw a circle around the word *I*. Next to the word *my* draw a picture of something or someone you love. Then draw a circle around the word *my*.

5 Unit 2
Review I, and, my

At Home: Together, make a card for a relative. Help the child write *I love my ____*. Have your child draw a picture to go with it.

89

Practice 90

Mm Name _____

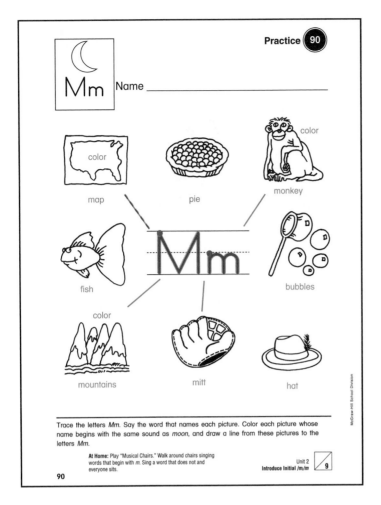

map   pie   monkey (color)

color

fish   bubbles

color   mountains   mitt   hat

Trace the letters *Mm*. Say the word that names each picture. Color each picture whose name begins with the same sound as *moon*, and draw a line from these pictures to the letters *Mm*.

At Home: Play "Musical Chairs." Walk around chairs singing words that begin with *m*. Sing a word that does not and everyone sits.

Unit 2
Introduce Initial /m/m   9

90

Practice 91

Name _____

blue   blue   yellow

blue

blue

yellow   yellow   yellow

Find the circles in the picture. Color them yellow. Find the triangles in the picture. Color them blue.

8   Unit 2
Introduce Shapes: Circle, Triangle

At Home: Together, draw and color your own picture. Use circles and triangles and choose one special color for each shape.

91

Practice 92

_m Name _____

color
ham   butterfly   m

color
dog   jam   m

color
broom   football   m

Say the name of each picture. Color the picture whose name has the same ending sound as *drum*. Write the letter *m*.

At Home: Play "Rhyme Time." Take turns. One player says a word that ends with *m*. The other says a rhyming word (for example, *jam*, *ham*).

Unit 2
Introduce Final /m/m   6

92

Practice 93

Name _____

Think about the story "The Chick and the Duckling." In each row, draw a circle around the picture that shows something from the story.

3   Unit 2
Review Story Details

At Home: As you read a story together, take turns asking each other a question about each page. For example, Did _____ happen?

93

I Am Sam! • PRACTICE

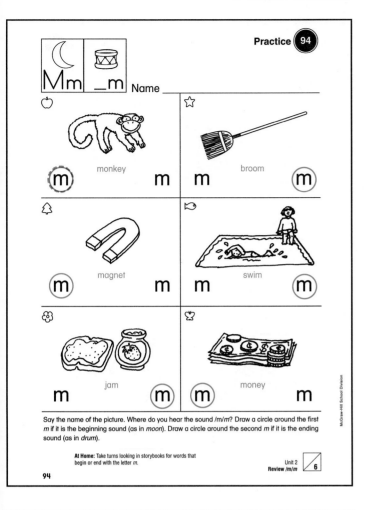

Practice 94

Mm _m Name _____

monkey m | broom m

magnet m | swim m

jam m | money m

Say the name of the picture. Where do you hear the sound /m/m? Draw a circle around the first *m* if it is the beginning sound (as in *moon*). Draw a circle around the second *m* if it is the ending sound (as in *drum*).

At Home: Take turns looking in storybooks for words that begin or end with the letter *m*.

94

Unit 2
Review /m/m 6

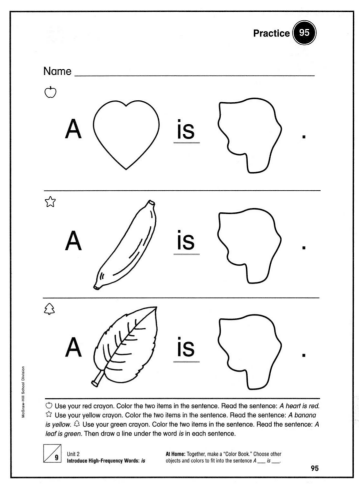

Practice 95

Name _____

A ♥ is ⬤ .

A 🍌 is ⬤ .

A 🍃 is ⬤ .

○ Use your red crayon. Color the two items in the sentence. Read the sentence: *A heart is red.*
☆ Use your yellow crayon. Color the two items in the sentence. Read the sentence: *A banana is yellow.* △ Use your green crayon. Color the two items in the sentence. Read the sentence: *A leaf is green.* Then draw a line under the word *is* in each sentence.

9 Unit 2
Introduce High-Frequency Words: *is*

At Home: Together, make a "Color Book." Choose other objects and colors to fit into the sentence A ___ is ___.

95

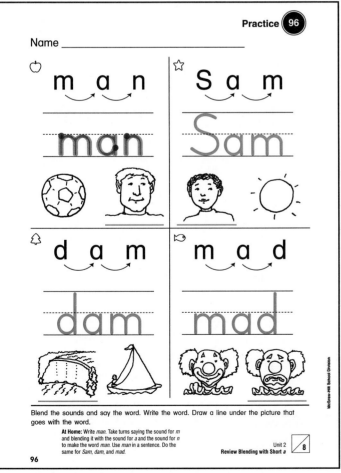

Practice 96

Name _____

m a n | S a m

man | Sam

d a m | m a d

dam | mad

Blend the sounds and say the word. Write the word. Draw a line under the picture that goes with the word.

At Home: Write *man*. Take turns saying the sound for *m* and blending it with the sound for *a* and the sound for *n* to make the word *man*. Use *man* in a sentence. Do the same for *Sam, dam,* and *mad.*

96

Unit 2
Review Blending with Short *a* 8

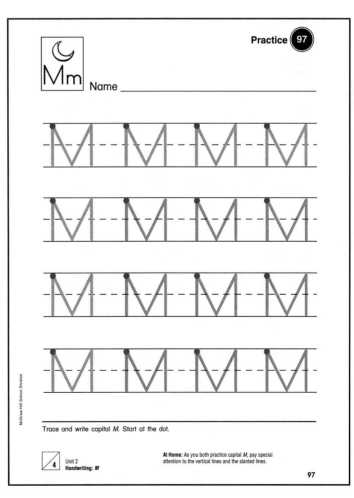

Practice 97

Mm Name _____

M M M M

M M M M

M M M M

M M M M

Trace and write capital *M*. Start at the dot.

4 Unit 2
Handwriting: *M*

At Home: As you both practice capital *M*, pay special attention to the vertical lines and the slanted lines.

97

T15

I Am Sam! • PRACTICE

Practice 98

Mm

Name _____

m m m m m m

m m m m m m

m m m m m m

Mm Mm Mm

Trace and write lowercase m. Start at the dot. On the last line, trace and write Mm.

At Home: As you practice writing Mm, guide the child to see that capital M has sharp angles, while lowercase m has curves.

Unit 2
Handwriting: M, m / 4

98

Practice 99

Name _____

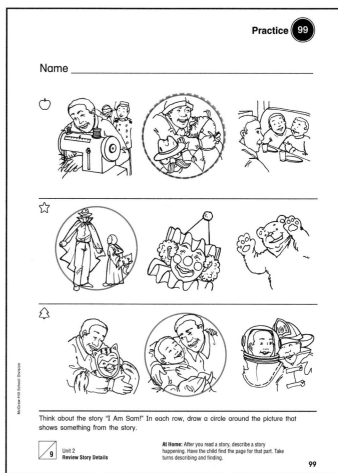

Think about the story "I Am Sam!" In each row, draw a circle around the picture that shows something from the story.

9 Unit 2
Review Story Details

At Home: After you read a story, describe a story happening. Have the child find the page for that part. Take turns describing and finding.

99

Practice 100

Name _____

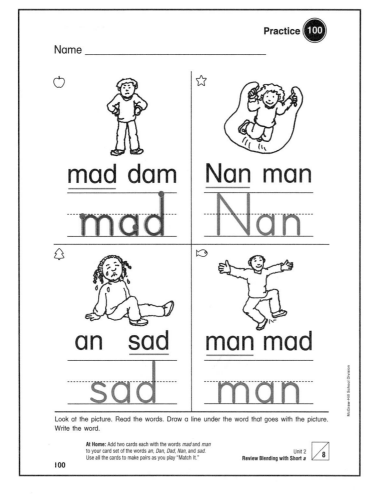

mad dam   Nan man

mad   Nan

an sad   man mad

sad   man

Look at the picture. Read the words. Draw a line under the word that goes with the picture. Write the word.

At Home: Add two cards each with the words mad and man to your card set of the words an, Dan, Dad, Nan, and sad. Use all the cards to make pairs as you play "Match It."

Unit 2
Review Blending with Short a / 8

100

Practice 101

Name _____

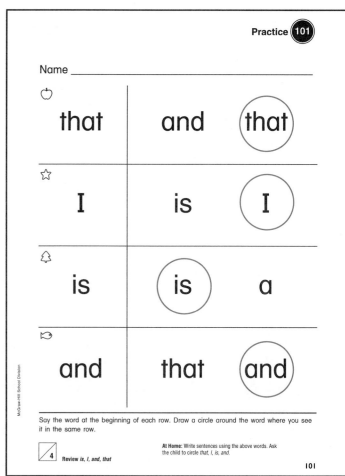

that	and	(that)
I	is	(I)
is	(is)	a
and	that	(and)

Say the word at the beginning of each row. Draw a circle around the word where you see it in the same row.

4 Review is, I, and, that

At Home: Write sentences using the above words. Ask the child to circle that, I, is, and and.

101

T16 *Annotated Workbooks*

Sid Said • PRACTICE

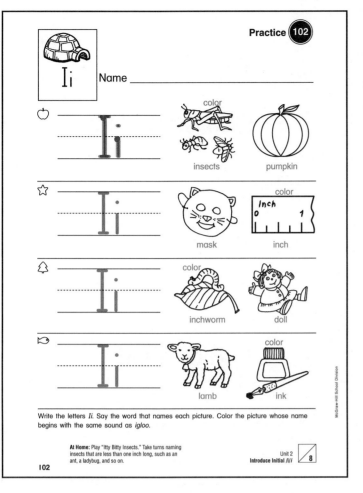

Name _____

color

insects

pumpkin

color

mask

inch

color

inchworm

doll

color

lamb

ink

Write the letters *Ii*. Say the word that names each picture. Color the picture whose name begins with the same sound as *igloo*.

At Home: Play "Itty Bitty Insects." Take turns naming insects that are less than one inch long, such as an ant, a ladybug, and so on.

Unit 2
Introduce Initial /i/i

8

102

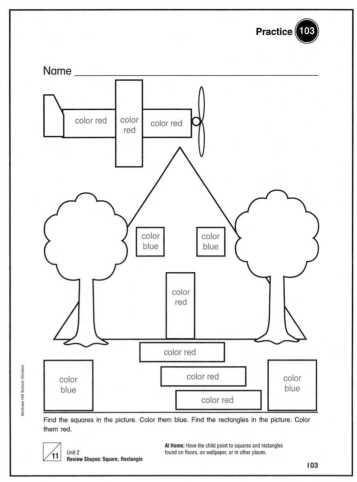

Name _____

color red   color red   color red

color blue   color blue

color red

color red

color blue   color red   color blue

color red

Find the squares in the picture. Color them blue. Find the rectangles in the picture. Color them red.

11 Unit 2
Review Shapes: Square, Rectangle

At Home: Have the child point to squares and rectangles found on floors, on wallpaper, or in other places.

103

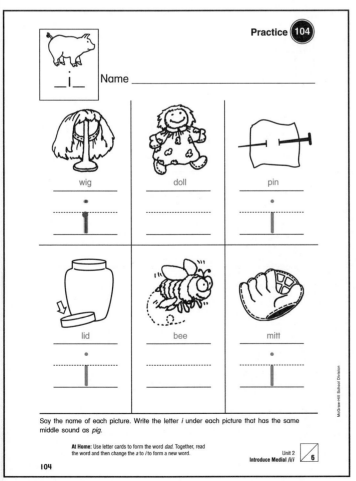

Name _____

| wig | doll | pin |
| lid | bee | mitt |

Say the name of each picture. Write the letter *i* under each picture that has the same middle sound as *pig*.

At Home: Use letter cards to form the word *dad*. Together, read the word and then change the *a* to *i* to form a new word.

Unit 2
Introduce Medial /i/i

6

104

Name _____

color   color   color

color   color   color

color   color   color

color   color   color

Color the three pictures that belong to the same group.

16 Unit 2
Review Classify and Categorize

At Home: Have the child help you organize kitchen utensils or silverware by categories.

105

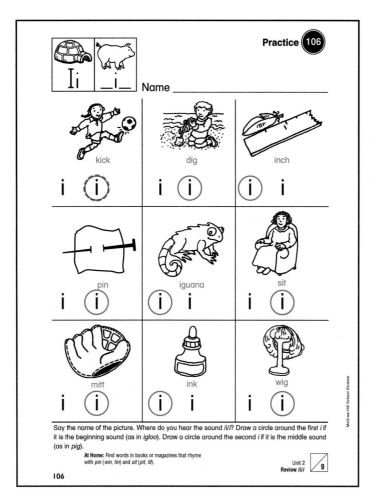

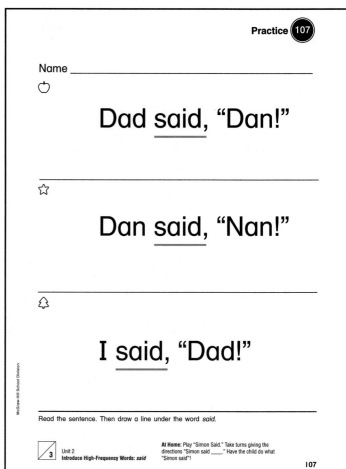

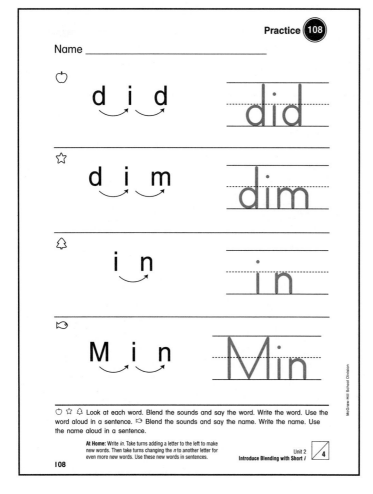

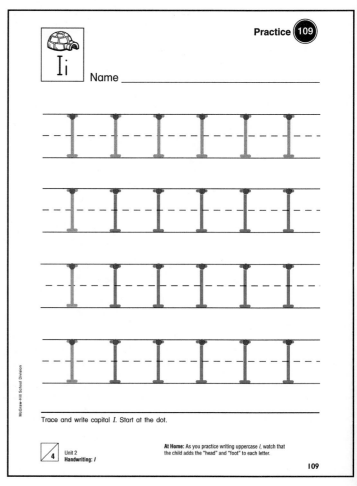

Sid Said • PRACTICE

Ii Name _____

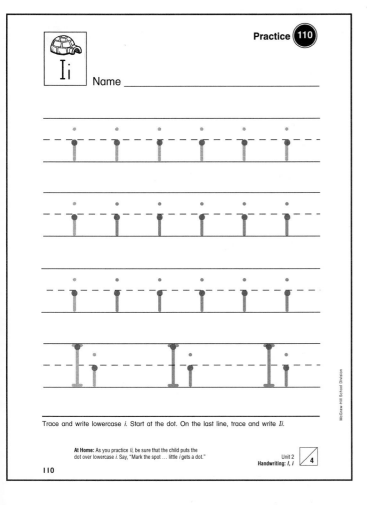

Trace and write lowercase *i*. Start at the dot. On the last line, trace and write *Ii*.

At Home: As you practice *Ii*, be sure that the child puts the dot over lowercase *i*. Say, "Mark the spot ... little *i* gets a dot."

Unit 2
Handwriting: *I, i* / 4

110

Name _____

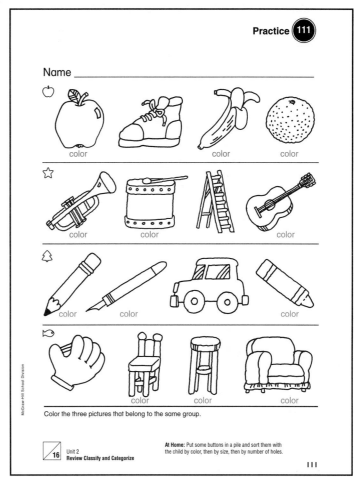

Color the three pictures that belong to the same group.

16 Unit 2
Review Classify and Categorize

At Home: Put some buttons in a pile and sort them with the child by color, then by size, then by number of holes.

111

Name _____

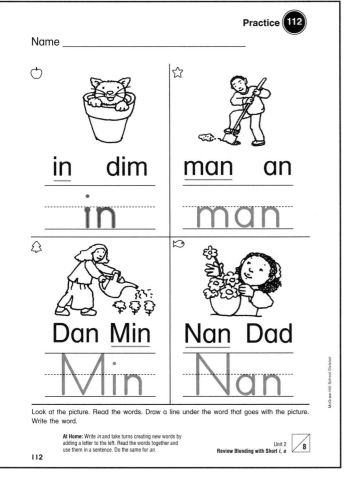

in dim

in

man an

man

Dan Min

Min

Nan Dad

Nan

Look at the picture. Read the words. Draw a line under the word that goes with the picture. Write the word.

At Home: Write *in* and take turns creating new words by adding a letter to the left. Read the words together and use them in a sentence. Do the same for *an*.

Unit 2
Review Blending with Short *i, a* / 8

112

Name _____

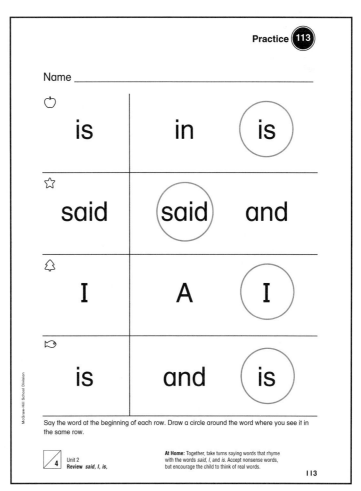

is	in	(is)
said	(said)	and
I	A	(I)
is	and	(is)

Say the word at the beginning of each row. Draw a circle around the word where you see it in the same row.

Unit 2
Review *said, I, is,* / 4

At Home: Together, take turns saying words that rhyme with the words *said, I,* and *is.* Accept nonsense words, but encourage the child to think of real words.

113

T19

Is Sam Mad? • PRACTICE

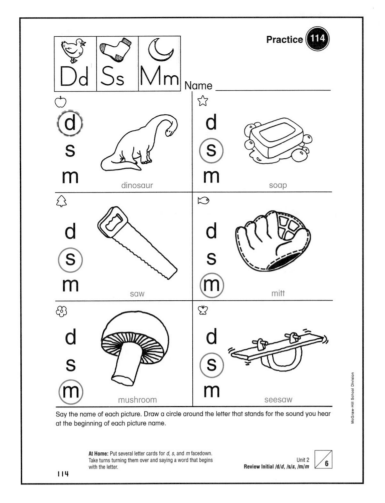

Practice 114

Dd   Ss   Mm   Name _____

- dinosaur — d / s / m (d circled)
- soap — d / s / m (s circled)
- saw — d / s / m (s circled)
- mitt — d / s / m (m circled)
- mushroom — d / s / m (m circled)
- seesaw — d / s / m (s circled)

Say the name of each picture. Draw a circle around the letter that stands for the sound you hear at the beginning of each picture name.

At Home: Put several letter cards for *d*, *s*, and *m* facedown. Take turns turning them over and saying a word that begins with the letter.

Unit 2
Review Initial /d/d, /s/s, /m/m   6

114

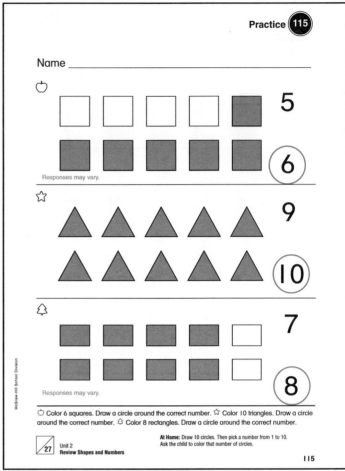

Practice 115

Name _____

- 5 squares (one shaded) — 5 / 6 (6 circled)
- 10 triangles — 9 / 10 (10 circled)
- rectangles — 7 / 8 (8 circled)

Responses may vary.

Color 6 squares. Draw a circle around the correct number. ☆ Color 10 triangles. Draw a circle around the correct number. △ Color 8 rectangles. Draw a circle around the correct number.

At Home: Draw 10 circles. Then pick a number from 1 to 10. Ask the child to color that number of circles.

27   Unit 2
Review Shapes and Numbers

115

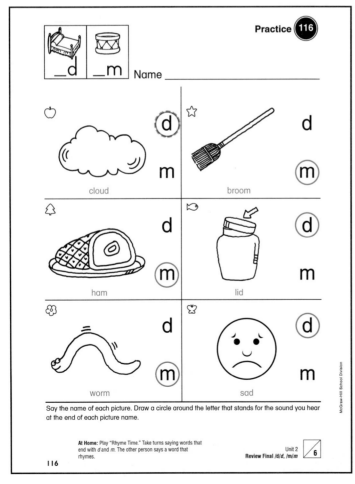

Practice 116

_d   _m   Name _____

- cloud — d / m (d circled)
- broom — d / m (m circled)
- ham — d / m (m circled)
- lid — d / m (d circled)
- worm — d / m (m circled)
- sad — d / m (d circled)

Say the name of each picture. Draw a circle around the letter that stands for the sound you hear at the end of each picture name.

At Home: Play "Rhyme Time." Take turns saying words that end with *d* and *m*. The other person says a word that rhymes.

Unit 2
Review Final /d/d, /m/m   6

116

Practice 117

Name _____

Think about the story "The Chick and the Duckling." In each row, draw a circle around the picture that shows something from the story.

9   Unit 2
Review Story Details

At Home: Play "Prove It." After you read a story, take turns asking questions that require a yes or no answer. One person asks "Can you prove it?" The other finds the page.

117

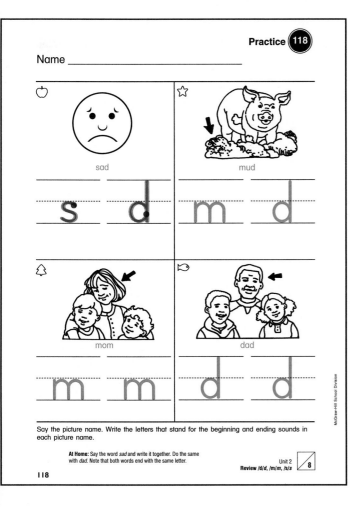

Name _____

Say the picture name. Write the letters that stand for the beginning and ending sounds in each picture name.

At Home: Say the word *sad* and write it together. Do the same with *dad*. Note that both words end with the same letter.

Unit 2
Review /d/d, /m/m, /s/s   8

118

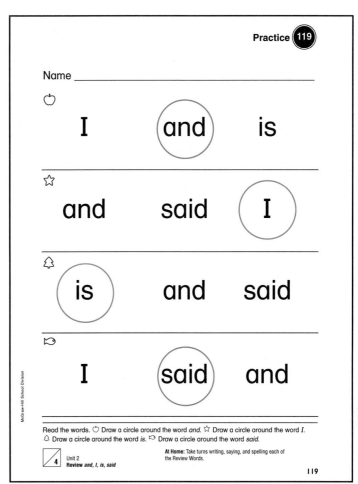

Name _____

Read the words. ○ Draw a circle around the word *and*. ☆ Draw a circle around the word *I*. ♧ Draw a circle around the word *is*. ⌕ Draw a circle around the word *said*.

4 Unit 2
Review *and, I, is, said*

At Home: Take turns writing, saying, and spelling each of the Review Words.

119

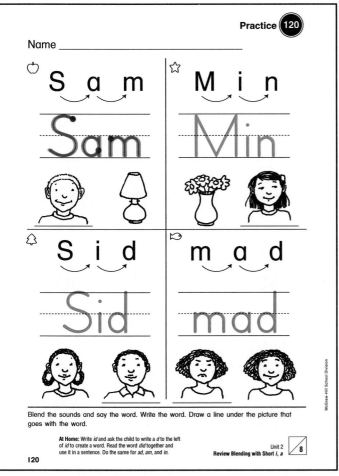

Name _____

Blend the sounds and say the word. Write the word. Draw a line under the picture that goes with the word.

At Home: Write *id* and ask the child to write a *d* to the left of *id* to create a word. Read the word *did* together and use it in a sentence. Do the same for *ad*, *am*, and *in*.

Unit 2
Review Blending with Short *i, a*   8

120

Name _____

and is man

and is man

I said Sam

I said Sam

Trace the words. Then write the words under their models.

4 Unit 2
Handwriting Review

At Home: Have the child show you how to make a capital *S* and how to make a lowercase *s*. How are they the same? How are they different?

121

Practice 122

Name _____

Sid am an

Sid am an

Dad did in

Dad did in

Trace the words. Then write the words under their models.

At Home: Have the child show you how to make a capital *D* and how to make a lowercase *d*. How are they different?

Unit 2
Handwriting Review / 4

122

Practice 123

Name _____

color   color   color

color   color   color

color   color   color

color   color   color

Color the three pictures that belong to the same group.

16 / Unit 2
Review Classify and Categorize

At Home: Have the child help you sort laundry into whites and colors by type of item (socks, towels, and so on).

123

Practice 124

Name _____

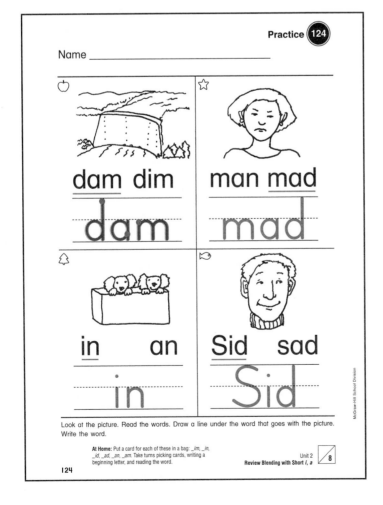

dam dim

dam

man mad

mad

in an

in

Sid sad

Sid

Look at the picture. Read the words. Draw a line under the word that goes with the picture. Write the word.

At Home: Put a card for each of these in a bag: _im, _in, _id, _ad, _an, _am. Take turns picking cards, writing a beginning letter, and reading the word.

Unit 2
Review Blending with Short *i, a* / 8

124

Practice 125

Name _____

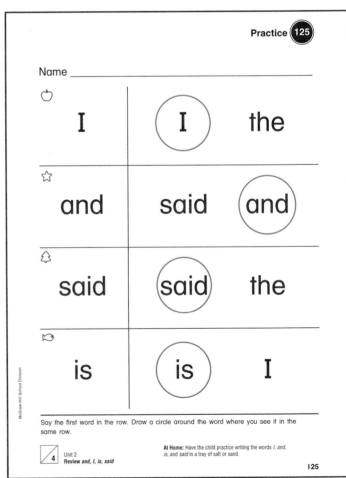

I   I   the

and   said   and

said   said   the

is   is   I

Say the first word in the row. Draw a circle around the word where you see it in the same row.

4 / Unit 2
Review *and, I, is, said*

At Home: Have the child practice writing the words *I, and, is,* and *said* in a tray of salt or sand.

125

Initial and Final *d*

OBJECTIVES Children will name pictures of objects whose names contain initial and final *d*.

Alternate

Visual

WHAT AM I?

 Materials: pictures of objects from magazines—some object's names should begin or end with *d*

Use the following activity to give children practice with *d*.

- Hold up the pictures, one at a time, and ask: *What am I?*

- After children have named the picture correctly, ask: *Does my name begin with* d? *Does my name end with* d? After each question, give children time to respond. ▶**Linguistic**

Auditory

THINK OF A WORD

 Use the following activity to give children practice with words beginning with *d*.

- Organize the class into groups of four. Give groups time to brainstorm as many words as possible that begin with *d*.

- Ask the first group to name one of its words. Write the word on the chalkboard. Do the same with the other groups. Continue until none of the groups can think of a *d* word. ▶**Interpersonal**

Kinesthetic

CONCENTRATION

Materials: crayons, drawing paper

Have children work in pairs to draw pictures of items whose names begin or end with *d*. Have them use the pictures in a game to review words containing initial or final *d*.

- Organize the class into pairs. Ask each pair to draw six small pictures of things whose names begin or end with *d*. You might suggest the following: *dot, mud, dinner, dog, doll, bread, bed, card, bird, duck, dime, desk.*

- Have partners use the pictures in a game of *Concentration*. Ask children to arrange the pictures in the middle of a table.

- The players study the pictures for a few minutes. The pictures are then turned face down. Players then take turns trying to remember the correct position of as many pictures as possible. ▶**Bodily/Kinesthetic**

 **CD-ROM**

Numbers 1–10

 **OBJECTIVES** Children will participate in games and
activities using the numbers 1 through 10.

Alternate Activities

Kinesthetic

NUMBER MARCH

 Materials: number cards as described
below, marching music

- Give each child a large card that shows a number from 1 to 10. (You may want to have children make the cards themselves.)

- Have children sit in a large circle. While the music is playing, call out, *One!* The child or children holding that number should march around inside the circle.

- Call out the rest of the numbers, until all the children are marching. ▶**Bodily/Kinesthetic**

Visual

MOBILE

 Materials: construction paper, crayons, drawing paper, scissors, string or yarn

Have children make mobiles that illustrate a number.

- Organize the class into ten small groups. Assign each group a number from 1 to 10.

- Tell each group to write their number on a sheet of construction paper.

- Have each group create a mobile that displays its number. For example, the group assigned the number 3 might draw three kittens, cut them out, and then use string or yarn to hang them from the construction paper with the number printed on it.

- Help groups hang their finished mobiles around the classroom. ▶**Spatial**

Auditory

MAKE A MATCH

 Materials: number cards

Use the following activity to give children added practice in recognizing the numbers 1 through 10.

- Assign each of ten children a number card from 1 to 10. They should keep their numbers a secret.

- Organize the rest of the class into pairs. The partners should take turns guessing the number that each of the first ten children is holding.

- If the guess is incorrect, the child with a number should give a clue. For example, if the incorrect guess is *4*, the child should say, *No, my number is less [or greater] than 4.* ▶**Interpersonal**

Story Details

☑OBJECTIVES Children will practice noting details in stories and pictures.

Alternate Activities

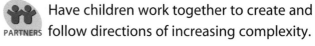

Auditory

DETAILS FROM A STORY

 GROUP

Materials: a storybook

Use this activity to give children practice in recognizing and remembering details from a story.

- Read several paragraphs from a story. After each paragraph, ask children questions based on details stated in the paragraph—for example, *How big was the dog? What game were the girls playing? In what room were the people talking?*
▶**Linguistic**

Visual

PICTURE DETAILS

GROUP

Materials: pictures from storybooks or magazines

This activity will give children practice in recognizing and remembering details in pictures.

- Hold up a picture from a book or magazine. Give children several minutes to look at it.

- Put down the picture, and ask children questions about its detail—for example, *What color was the girl's sweater? Was the window open or closed?*
▶**Spatial**

Kinesthetic

FOLLOW DIRECTIONS

PARTNERS Have children work together to create and follow directions of increasing complexity.

- Have pairs of children take turns giving each other directions that become more and more complicated. For example, *Hop on one foot. Now hop on one foot with your hand on your hip. Now hop on one foot with one hand on your hip and one on your head.*

- Alternatively, you may want to work with the entire class, calling on individuals to carry out your directions. ▶**Bodily/Kinesthetic**

High-Frequency Words
and, I, is, said

OBJECTIVES Children will read, listen to, and complete the high-frequency words *and, I, is,* and *said.*

Alternate

Visual

COMPLETE THE WORDS

Use the following activity to allow children to practice the high-frequency words *and, I, is,* and *said.*

- Write the following incomplete words in a column on the chalkboard: _aid, i_, _nd.

- Point to each word and ask these questions:
What letter can I add to make this word said?
What letter can I add to make this word is?
What letter can I add to make this word and?

- After each correct response, complete the word. Then ask: *Which of the letters in these words is a word all by itself?* ▶**Linguistic**

Auditory

Materials: word cards for *and, I, is,* and *said*
Have children practice recognizing these high-frequency words in spoken sentences.

- Arrange the word cards along the chalk tray.

- Use each word in a sentence, such as *Jay* is *jumping.* I *am talking. José* and *Cammy like to read.* "*This* is *a good book,*" said *Maria.*

- After reading each sentence aloud, ask a volunteer to point to the card on the chalk tray that shows a word used in that sentence.

- Continue until all children have had a chance to participate. Alternatively, you could ask volunteers to create appropriate sentences.
▶**Linguistic**

Kinesthetic

CROSSWORD PUZZLE

Materials: letter cards for the words *and, is,* and *said*

Children will use letter cards to complete a crossword puzzle.

- Organize the class into pairs. Distribute the following letter cards to each pair:
i (2), *s* (2), *a* (2), *d, n.*

- Write the words *and, is,* and *said* on the chalkboard.

- Challenge partners to use letter cards to connect the words *and, is,* and *said.* You might offer as an example the following solution:

a

n

s a i d

s

▶**Bodily/Kinesthetic**

Initial *s*

 OBJECTIVES Children will answer riddles with words that begin with *s*. They will play games that reinforce this sound.

Alternate Activities

Auditory

RIDDLES

 Use this activity to give children practice with initial *s*.

- Ask children riddles whose answers begin with *s*.

- Possible riddles: *I am a huge body of water. Look for ships on me.* (sea) *I am a little animal you might see at the beach. I have a shell and crawl very slowly.* (snail) *Put me in the ground and I will grow into a plant.* (seed) *Use me to weigh things.* (scale)

- Encourage children to invent riddles of their own and present them to their classmates.
▶**Logical/Mathematical**

Visual

PICTURE PAGE

 Materials: old magazines, glue, pencils or crayons, drawing paper, scissors

Have children create a puzzle for a partner to complete.

- Give each child a piece of paper and some magazines. Ask children to cut out pictures of some things whose names begin with *s* and some things whose names do not begin with *s*.

 Have them print *s* in the middle of their papers. They should then paste around the *s* the pictures they have cut out.

- Have children give their pages to a partner, who should then draw a line from the *s* to each picture on the page whose name begins with that letter. ▶**Spatial**

Kinesthetic

RACE ACROSS THE ROOM

 Have children play a game that reinforces the *s* sound.

- Have children line up along one side of the room.

- Play a game in which each child is asked to say a word that begins with *s*. Each child who does so advances one step toward a finish line.

- Continue the game until all children have crossed the finish line. You may want to give hints to children who have difficulty thinking of an *s* word. ▶**Bodily/Kinesthetic**

 **CD-ROM**

Classify and Categorize

OBJECTIVES Children will classify and categorize according to different criteria.

Alternate Activities

Visual

MAKE A BOOK

 GROUP **Materials:** old magazines, drawing paper, scissors, glue

Children will create a book, classifying different types of pictures.

- Organize the class into small groups. Ask groups to decide on a kind of picture to look for in magazines—for example, animals, ways of going places (such as bike, car, and plane), things to wear, toys, or buildings.

- Have group members cut out the pictures they have decided on and glue them to a piece of paper.

- When all groups have finished, have them share their pages. Encourage children to discuss what the pictures on each page have in common. Then help each group label its page according to what its pictures have in common. Organize the pages into a class book. ▶**Logical/Mathematical**

Auditory

WHAT SHOULD I WEAR?

 GROUP Have children discuss types of clothing people wear for various types of weather and activities.

- Describe several weather scenarios to children.

- After each description, encourage children to discuss what clothing someone should wear in that situation. For example, a description of a winter scene with a child building a snowman might lead children to list scarves, gloves, hats, boots, and big coats. ▶**Linguistic**

Kinesthetic

GROUPINGS

 GROUP Use this activity to give children more practice with classifying and categorizing.

- Have children group themselves according to categories you suggest—for example, *Boys, go to one side of the room, and girls, go to the other. Now, anybody wearing a sweater, go to the back of the room. Anybody wearing something with red, stand by me.*

- End the activity by discussing why children moved from one group to another. ▶**Bodily/Kinesthetic**

T29

Initial and Final *m*

 OBJECTIVES Children will develop awareness of the *m* sound at the beginning and end of words. They will rearrange known letters to make words.

Alternate Activities

Auditory

COMPLETE THE SENTENCE

 ONE Have children complete sentences with words beginning or ending with *m*.

- Say the following incomplete sentences. Have children complete each sentence with a word that begins or ends with *m*.
  "I love your necktie," she said to the _____. (man)
  If a dog growls, it means he's _____. (mad)
  My favorite book is Green Eggs and _____. (Ham)
  Will you sweep the floor with a _____? (broom)
  You play the piano, and I'll beat the _____. (drum)

- Encourage children to make up their own incomplete sentences for their classmates to fill in missing words. ▶**Linguistic**

Visual

NONSENSE

 PARTNERS **Materials:** pictures from magazines or illustrations from stories

Have children work with partners to create nonsense words beginning or ending with *m*.

- Organize the class into pairs. Give each pair of children a magazine with pictures, or a book with illustrations.

- Have partners name an item in the picture and then change the first or last letter to *m* to create a different word or a nonsense word. For example, *rug* becomes *mug, wall* becomes *mall* or *wam, dog* becomes *mog* or *dom, cat* becomes *mat* or *cam,* and so on. ▶**Linguistic**

Kinesthetic

REARRANGE

GROUP **Materials:** upper-case letter cards for *N, A, D, S, M*

Have children rearrange letter cards to make words.

- Invite five children to stand before the class, each one holding one of the letter cards.

- Encourage the rest of the children to discuss how the letters can be rearranged to form words, including names.

- Invite individuals to form the words and names by rearranging the children holding letters. Possibilities include: DAN, SAM, SAD, MAD, MAN, A, AM, AND, ANA, AS. ▶**Linguistic**

 **CD-ROM**

Shapes

OBJECTIVES Children will learn to recognize a triangle, a square, a circle, and a rectangle.

Alternate

Auditory

MAKING SHAPES

 Materials: construction paper in a variety of colors, scissors, pencils

Have children make different shapes.

- Organize the class into groups of four. Have each group member make a different shape: a triangle, a square, a circle, or a rectangle.

- When groups have finished, call out the following: *Show me a circle!* All the children who made circles should hold them up. Do the same with the rest of the shapes. ▶**Bodily/Kinesthetic**

Visual

STRING SHAPES TOGETHER

 Materials: the shapes children made in the Kinesthetic Activity, yarn or string, tape

Have children use yarn or string to connect the shapes they created in the previous activity. Use the connected shapes to make a decorative garland for the classroom.

- Have children in each group string their shapes together with yarn.

- The groups should then combine the strings of shapes together into one long string and hang it somewhere in the classroom. ▶**Spatial**

Kinesthetic

TWIST AND BEND

Have children use their bodies to make shapes.

- Organize the class into groups of four.

- Have each group work together to form their bodies into a circle, a square, a triangle, and a rectangle.

- Point out to children that they will have to lie on the floor to make the shapes and that not all four children will be needed to make all the shapes. ▶**Bodily/Kinesthetic**

Initial and Medial *i*

 OBJECTIVES Children will work with words containing initial and medial *i*.

Alternate Activities

Auditory

THE RIGHT SOUND

 GROUP Use the following activity to develop children's awareness of *i*.

- Say words such as the following: *bit, bat, lid, hid, sat, is, not, an, in, dim, get, off, if, hum.* After each word, ask children to raise their hands if it contains the short *i* sound. ▶**Intrapersonal**

Kinesthetic

RIDDLES

 GROUP Have children challenge their classmates with a game of *Charades.*

- Organize children into small groups. Assign each group a word that contains short *i* in the middle, such as *bit, hit, kiss, kick, swim,* or *rip.*

- Challenge groups to create riddles for their classmates. Children will give a clue, such as *This is what the mouse did to the piece of cheese,* and then pantomime the short *i* word that answers the riddle, *bit.* ▶**Bodily/Kinesthetic**

Visual

ADD A LETTER

 **GROUP** Have children complete words with the short *i* sound.

- Write on the chalkboard the following letters, leaving a space in between them: *d_m.*

- Tell children that if you put *i* between these letters, you will make a word that describes a light that is not bright. Ask what the word is. When children have suggested *dim,* add the missing *i*.

- Do the same with other letter combinations, such as *k_d*—a young goat or a young person (kid); *l_d*—something that goes on top of a jar (lid); *h_d*—what the child did when playing *Hide-and-Seek* (hid). ▶**Linguistic**

Phonics CD-ROM

Writing Readiness

Before children begin to write, fine motor skills need to be developed. Here are examples of activities that can be used:

- **Simon Says** Play Simon Says using just finger positions.
- **Finger Plays and Songs** Sing songs such as "Where Is Thumbkin" or "The Eensie, Weensie, Spider" or songs that use Signed English or American Sign Language.
- **Mazes** Use or create mazes, especially ones that require moving the writing instruments from left to right.

The Mechanics of Writing

POSTURE

- Chair height should allow for the feet to rest flat on the floor.
- Desk height should be two inches above the elbows.
- There should be an inch between the child and the desk.
- Children sit erect with the elbows resting on the desk.
- Letter models should be on the desk or at eye level.

PAPER POSITION

- **Right-handed children** should turn the paper so that the lower left-hand corner of the paper points to the abdomen.

- **Left-handed children** should turn the paper so that the lower right-hand corner of the paper points to the abdomen.

- The nondominant hand should anchor the paper near the top so that the paper doesn't slide.

- The paper should be moved up as the child nears the bottom of the paper. Many children won't think of this.

The Writing Instrument Grasp

For handwriting to be functional, the writing instrument must be held in a way that allows for fluid dynamic movement.

FUNCTIONAL GRASP PATTERNS

- **Tripod Grasp** The writing instrument is held with the tip of the thumb and the index finger and rests against the side of the third finger. The thumb and index finger form a circle.

- **Quadrupod Grasp** The writing instrument is held with the tip of the thumb and index finger and rests against the fourth finger. The thumb and index finger form a circle.

INCORRECT GRASP PATTERNS

- **Fisted Grasp** The writing instrument is held in a fisted hand.

- **Pronated Grasp** The instrument is held diagonally within the hand with the tips of the thumb and index finger but with no support from other fingers.

- **Five-Finger Grasp** The writing instrument is held with the tips of all five fingers.

- **Flexed or Hooked Wrist** Flexed or bent wrist is typically seen with left-handed writers but is also present in some right-handed writers.

- To correct wrist position, have children check their writing posture and paper placement.

TO CORRECT GRASPS

- Have children play counting games with an eye dropper and water.
- Have children pick up small objects with a tweezer.
- Do counting games with children picking up small coins using just the thumb and index finger.

Evaluation Checklist

Formation and Strokes

- ☑ Does the child begin letters at the top?
- ☑ Do circles close?
- ☑ Are the horizontal lines straight?
- ☑ Do circular shapes and extender and descender lines touch?
- ☑ Are the heights of all upper-case letters equal?
- ☑ Are the heights of all lower-case letters equal?
- ☑ Are the lengths of the extenders and descenders the same for all letters?

Directionality

- ☑ Do the children form letters starting at the top and moving to the bottom?
- ☑ Are letters formed from left to right?

Spacing

- ☑ Are the spaces between letters equidistant?
- ☑ Are the spaces between words equidistant?
- ☑ Do the letters rest on the line?
- ☑ Are the top, bottom and side margins on the paper even?

Write the Alphabet

Trace and write the letters.

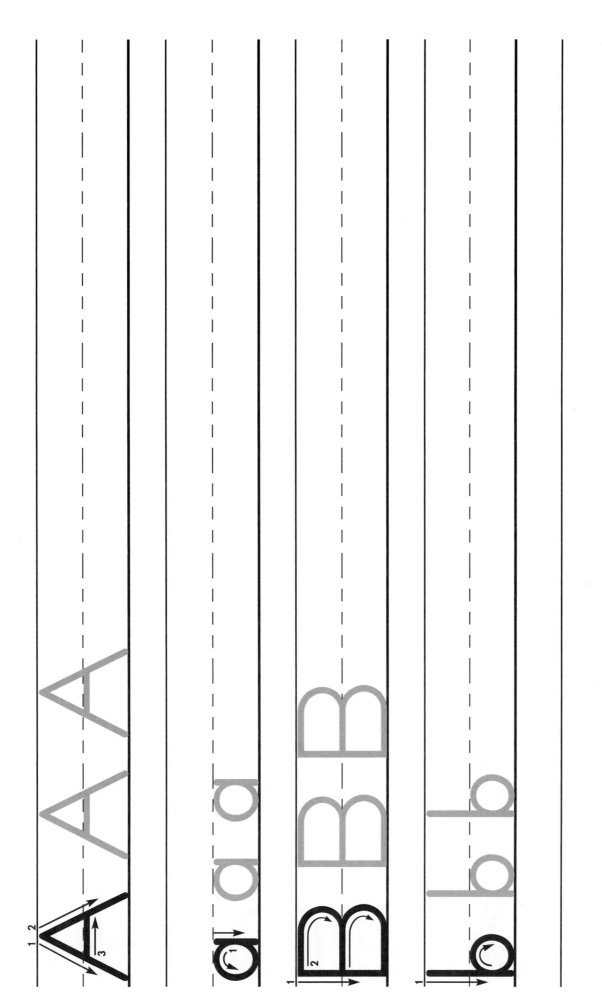

Trace and write the letters.

C C C

c c c

D D D

d d d

Trace and write the letters.

E E E

e e e

F F F

f f f

Trace and write the letters.

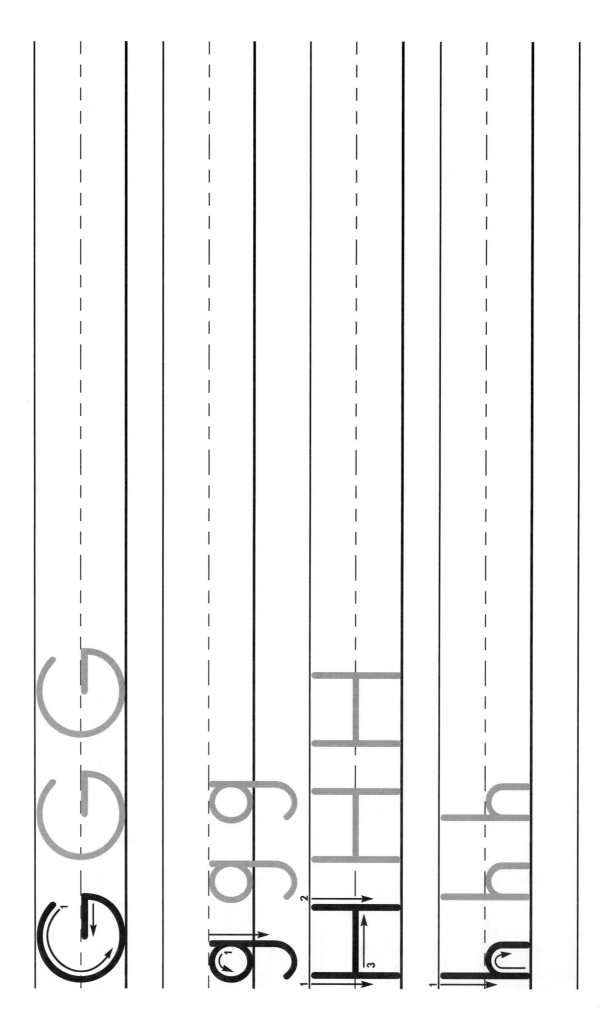

Trace and write the letters.

Trace and write the letters.

Trace and write the letters.

Trace and write the letters.

Trace and write the letters.

Trace and write the letters.

Trace and write the letters.

1 U U U

1 u u u

1 V V V

1 v v v

Trace and write the letters.

Trace and write the letters.

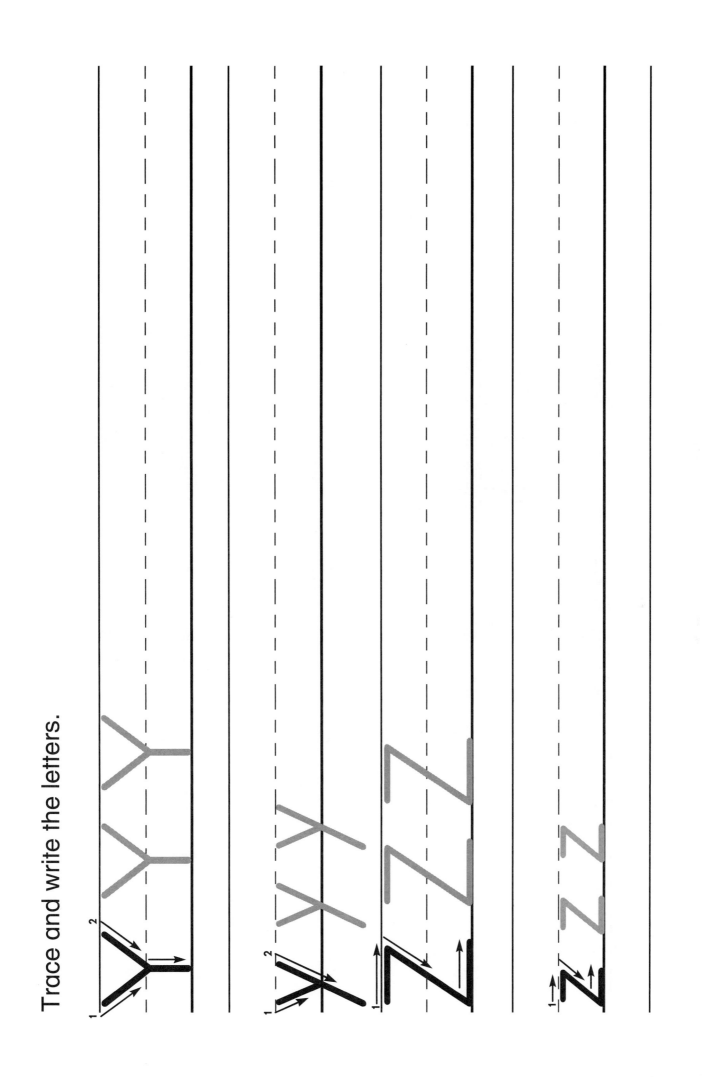

T47

Pamela Duncan Edwards ● Henry Cole

WARTHOGS in the Kitchen

A Sloppy Counting Book

McGraw Hill

Warthogs
in the Kitchen

A Sloppy Counting Book

Pamela Duncan Edwards
Illustrated by Henry Cole

McGraw-Hill
School Division
New York   Farmington

1

One little chef thinks
he'll cook today.

4

2

Two clean hooves.
All the germs washed away.

5

"I want to help.
I won't make a mess."

6

"Better find some measures.
We can't just guess."

7

3

Three cake makers read the
book to check how.

8

4

Four scoops of sugar should
go in now.

9

T49

There's something in the bowl
that shouldn't be there!

10

"Get out this instant, you greedy
little bear."

11

5
Five scoops of butter.
Beat and beat some more.

12

6
Six cracked eggs.
How many on the floor?

13

"I've found a jar of pickles!
Should pickles go in, too?"

14

"Pickles in cupcakes!
Well, perhaps just a few!"

15

7

Seven scoops of flour should
make the mixture just right.

16

8

Eight pink tongues lick lips
at the sight.

17

"Put them in the cupcake pans.
Let's each have a turn."

18

"Pop them in the oven.
Don't let them burn!"

19

9

Nine minutes cooking and
our cakes will be ready.

20

10

Ten cupcakes—the two tiny
ones for Teddy.

21

O

Zero cakes left.
They're down in each tummy.

22

"We're excellent cooks.
Those cupcakes were YUMMY!"

23

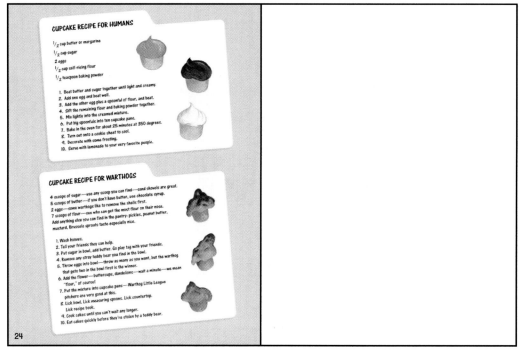

CUPCAKE RECIPE FOR HUMANS

1/2 cup butter or margarine
1/2 cup sugar
2 eggs
1/2 cup self-rising flour
1/2 teaspoon baking powder

1. Beat butter and sugar together until light and creamy.
2. Add one egg and beat well.
3. Add the other egg plus a spoonful of flour, and beat.
4. Sift the remaining flour and baking powder together.
5. Mix lightly into the creamed mixture.
6. Put big spoonfuls into ten cupcake pans.
7. Bake in the oven for about 25 minutes at 350 degrees.
8. Turn out onto a cookie sheet to cool.
9. Decorate with some frosting.
10. Serve with lemonade to your very favorite people.

CUPCAKE RECIPE FOR WARTHOGS

4 scoops of sugar—use any scoop you can find—sand shovels are great.
5 scoops of butter—if you don't have butter, use chocolate syrup.
2 eggs—some warthogs like to remove the shells first.
7 scoops of flour—see who can get the most flour on their nose.
Add anything else you can find in the pantry: pickles, peanut butter,
mustard, Brussels sprouts taste especially nice.

1. Wash hooves.
2. Tell your friends they can help. Go play tag with your friends.
3. Put sugar in bowl, add butter.
4. Remove any stray teddy bear you find in the bowl.
5. Throw eggs into bowl—throw as many as you want, but the warthog
   that gets two in the bowl first is the winner.
6. Add the flower—buttercups, dandelions—wait a minute—we mean
   "flour," of course!
7. Put the mixture into cupcake pans—Warthog Little League
   pitchers are very good at this.
8. Lick bowl. Lick measuring spoons. Lick countertop.
   Lick recipe book.
9. Cook cakes until you can't wait any longer.
10. Eat cakes quickly before they're stolen by a teddy bear.

24

The Chick and the Duckling

Translated from the Russian of V. Suteyev

by Mirra Ginsburg
Pictures by Jose Aruego & Ariane Dewey

McGraw Hill

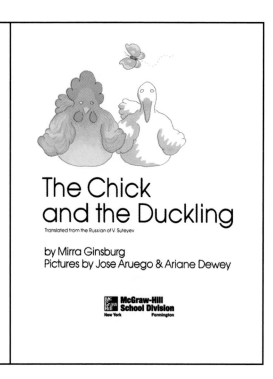

The Chick and the Duckling

Translated from the Russian of V. Suteyev

by Mirra Ginsburg
Pictures by Jose Aruego & Ariane Dewey

McGraw-Hill School Division
New York   Farmington

A Duckling came out
of the shell.

"I am out!" he said.

"Me too," said the Chick.

"I am taking a walk,"
said the Duckling.

"Me too,"
said the Chick.

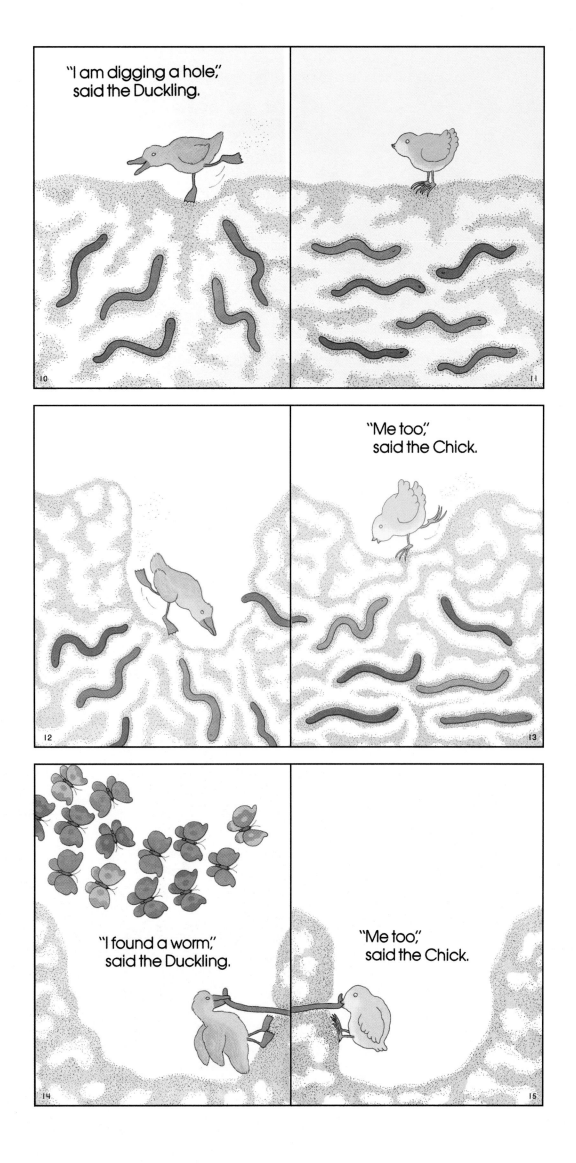

"I am digging a hole," said the Duckling.

"Me too," said the Chick.

"I found a worm," said the Duckling.

"Me too," said the Chick.

"I caught a butterfly," said the Duckling.

16

17

"Me too," said the Chick.

18

19

"I am going for a swim," said the Duckling.

20

21

"Me too,"
said the Chick.

"I am swimming,"
said the Duckling.

"Me too!"
cried the Chick.

The Duckling pulled
the Chick out.

28

29

"I'm going for another swim,"
said the Duckling.

30

31

"Not me,"
said the Chick.

32

The ABC Street Fair

Written By Constance Keremes

Illustrated By Lindy Burnett

The ABC Street Fair

Written by Constance Keremes
Illustrated by Lindy Burnett

McGraw-Hill
School Division
New York   Farmington

Beautiful balloons

Bb

Cc Colorful **c**ostumes

Dd Delicious **d**esserts — Eddi**e**'s **e**ggs **Ee**

Ff **F**unny **f**aces

Gg Good game

Hh Happy hippos

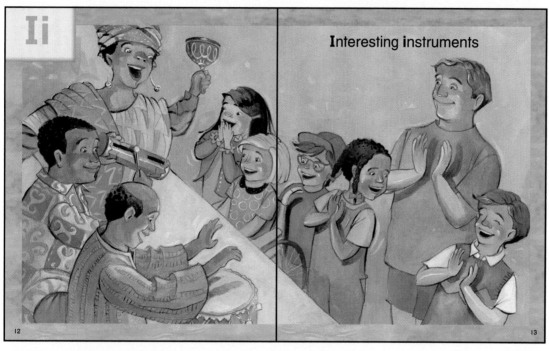

Ii

Interesting instruments

Jj Jolly juggler

Kk Keisha's kites

Qq Quincy's **q**uilts

22

Red **r**oses **Rr**

23

Ss **S**uper **s**andwiches

24

Tasty **t**acos **Tt**

25

Uu **U**nusual **u**mbrellas

26

Valuable **v**ases **Vv**

27

Ww Warm waffles

Six boxes **X**x

28

29

Yy Yellow yo-yos

Zany zebra **Z**z

30

31

The ABC Street Fair

32

Selection Titles

Honors, Prizes, and Awards

SHOW AND TELL DAY
by **Anne Rockwell**

Author/Ilustrator Anne Rockwell, winner of American Booksellers' Award Pick of the List for *Boats* (1985) and *Cars* (1986); National Science Teachers Association Award for Outstanding Science Trade Book for Children (1988) for *Trains*

CHICK AND THE DUCKLING
by **Mirra Ginsburg**
Illustrated by **Jose Aruego and Ariane Dewey**

Illustrators: Jose Aruego and Ariane Dewey, winners of Boston Globe-Horn Book Honor (1974) for *Herman the Helper*

FLOWER GARDEN
by **Eve Bunting**
Illustrated by **Kathryn Hewitt**

Author: Eve Bunting, winner of ALA Notable Book (1990), IRA-CBC Children's Choice, IRA-Teachers' Choice, School Library Journal Best Book (1989) for *The Wednesday Surprise;* Mark Twain Award (1989) for *Sixth Grade Sleepover;* ALA Notable (1990) for *Wall;* ALA Notable (1992) for *Fly Away Home;* Edgar Allen Poe Juvenile Award (1993) for *Coffin on a Case;* ALA Notable, Caldecott Medal (1995) for *Smoky Night;* Booklist Editors' Choice (1995) for *Spying on Miss Müller;* ALA Notable, Booklist Editors' Choice (1997) for *Train to Somewhere;* National Council for Social Studies Notable Children's Book Award (1998) for *Moonstick,* and *I Am the Mummy Heb-Nefert,* and *On Call Back Mountain;* Young Reader's Choice Award (1997) for *Nasty Stinky Sneakers*
Illustrator: Kathryn Hewitt, winner of Association of Booksellers for Children, Children's Choice Award (1998) for *Lives of the Athletes: Thrills, Spills (And What the Neighbors Thought);* ALA Notable (1994) Boston Globe-Horn Book Honor (1993) for *Lives of the Musicians: Good Times, Bad Times (and What the Neighbors Thought)*

PRETEND YOU'RE A CAT
by **Jean Marzolla**
Illustrated by **Jerry Pinkney**

Author: Jean Marzolla, winner of 1998 Association of Booksellers for Children, Children's Choice Award for *I Spy Little Book*
Illustrator: Jerry Pinkney, winner of Coretta Scott King Award, ALA Notable, Christopher Award (1986) for *Patchwork Quilt;* Newbery Medal, Boston Globe-Horn Book Honor (1977) for *Roll of Thunder, Hear My Cry;* Boston Globe-Horn Book Honor (1980) *Childtimes: A Three Generation Memoir;* Coretta Scott King Award (1987) for *Half a Moon and One Whole Star;* ALA Notable (1988) for

Selection Titles	Honors, Prizes, and Awards

 **PRETEND YOU'RE A CAT (CONTINUED)**
by *Jean Marzolla*
Illustrated by *Jerry Pinkney*

Tales of Uncle Remus: The Adventures of Brer Rabbit; ALA Notable, Caldecott Honor, Coretta Scott King Award (1989) for *Mirandy and Brother Wind;* ALA Notable, Caldecott Honor, Coretta Scott King Honor (1990) for *Talking Eggs: A Folktale for the American South;* Golden Kite Award Book (1990) for *Home Place;* ALA Notable (1991) for *Further Tales of Uncle Remus: The Misadventures of Brer Rabbit, Brer Fox . . .;* ALA Notable (1993) for *Back Home;* ALA Notable, Boston Globe-Horn Book Award, Caldecott Honor (1995) for *John Henry;* ALA Notable, Blue Ribbon, Booklist Editors' Choice (1997) for *Sam and the Tigers;* ALA Notable, Christopher Award, Coretta Scott King Award, Golden Kite Honor Book (1997) for *Minty: A Story of Young Harriet Tubman;* Aesop Prize (1997) for *The Hired Hand;* National Council for Social Studies Notable Children's Book Award (1998) for *The Hired Hand* and *Rikki-Tikki-Tavi* (also Children's Choice Award, Association of Booksellers for Children, and Booklist Editors' Choice, 1998); Rip Van Winkle Award (1998); 1998 Hans Christian Andersen nominee

 **ANY KIND OF DOG**
by *Lynn Reiser*

Author/Illustrator: *Lynn Reiser,* winner of ALA Notable (1995) for *The Surprise Family*

 **THE EARTH AND I**
by *Frank Asch*

Author/Illustrator: *Frank Asch,* winner of American Book Award Pick of the List Award (1997) for *Barnyard Animals*

Theme Bibliography

Trade Books

Additional fiction and nonfiction trade books related to each selection can be shared with children throughout the unit.

Best Friends Together, Again
by Aliki (Greenwillow Books, 1995)

When Robert's best friend, Peter, who moved away, comes back to visit, the boys rediscover their friendship.

Friends
Nicola Baxter, illustrated by Michael Evans (Children's Press, 1997)

An introduction to the concept of friends and friendship that includes photographs and cartoons.

May I Bring a Friend?
Beatrice Schenk DeRegniers, illustrated by Beni Montresor (Atheneum, 1964)

A little boy brings his animal friends for a visit with the king and queen. (1965 Caldecott Medal winner)

Building a Bridge
Lisa Shook Begaye, illustrated by Libba Tracy (Northland, 1993)

Two girls of different cultures learn to overlook their differences and work together.

Jobs People Do
Christopher Maynard (Dorling Kindersley, 1996)

Lively photographs of children dressed in detailed costumes present key aspects of various professions.

Music, Music for Everyone
Vera B. Williams (Greenwillow, 1984)

Rosa and her friends work together in a band to earn money to help her mother.

Technology

Multimedia resources can be used to enhance children's understanding of the selections.

Frog and Toad Together (Pied Piper) Video, 18 min. In this award-winning film, Frog and Toad learn from their friendship about the world and each other.

I Can Make Friends (National Geographic Educational Services) Video, 15 min. A look at how to make and keep friends.

Cannonball (BFA Educational Media) Video, 28 min. Hugo the Clown needs a new circus act, and when he befriends a homeless puppy, they learn to work and make a better life together.

Whazzat! (Adapted from "The Three Blind Men and the Elephant") (Brittanica) Video, 10 min. Six blind men each "see" something different when they meet an elephant, but only when they share their ideas and work together do they understand that what they are "seeing" is an elephant.

Jamaica Tag-Along
Juanita Havill, illustrated by Anne S. O'Brien (Houghton Mifflin, 1989)

When her older brother refuses to let her play with him, Jamaica befriends a younger child.

Play with Me
Marie Hall Ets (Viking, 1955)

A little girl goes to the meadow to play and learns how to befriend the animals who live there.

Playgrounds
Gail Gibbons (Holiday House, 1985)

Simple text and pictures introduce various types of playground equipment, games, and toys.

A Boy, a Dog and a Frog (BFA Educational Media) Video, 9 min. A boy and his dog discover a new playmate, a frog.

I Can Make Friends (National Geographic Educational Services) Video, 15 min. A look at how to make and keep friends.

Abdo & Daughters
4940 Viking Drive, Suite 622
Edina, MN 55435
(800) 458-8399 • www.abdopub.com

Aladdin Paperbacks
(Imprint of Simon & Schuster Children's
Publishing)

Atheneum
(Imprint of Simon & Schuster Children's
Publishing)

**Bantam Doubleday Dell Books for
Young Readers**
(Imprint of Random House)

Blackbirch Press
1 Bradley Road, Suite 205
Woodbridge, CT 06525
(203) 387-7525 • (800) 831-9183

Blue Sky Press
(Imprint of Scholastic)

Boyds Mills Press
815 Church Street
Honesdale, PA 18431
(570) 253-1164 • Fax (570) 251-0179 •
(800) 949-7777

Bradbury Press
(Imprint of Simon & Schuster Children's
Publishing)

BridgeWater Books
(Distributed by Penguin Putnam)

Candlewick Press
2067 Masssachusetts Avenue
Cambridge, MA 02140
(617) 661-3330 • Fax (617) 661-0565

Carolrhoda Books
(Division of Lerner Publications Co.)

Charles Scribners's Sons
(Imprint of Simon & Schuster Children's
Publishing)

Children's Press (Division of Grolier, Inc.)
P.O. Box 1796
Danbury, CT 06813-1333
(800) 621-1115 • www.grolier.com

Child's World
P.O. Box 326
Chanhassen, MN 55317-0326
(612) 906-3939 • (800) 599-READ •
www.childsworld.com

Chronicle Books
85 Second Street, Sixth Floor
San Francisco, CA 94105
(415) 537-3730 • (415) 537-4460 • (800)
722-6657 • www.chroniclebooks.com

Clarion Books
(Imprint of Houghton Mifflin, Inc.)
215 Park Avenue South
New York, NY 10003
(212) 420-5800 • (800) 726-0600 •
www.hmco.com/trade/childrens/
shelves.html

Crowell (Imprint of HarperCollins)

Crown Publishing Group
(Imprint of Random House)

Dial Books
(Imprint of Penguin Putnam Inc.)

Dorling Kindersley (DK Publishing)
95 Madison Avenue
New York, NY 10016
(212) 213-4800 • Fax (800) 774-6733 •
(888) 342-5357 • www.dk.com

Doubleday (Imprint of Random House)

E. P. Dutton Children's Books
(Imprint of Penguin Putnam Inc.)

Farrar Straus & Giroux
19 Union Square West
New York, NY 10003
(212) 741-6900 • Fax (212) 633-2427 •
(888) 330-8477

Four Winds Press
(Imprint of Macmillan, see Simon &
Schuster Children's Publishing)

Greenwillow Books
(Imprint of William Morrow & Co, Inc.)

Grosset & Dunlap
(Imprint of Penguin Putnam, Inc.)

Harcourt Brace & Co.
525 "B" Street
San Diego, CA 92101
(619) 231-6616 • (800) 543-1918 •
www.harcourtbooks.com

Harper & Row (Imprint of HarperCollins)

HarperCollins Children's Books
10 East 53rd Street
New York, NY 10022
(212) 207-7000 • Fax (212) 202-7044 •
(800) 242-7737 •
www.harperchildrens.com

Henry Holt and Company
115 West 18th Street
New York, NY 10011
(212) 886-9200 • (212) 633-0748 • (888)
330-8477 • www.henryholt.com/byr/

Holiday House
425 Madison Avenue
New York, NY 10017
(212) 688-0085 • Fax (212) 421-6134

Houghton Mifflin
222 Berkeley Street
Boston, MA 02116
(617) 351-5000 • Fax (617) 351-1125 •
(800) 225-3362 • www.hmco.com/trade

Hyperion Books
(Imprint of Buena Vista Publishing Co.)
114 Fifth Avenue
New York, NY 10011
(212) 633-4400 • (800) 759-0190 •
www.disney.com

Ideals Children's Books
(Imprint of Hambleton-Hill Publishing, Inc.)
1501 County Hospital Road
Nashville, TN 37218
(615) 254-2480 • (800) 336-6438

Joy Street Books
(Imprint of Little, Brown & Co.)

Just Us Books
356 Glenwood Avenue
E. Orange, NJ 07017
(973) 672-0304 • Fax (973) 677-7570

Alfred A. Knopf
(Imprint of Random House)

Lee & Low Books
95 Madison Avenue
New York, NY 10016
(212) 779-4400 • Fax (212) 683-1894

Lerner Publications Co.
241 First Avenue North
Minneapolis, MN 55401
(612) 332-3344 • Fax (612) 332-7615 •
(800) 328-4929 • www.lernerbooks.com

Little, Brown & Co.
3 Center Plaza
Boston, MA 02108
(617) 227-0730 • Fax (617) 263-2864 •
(800) 343-9204 • www.littlebrown.com

Lothrop Lee & Shepard
(Imprint of William Morrow & Co.)

Macmillan
(Imprint of Simon & Schuster
Children's Publishing)

Marshall Cavendish
99 White Plains Road
Tarrytown, NY 10591
(914) 332-8888 • Fax (914) 332-1082 •
(800) 821-9881 •
www.marshallcavendish.com

William Morrow & Co.
1350 Avenue of the Americas
New York, NY 10019
(212) 261-6500 • Fax (212) 261-6619 •
(800) 843-9389 •
www.williammorrow.com

Morrow Junior Books
(Imprint of William Morrow & Co.)

Mulberry Books
(Imprint of William Morrow & Co.)

National Geographic Society
1145 17th Street, NW
Washington, DC 20036
(202) 828-5667 • (800) 368-2728 •
www.nationalgeographic.com

Northland Publishing
(Division of Justin Industries)
P.O. Box 62
Flagstaff, AZ 86002
(520) 774-5251 • Fax (800) 257-9082 •
(800) 346-3257 • www.northlandpub.com

North-South Books
1123 Broadway, Suite 800
New York, NY 10010
(212) 463-9736 • Fax (212) 633-1004 •
(800) 722-6657 • www.northsouth.com

Orchard Books (A Grolier Company)
95 Madison Avenue
New York, NY 10016
(212) 951-2600 • Fax (212) 213-6435 •
(800) 621-1115 • www.grolier.com

Owlet (Imprint of Henry Holt & Co.)

Willa Perlman Books
(Imprint of Simon & Schuster
Children's Publishing)

Philomel Books
(Imprint of Putnam Penguin, Inc.)

Puffin Books
(Imprint of Penguin Putnam, Inc.)

G.P. Putnam's Sons Publishing
(Imprint of Penguin Putnam, Inc.)

Penguin Putnam, Inc.
345 Hudson Street
New York, NY 10014
(212) 366-2000 • Fax (212) 366-2666 •
(800) 631-8571 •
www.penguinputnam.com

Random House
201 East 50th Street
New York, NY 10022
(212) 751-2600 • Fax (212) 572-2593 •
(800) 726-0600 • www.randomhouse/kids

Rourke Corporation
P.O. Box 3328
Vero Beach, FL 32964
(561) 234-6001 • (800) 394-7055 •
www.rourkepublishing.com

Scholastic
555 Broadway
New York, NY 10012
(212) 343-6100 • Fax (212) 343-6930 •
(800) SCHOLASTIC • www.scholastic.com

Sierra Junior Club
85 Second Street, Second Floor
San Francisco, CA 94105-3441
(415) 977-5500 • Fax (415) 977-5799 •
(800) 935-1056 • www.sierraclub.org

Simon & Schuster Children's Books
1230 Avenue of the Americas
New York, NY 10020
(212) 698-7200 • (800) 223-2336 •
www.simonsays.com/kidzone

Smith & Kraus
4 Lower Mill Road
N. Stratford, NH 03590
(603) 643-6431 • Fax (603) 643-1831 •
(800) 895-4331 • www.smithkraus.com

Teacher Ideas Press
(Division of Libraries Unlimited)
P.O. Box 6633
Englewood, CO 80155-6633
(303) 770-1220 • Fax (303) 220-8843 •
(800) 237-6124 • www.lu.com

Ticknor & Fields
(Imprint of Houghton Mifflin, Inc.)

Usborne (Imprint of EDC Publishing)
10302 E. 55th Place, Suite B
Tulsa, OK 74146-6515
(918) 622-4522 • (800) 475-4522 •
www.edcpub.com

Viking Children's Books
(Imprint of Penguin Putnam Inc.)

Watts Publishing
(Imprint of Grolier Publishing;
see Children's Press)

Walker & Co.
435 Hudson Street
New York, NY 10014
(212) 727-8300 • (212) 727-0984 • (800)
AT-WALKER

Whispering Coyote Press
300 Crescent Court, Suite 860
Dallas, TX 75201
(800) 929-6104 • Fax (214) 319-7298

Albert Whitman
6340 Oakton Street
Morton Grove, IL 60053-2723
(847) 581-0033 • Fax (847) 581-0039 •
(800) 255-7675 • www.awhitmanco.com

Workman Publishing Co., Inc.
708 Broadway
New York, NY 10003
(212) 254-5900 • Fax (800) 521-1832 •
(800) 722-7202 • www.workman.com

Multimedia Resources

AGC/United Learning
6633 West Howard Street
Niles, IL 60714-3389
(800) 424-0362 • www.unitedlearning.com

AIMS Multimedia
9710 DeSoto Avenue
Chatsworth, CA 91311-4409
(800) 367-2467 •
www.AIMS-multimedia.com

BFA Educational Media
(see Phoenix Learning Group)

Broderbund
(Parsons Technology;
also see The Learning Company)
500 Redwood Blvd
Novato, CA 94997
(800) 521-6263 • Fax (800) 474-8840 •
www.broderbund.com

Carousel Film and Video
260 Fifth Avenue, Suite 705
New York, NY 10001
(212) 683-1660 • e-mail:
carousel@pipeline.com

Cloud 9 Interactive
(888) 662-5683 • www.cloud9int.com

Computer Plus (see ESI)

Coronet/MTI
(see Phoenix Learning Group)

Davidson (see Knowledge Adventure)

Direct Cinema, Ltd.
P.O. Box 10003
Santa Monica, CA 90410-1003
(800) 525-0000

Disney Interactive
(800) 900-9234 •
www.disneyinteractive.com

DK Multimedia (Dorling Kindersley)
95 Madison Avenue
New York, NY 10016
(212) 213-4800 • Fax: (800) 774-6733 •
(888) 342-5357 • www.dk.com

Edmark Corp.
P.O. Box 97021
Redmond, CA 98073-9721
(800) 362-2890 • www.edmark.com

Encyclopaedia Britannica Educational Corp.
310 South Michigan Avenue
Chicago, IL 60604
(800) 554-9862 • www.eb.com

ESI/Educational Software
4213 S. 94th Street
Omaha, NE 68127
(800) 955-5570 • www.edsoft.com

GPN/Reading Rainbow
University of Nebraska-Lincoln
P.O. Box 80669
Lincoln, NE 68501-0669
(800) 228-4630 • www.gpn.unl.edu

Hasbro Interactive
(800) 683-5847 • www.hasbro.com

Humongous
13110 NE 177th Pl., Suite B101, Box 180
Woodenville, WA 98072
(800) 499-8386 • www.humongous.com

IBM Corp.
1133 Westchester Ave.
White Plains, NY 10604
(770) 863-1234 • Fax (770) 863-3030 •
(888) 411-1932 •
www.pc.ibm.com/multimedia/crayola

ICE, Inc.
(Distributed by Arch Publishing)
12B W. Main St.
Elmsford, NY 10523
(914) 347-2464 • (800) 843-9497 •
www.educorp.com

Knowledge Adventure
19840 Pioneer Avenue
Torrence, CA 90503
(800) 542-4240 • (800) 545-7677 •
www.knowledgeadventure.com

The Learning Company
6160 Summit Drive North
Minneapolis, MN 55430
(800) 685-6322 • www.learningco.com

Listening Library
One Park Avenue
Greenwich, CT 06870-1727
(800) 243-4504 • www.listeninglib.com

Macmillan/McGraw-Hill
(see SRA/McGraw-Hill)

Maxis
2121 N. California Blvd
Walnut Creek, CA 94596-3572
(925) 933-5630 • Fax (925) 927-3736 •
(800) 245-4525 • www.maxis.com

MECC
(see the Learning Company)

Microsoft
One Microsoft Way
Redmond, WA 98052-6399
(800) 426-9400 • www.microsoft.com/kids

National Geographic Society Educational Services
P.O. Box 10597
Des Moines, IA 50340-0597
(800) 368-2728 •
www.nationalgeographic.com

National School Products
101 East Broadway
Maryville, TN 37804
(800) 251-9124 • www.ierc.com

PBS Video
1320 Braddock Place
Alexandria, VA 22314
(800) 344-3337 • www.pbs.org

Phoenix Films
(see Phoenix Learning Group)

The Phoenix Learning Group
2348 Chaffee Drive
St. Louis, MO 63146
(800) 221-1274 • e-mail:
phoenixfilms@worldnet.att.net

Pied Piper (see AIMS Multimedia)

Scholastic New Media
555 Broadway
New York, NY 10003
(800) 724-6527 • www.scholastic.com

Simon & Schuster Interactive
(see Knowledge Adventure)

SRA/McGraw-Hill
220 Daniel Dale Road
De Soto, TX 75115
(800) 843-8855 • www.sra4kids.com

SVE/Churchill Media
6677 North Northwest Highway
Chicago, IL 60631
(800) 829-1900 •www.svemedia.com

Tom Snyder Productions (also see ESI)
80 Coolidge Hill Rd.
Watertown, MA 02472
(800) 342-0236 • www.teachtsp.com

Troll Associates
100 Corporate Drive
Mahwah, NJ 07430
(800) 929-8765 • Fax (800) 979-8765 •
www.troll.com

Voyager (see ESI)

Weston Woods
12 Oakwood Avenue
Norwalk, CT 06850
(800) 243-5020 • Fax (203) 845-0498

Zenger Media
10200 Jefferson Blvd., Room 94,
P.O. Box 802
Culver City, CA 90232-0802
(800) 421-4246 • (800) 944-5432 •
www.Zengermedia.com

UNIT 1

	Decodable Words	Vocabulary
THE HOUSE		High-Frequency Words the
A PRESENT		High-Frequency Words a
MY SCHOOL		High-Frequency Words my
NAN	an **Nan**	High-Frequency Words that
THAT NAN!	Review	High-Frequency Words Review

UNIT 2

	Decodable Words	Vocabulary
DAN AND DAD	**Dad** **Dan**	High-Frequency Words and
DAD, DAN, AND I	**sad**	High-Frequency Words I
I AM SAM!	**am** mad man **Sam** dam	High-Frequency Words is
SID SAID	did in **Min** **Sid** dim	High-Frequency Words said
IS SAM MAD?	Review	High-Frequency Words Review

Boldfaced words appear in the selection.

UNIT 3

	Decodable Words				Vocabulary
THAT TAM!	at it mat	Nat **sat** **sit**	**Tam** tan	**Tim** tin	**High-Frequency Words** **we**
NAT IS MY CAT	**can**	**cat**			**High-Frequency Words** **are**
ON THE DOT	cot Dom **Don**	**dot** **Mom**	**not** **on**	**Tom** tot	**High-Frequency Words** **you**
WE FIT!	fan	fat	fin	**fit**	**High-Frequency Words** **have**
THE TAN CAT	Review				**High-Frequency Words** Review

UNIT 4

	Decodable Words				Vocabulary
YOU ARE IT!	**ran** rat	rod	**Ron**	rot	**High-Frequency Words** **to**
TAP THE SAP	**cap** dip map mop nap	pad **Pam** **pan** pat	pod **pot** rip **sap**	**sip** **tap** tip **top**	**High-Frequency Words** **me**
NAP IN A LAP	lad **lap**	lid lip	lit	lot	**High-Frequency Words** **go**
MUD FUN	**cup** cut **fun**	**mud** nut pup	run rut	sun up	**High-Frequency Words** **do**
FUN IN THE SUN	Review				**High-Frequency Words** Review

UNIT 5

Decodable Words | Vocabulary

TOM IS SICK

dock	lock	**pick**	**sock**
duck	luck	rack	tack
kid	Mack	rock	tick
Kim	Mick	sack	tock
kit	muck	**sick**	tuck
lick	pack		

High-Frequency Words

for

PUG

dug	gum	**Pug**	tag
fog	log	rag	tug
got	**mug**	rug	

High-Frequency Words

he

A PET FOR KEN

den	leg	Ned	**red**
fed	**let**	net	set
get	Meg	pen	Ted
Ken	men	**pet**	ten
led	met		

High-Frequency Words

she

A BIG BUG

bad	bet	bog	cub
bag	**big**	bud	Rob
bat	bin	**bug**	rub
bed	bit	but	tub
Ben			

High-Frequency Words

has

A PUP AND A CAT

Review

High-Frequency Words

Review

UNIT 6

	Decodable Words				**Vocabulary**

Hop with a Hog

had	him	**hog**	**hug**
ham	hip	**hop**	**hum**
hat	**hit**	hot	hut
hen			

High-Frequency Words
with

We Win!

wag	wed	wig	**win**
web	wet		

High-Frequency Words
was

The Vet Van

ax	fox	ox	**van**
box	**Max**	**Rex**	**vet**
fix	mix	six	wax

High-Frequency Words
not

Jen and Yip

jam	job	quit	yum
Jan	**jog**	yam	Zack
Jen	jot	yet	Zeb
jet	jug	**Yip**	**zigzag**
jig	**quack**	yuck	zip
Jim	**quick**		

High-Frequency Words
of

Zack and Jan

Review

High-Frequency Words
Review

Listening, Speaking, Viewing, Representing

☑ Tested Skill

Tinted panels show skills, strategies, and other teaching opportunities

	K	1	2	3	4	5	6
LISTENING							
Learn the vocabulary of school (numbers, shapes, colors, directions, and categories)							
Identify the musical elements of literary language, such as rhymes, repeated sounds, onomatopoeia							
Determine purposes for listening (get information, solve problems, enjoy and appreciate)							
Listen critically and responsively							
Ask and answer relevant questions							
Listen critically to interpret and evaluate							
Listen responsively to stories and other texts read aloud, including selections from classic and contemporary works							
Connect own experiences, ideas, and traditions with those of others							
Apply comprehension strategies in listening activities							
Understand the major ideas and supporting evidence in spoken messages							
Participate in listening activities related to reading and writing (such as discussions, group activities, conferences)							
Listen to learn by taking notes, organizing, and summarizing spoken ideas							
SPEAKING							
Learn the vocabulary of school (numbers, shapes, colors, directions, and categories)							
Use appropriate language and vocabulary learned to describe ideas, feelings, and experiences							
Ask and answer relevant questions							
Communicate effectively in everyday situations (such as discussions, group activities, conferences)							
Demonstrate speaking skills (audience, purpose, occasion, volume, pitch, tone, rate, fluency)							
Clarify and support spoken messages and ideas with objects, charts, evidence, elaboration, examples							
Use verbal and nonverbal communication in effective ways when, for example, making announcements, giving directions, or making introductions							
Retell a spoken message by summarizing or clarifying							
Connect own experiences, ideas, and traditions with those of others							
Determine purposes for speaking (inform, entertain, give directions, persuade, express personal feelings and opinions)							
Demonstrate skills of reporting and providing information							
Demonstrate skills of interviewing, requesting and providing information							
Apply composition strategies in speaking activities							
Monitor own understanding of spoken message and seek clarification as needed							
VIEWING							
Demonstrate viewing skills (focus attention, organize information)							
Respond to audiovisual media in a variety of ways							
Participate in viewing activities related to reading and writing							
Apply comprehension strategies in viewing activities							
Recognize artists' craft and techniques for conveying meaning							
Interpret information from various formats such as maps, charts, graphics, video segments, technology							
Evaluate purposes of various media (information, appreciation, entertainment, directions, persuasion)							
Use media to compare ideas and points of view							
REPRESENTING							
Select, organize, or produce visuals to complement or extend meanings							
Produce communication using appropriate media to develop a class paper, multimedia or video reports							
Show how language, medium, and presentation contribute to the message							

Reading: Alphabetic Principle, Sounds/Symbols

☑ Tested Skill

Tinted panels show skills, strategies, and other teaching opportunities

PRINT AWARENESS

	K	1	2	3	4	5	6
Know the order of the alphabet							
Recognize that print represents spoken language and conveys meaning							
Understand directionality (tracking print from left to right; return sweep)							
Understand that written words are separated by spaces							
Know the difference between individual letters and printed words							
Understand that spoken words are represented in written language by specific sequence of letters							
Recognize that there are correct spellings for words							
Know the difference between capital and lowercase letters							
Recognize how readers use capitalization and punctuation to comprehend							
Recognize the distinguishing features of a paragraph							
Recognize that parts of a book (such as cover/title page and table of contents) offer information							

PHONOLOGICAL AWARENESS

	K	1	2	3	4	5	6
Identify letters, words, sentences							
Divide spoken sentence into individual words							
Produce rhyming words and distinguish rhyming words from nonrhyming words							
Identify, segment, and combine syllables within spoken words							
Identify and isolate the initial and final sound of a spoken word							
Add, delete, or change sounds to change words (such as *cow* to *how*, *pan* to *fan*)							
Blend sounds to make spoken words							
Segment one-syllable spoken words into individual phonemes							

PHONICS AND DECODING

	K	1	2	3	4	5	6
Alphabetic principle: Letter/sound correspondence	☑	☑	☑				
Blending CVC words	☑						
Segmenting CVC words	☑						
Blending CVC, CVCe, CCVC, CVCC, CVVC words	☑	☑	☑				
Segmenting CVC, CVCe, CCVC, CVCC, CVVC words	☑	☑	☑				
Initial and final consonants: /n/n, /d/d, /s/s, /m/m, /t/t, /k/c, /f/f, /r/r, /p/p, /l/l, /k/k, /g/g, /b/b, /h/h, /w/w, /v/v, /ks/x, /kw/qu, /j/j, /y/y, /z/z	☑	☑					
Initial and medial short vowels: *a, i, u, o, e*	☑	☑	☑				
Long vowels: *a-e, i-e, o-e, u-e* (vowel-consonant-e)		☑	☑				
Long vowels, including *ay, ai; e, ee, ie, ea, o, oa, oe, ow; i, y, igh*		☑	☑				
Consonant Digraphs: *sh, th, ch, wh*		☑					
Consonant Blends: continuant/continuant, including *sl, sm, sn, fl, fr, ll, ss, ff*		☑					
Consonant Blends: continuant/stop, including *st, sk, sp, ng, nt, nd, mp, ft*		☑					
Consonant Blends: stop/continuant, including *tr, pr, pl, cr, tw*		☑					
Variant vowels: including /u/oo; /ô/a, aw, au; /ü/ue, ew		☑	☑				
Diphthongs, including /ou/ou, ow; /oi/oi, oy		☑	☑				
r-controlled vowels, including /âr/are; /ôr/or, ore; /îr/ear			☑				
Soft *c* and soft *g*			☑				
nk		☑	☑				
Consonant Digraphs: *ck*	☑	☑					
Consonant Digraphs: *ph, tch, ch*			☑				
Short *e: ea*			☑				
Long *e: y, ey*			☑				
/ü/oo		☑	☑				
/är/ar; /ûr/ir, ur, er		☑	☑				
Silent letters: including *l, b, k, w, g, h, gh*			☑				
Schwa: /ər/er; /ən/en; /əl/le;			☑				
Reading/identifying multisyllabic words		☑	☑				

Reading: Vocabulary/Word Identification

WORD STRUCTURE	K	1	2	3	4	5	6
Common spelling patterns							
Syllable patterns							
Plurals							
Possessives							
Contractions							
Root, or base, words and inflectional endings (-s, -es, -ed, -ing)							
Compound Words							
Prefixes and suffixes (such as un-, re-, dis-, non-; -ly, -y, -ful, -able, -tion)							
Root words and derivational endings							
WORD MEANING							
Develop vocabulary through concrete experiences							
Develop vocabulary through selections read aloud							
Develop vocabulary through reading							
Cueing systems: syntactic, semantic, phonetic							
Context clues, including semantic clues (word meaning), syntactical clues (word order), and phonetic clues	☑	☑	☑	☑	☑	☑	☑
High-frequency words (such as the, a, an, and, said, was, where, is)							
Identify words that name persons, places, things, and actions							
Automatic reading of regular and irregular words							
Use resources and references dictionary, glossary, thesaurus, synonym finder, technology and software, and context)							
Synonyms and antonyms							
Multiple-meaning words							
Figurative language							
Decode derivatives (root words, such as like, pay, happy with affixes, such as dis-, pre-, -un)							
Systematic study of words across content areas and in current events							
Locate meanings, pronunciations, and derivations (including dictionaries, glossaries, and other sources)							
Denotation and connotation							
Word origins as aid to understanding historical influences on English word meanings							
Homophones, homographs							
Analogies							
Idioms							

Reading: Comprehension

PREREADING STRATEGIES	K	1	2	3	4	5	6
Preview and Predict							
Use prior knowledge							
Establish and adjust purposes for reading							
Build background							
MONITORING STRATEGIES							
Adjust reading rate							
Reread, search for clues, ask questions, ask for help							
Visualize							
Read a portion aloud, use reference aids							
Use decoding and vocabulary strategies							
Paraphrase							
Create story maps, diagrams, charts, story props to help comprehend, analyze, synthesize and evaluate texts							

(continued on next page)

(Reading: Comprehension continued)

SKILLS AND STRATEGIES	K	1	2	3	4	5	6
Story details	☑						
Use illustrations	☑	☑					
Reality and fantasy	☑	☑	☑	☑			
Classify and categorize	☑						
Make predictions	☑	☑	☑	☑	☑	☑	☑
Sequence of events (tell or act out)	☑	☑	☑	☑	☑	☑	☑
Cause and effect		☑	☑	☑	☑	☑	☑
Compare and contrast	☑	☑	☑	☑	☑	☑	☑
Summarize	☑	☑	☑	☑	☑	☑	☑
Make and explain inferences		☑	☑	☑	☑	☑	☑
Draw conclusions		☑	☑	☑	☑	☑	☑
Important and unimportant information				☑	☑	☑	☑
Main idea and supporting details	☑	☑	☑	☑	☑	☑	☑
Form conclusions or generalizations and support with evidence from text			☑	☑	☑	☑	☑
Fact and opinion (including news stories and advertisements)			☑	☑	☑	☑	☑
Problem and solution			☑	☑	☑	☑	☑
Steps in a process		☑	☑	☑	☑	☑	☑
Make judgments and decisions				☑	☑	☑	☑
Fact and nonfact				☑	☑	☑	☑
Recognize techniques of persuasion and propaganda					☑	☑	☑
Evaluate evidence and sources of information					☑	☑	☑
Identify similarities and differences across texts (including topics, characters, problems, themes, treatment, scope, or organization)							
Practice various questions and tasks (test-like comprehension questions)							
Paraphrase and summarize to recall, inform, and organize							
Answer various types of questions (open-ended, literal, interpretive, test-like such as true-false, multiple choice, short-answer)							
Use study strategies to learn and recall (preview, question, reread, and record)							
LITERARY RESPONSE							
Listen to stories being read aloud							
React, speculate, join in, read along when predictable and patterned selections are read aloud							
Respond through talk, movement, music, art, drama, and writing to a variety of stories and poems							
Show understanding through writing, illustrating, developing demonstrations, and using technology							
Connect ideas and themes across texts							
Support responses by referring to relevant aspects of text and own experiences							
Offer observations, make connections, speculate, interpret, and raise questions in response to texts							
Interpret text ideas through journal writing, discussion, enactment, and media							
TEXT STRUCTURE/LITERARY CONCEPTS							
Distinguish forms of texts and the functions they serve (lists, newsletters, signs)							
Understand story structure							
Identify narrative (for entertainment) and expository (for information)							
Distinguish fiction from nonfiction, including fact and fantasy							
Understand literary forms (stories, poems, plays, and informational books)							
Understand literary terms by distinguishing between roles of author and illustrator							
Understand title, author, and illustrator across a variety of texts							
Analyze character, character's point of view, plot, setting, style, tone, mood		☑	☑	☑	☑	☑	☑
Compare communication in different forms							
Understand terms such as *title, author, illustrator, playwright, theater, stage, act, dialogue,* and *scene*							
Recognize stories, poems, myths, folktales, fables, tall tales, limericks, plays, biographies, and autobiographies							
Judge internal logic of story text							
Recognize that authors organize information in specific ways							
Identify texts to inform, influence, express, or entertain							
Describe how author's point of view affects text							
Recognize biography, historical fiction, realistic fiction, modern fantasy, informational texts, and poetry							
Analyze ways authors present ideas (cause/effect, compare/contrast, inductively, deductively, chronologically)							
Recognize flashback, foreshadowing, symbolism							

(continued on next page)

(Reading: Comprehension continued)

VARIETY OF TEXT	K	1	2	3	4	5	6
Read a variety of genres							
Use informational texts to acquire information							
Read for a variety of purposes							
Select varied sources when reading for information or pleasure							
FLUENCY							
Read regularly in independent-level and instructional-level materials							
Read orally with fluency from familiar texts							
Self-select independent-level reading							
Read silently for increasing periods of time							
Demonstrate characteristics of fluent and effective reading							
Adjust reading rate to purpose							
Read aloud in selected texts, showing understanding of text and engaging the listener							
CULTURES							
Connect own experience with culture of others							
Compare experiences of characters across cultures							
Articulate and discuss themes and connections that cross cultures							
CRITICAL THINKING							
Experiences (comprehend, apply, analyze, synthesize, evaluate)							
Make connections (comprehend, apply, analyze, synthesize, evaluate)							
Expression (comprehend, apply, analyze, synthesize, evaluate)							
Inquiry (comprehend, apply, analyze, synthesize, evaluate)							
Problem solving (comprehend, apply, analyze, synthesize, evaluate)							
Making decisions (comprehend, apply, analyze, synthesize, evaluate)							

Study Skills

INQUIRY/RESEARCH	K	1	2	3	4	5	6
Follow directions							
Use alphabetical order							
Identify/frame questions for research							
Obtain, organize, and summarize information: classify, take notes, outline							
Evaluate research and raise new questions							
Use technology to present information in various formats							
Follow accepted formats for writing research, including documenting sources							
Use test-taking strategies							
Use text organizers (book cover; title page—title, author, illustrator; contents; headings; glossary; index)		☑	☑	☑	☑	☑	☑
Use graphic aids, including maps, diagrams, charts, graphs		☑	☑	☑	☑	☑	☑
Read and interpret varied texts including environmental print, signs, lists, encyclopedia, dictionary, glossary, newspaper, advertisement, magazine, calendar, directions, floor plans		☑	☑	☑	☑	☑	☑
Use reference sources, such as glossary, dictionary, encyclopedia, telephone directory, technology resources		☑	☑	☑	☑	☑	☑
Recognize Library/Media center resources, such as computerized references; catalog search—subject, author, title; encyclopedia index		☑	☑	☑	☑	☑	☑

Writing

MODES AND FORMS	K	1	2	3	4	5	6
Interactive writing							
Personal narrative (Expressive narrative)			☑	☑	☑	☑	☑
Writing that compares (Informative classificatory)			☑	☑	☑	☑	☑
Explanatory writing (Informative narrative)		☑	☑	☑	☑	☑	☑
Persuasive writing (Persuasive descriptive)			☑	☑	☑	☑	☑
Writing a story		☑	☑	☑	☑	☑	☑
Expository writing		☑	☑	☑	☑	☑	☑
Write using a variety of formats, such as advertisement, autobiography, biography, book report/report, comparison-contrast, critique/review/editorial, description, essay, how-to, interview, invitation, journal/log/notes, message/list, paragraph/multi-paragraph composition, picture book, play (scene), poem/rhyme, story, summary, note, letter							

PURPOSES/AUDIENCES	K	1	2	3	4	5	6
Dictate messages such as news and stories for others to write							
Write labels, notes, and captions for illustrations, possessions, charts, and centers							
Write to record, to discover and develop ideas, to inform, to influence, to entertain							
Exhibit an identifiable voice in personal narratives and stories							
Use literary devices (suspense, dialogue, and figurative language)							
Produce written texts by organizing ideas, using effective transitions, and choosing precise wording							

PROCESSES	K	1	2	3	4	5	6
Generate ideas for self-selected and assigned topics using prewriting strategies							
Develop drafts							
Revise drafts for varied purposes							
Edit for appropriate grammar, spelling, punctuation, and features of polished writings							
Proofread own writing and that of others							
Bring pieces to final form and "publish" them for audiences							
Use technology to compose text							
Select and use reference materials and resources for writing, revising, and editing final drafts							

SPELLING	K	1	2	3	4	5	6
Spell own name and write high-frequency words							
Words with short vowels (including CVC and one-syllable words with blends CCVC, CVCC, CCVCC)							
Words with long vowels (including CVCe)							
Words with digraphs, blends, consonant clusters, double consonants							
Words with diphthongs							
Words with variant vowels							
Words with r-controlled vowels							
Words with /ər/, /əl/, and /ən/							
Words with silent letters							
Words with soft c and soft g							
Inflectional endings (including plurals and past tense and words that drop the final e when adding -ing, -ed)							
Compound words							
Contractions							
Homonyms							
Suffixes including -able, -ly, or -less, and prefixes including dis-, re-, pre-, or un-							
Spell words ending in -tion and -sion, such as station and procession							
Accurate spelling of root or base words							
Orthographic patterns and rules such as keep/can; sack/book; out/now; oil/toy; match/speech; ledge/cage; consonant doubling, dropping e, changing y to i							
Multisyllabic words using regularly spelled phonogram patterns							
Syllable patterns (including closed, open, syllable boundary patterns)							
Synonyms and antonyms							
Words from Social Studies, Science, Math, and Physical Education							
Words derived from other languages and cultures							
Use resources to find correct spellings, synonyms, and replacement words							
Use conventional spelling of familiar words in writing assignments							
Spell accurately in final drafts							

(continued on next page)

✓ Tested Skill

Tinted panels show skills, strategies, and other teaching opportunities

GRAMMAR AND USAGE	K	1	2	3	4	5	6
Understand sentence concepts (word order, statements, questions, exclamations, commands)							
Recognize complete and incomplete sentences							
Nouns (common; proper; singular; plural; irregular plural; possessives)							
Verbs (action; helping; linking; irregular)							
Verb tense (present, past, future, perfect, and progressive)							
Pronouns (possessive, subject and object, pronoun-verb agreement)							
Use objective case pronouns accurately							
Adjectives							
Adverbs that tell how, when, where							
Subjects, predicates							
Subject-verb agreement							
Sentence combining							
Recognize sentence structure (simple, compound, complex)							
Synonyms and antonyms							
Contractions							
Conjunctions							
Prepositions and prepositional phrases							

PENMANSHIP	K	1	2	3	4	5	6
Write each letter of alphabet (capital and lowercase) using correct formation, appropriate size and spacing							
Write own name and other important words							
Use phonological knowledge to map sounds to letters to write messages							
Write messages that move left to right, top to bottom							
Gain increasing control of penmanship, pencil grip, paper position, beginning stroke							
Use word and letter spacing and margins to make messages readable							
Write legibly by selecting cursive or manuscript as appropriate							

MECHANICS	K	1	2	3	4	5	6
Use capitalization in sentences, proper nouns, titles, abbreviations and the pronoun I							
Use end marks correctly (period, question mark, exclamation point)							
Use commas (in dates, in addresses, in a series, in letters, in direct address)							
Use apostrophes in contractions and possessives							
Use quotation marks							
Use hyphens, semicolons, colons							

EVALUATION	K	1	2	3	4	5	6
Identify the most effective features of a piece of writing using class/teacher generated criteria							
Respond constructively to others' writing							
Determine how his/her own writing achieves its purpose							
Use published pieces as models for writing							
Review own written work to monitor growth as writer							

For more detailed scope and sequence including page numbers and additional phonics information, see McGraw-Hill Reading Program scope and sequence (K–6)

T89

Scoring Chart

The Scoring Chart is provided for your convenience in grading your students' work.

- Find the column that shows the total number of items.
- Find the row that matches the number of items answered correctly.
- The intersection of the two rows provides the percentage score.

TOTAL NUMBER OF ITEMS

NUMBER CORRECT

	1	2	3	4	5	6	7	8	9	10	11	12	13	14	15	16	17	18	19	20	21	22	23	24	25	26	27	28	29	30
1	100	50	33	25	20	17	14	13	11	10	9	8	8	7	7	6	6	6	5	5	5	5	4	4	4	4	4	4	3	3
2		100	66	50	40	33	29	25	22	20	18	17	15	14	13	13	12	11	11	10	10	9	9	8	8	8	7	7	7	7
3			100	75	60	50	43	38	33	30	27	25	23	21	20	19	18	17	16	15	14	14	13	13	12	12	11	11	10	10
4				100	80	67	57	50	44	40	36	33	31	29	27	25	24	22	21	20	19	18	17	17	16	15	15	14	14	13
5					100	83	71	63	56	50	45	42	38	36	33	31	29	28	26	25	24	23	22	21	20	19	19	18	17	17
6						100	86	75	67	60	55	50	46	43	40	38	35	33	32	30	29	27	26	25	24	23	22	21	21	20
7							100	88	78	70	64	58	54	50	47	44	41	39	37	35	33	32	30	29	28	27	26	25	24	23
8								100	89	80	73	67	62	57	53	50	47	44	42	40	38	36	35	33	32	31	30	29	28	27
9									100	90	82	75	69	64	60	56	53	50	47	45	43	41	39	38	36	35	33	32	31	30
10										100	91	83	77	71	67	63	59	56	53	50	48	45	43	42	40	38	37	36	34	33
11											100	92	85	79	73	69	65	61	58	55	52	50	48	46	44	42	41	39	38	37
12												100	92	86	80	75	71	67	63	60	57	55	52	50	48	46	44	43	41	40
13													100	93	87	81	76	72	68	65	62	59	57	54	52	50	48	46	45	43
14														100	93	88	82	78	74	70	67	64	61	58	56	54	52	50	48	47
15															100	94	88	83	79	75	71	68	65	63	60	58	56	54	52	50
16																100	94	89	84	80	76	73	70	67	64	62	59	57	55	53
17																	100	94	89	85	81	77	74	71	68	65	63	61	59	57
18																		100	95	90	86	82	78	75	72	69	67	64	62	60
19																			100	95	90	86	83	79	76	73	70	68	66	63
20																				100	95	91	87	83	80	77	74	71	69	67
21																					100	95	91	88	84	81	78	75	72	70
22																						100	96	92	88	85	81	79	76	73
23																							100	96	92	88	85	82	79	77
24																								100	96	92	89	86	83	80
25																									100	96	93	89	86	83
26																										100	96	93	90	87
27																											100	96	93	90
28																												100	97	93
29																													100	97
30																														100

Notes

Notes

Notes

Notes